MW00355932

THE CISO HANDBOOK

THE CISO HANDBOOK

A PRACTICAL GUIDE
TO SECURING YOUR COMPANY

MICHAEL GENTILE, CISSP
RONALD D. COLLETTE, CISSP
THOMAS D. AUGUST, CISSP

Auerbach Publications
Taylor & Francis Group
Boca Raton   New York

Published in 2006 by
Auerbach Publications
Taylor & Francis Group
6000 Broken Sound Parkway NW, Suite 300
Boca Raton, FL 33487-2742

© 2006 by Taylor & Francis Group, LLC
Auerbach is an imprint of Taylor & Francis Group

No claim to original U.S. Government works
Printed in the United States of America on acid-free paper
10 9 8 7 6 5 4 3 2 1

International Standard Book Number-10: 0-8493-1952-8 (Hardcover)
International Standard Book Number-13: 978-0-8493-1952-5 (Hardcover)
Library of Congress Card Number 2005047425

Library of Congress Cataloging-in-Publication Data

Gentile, Michael.
   The CISO handbook : a practical guide to securing your company / Michael Gentile, Ronald D. Collette, Thomas D. August.
      p. cm.
   Includes bibliographical references and index.
   ISBN 0-8493-1952-8 (alk. paper)
   1. Electronic data processing departments--security measures. 2. Computer security. 3. Data protection. I. Collette, Ronald D. II. August, Thomas D. III. Title

HF5548.37.G46 2005
658.4'78--dc22
                                                         2005047425

Taylor & Francis Group
is the Academic Division of T&F Informa plc.

Visit the Taylor & Francis Web site at
http://www.taylorandfrancis.com

and the Auerbach Publications Web site at
http://www.auerbach-publications.com

Table of Contents

Forward..xiii
Acknowledgments...xv
Team Acknowledgment...xv
Organizations We Would Like to Thank...xvi
Introduction...xvii
Overview xvii

1 Assess...1
Overview 1
Foundation Concepts..2
   Critical Skills...2
      Consultative Sales Skills...2
      Enabling New Business Opportunities..2
      Reducing Business Risk 3
   Critical Knowledge..4
   Understanding Your Business 4
   Understanding Risk 6
   Understanding Your Enterprise Differentiators...8
      Understanding Your Legal and Regulatory Environment 9
      Understanding Your Organizational Structure 10
      Understanding Your Organizational Dynamics....................................11
      Enterprise Culture..14
      Understanding Your Enterprise's View of Technology 15
      Assessment Methodology..16
   Identifying Your Program's Primary Driver 17
      Why Are You Here?..17
      Stakeholders..18
      Types of Stakeholders 18
      Identifying Your External Drivers...22
      Regulatory/Audit Environment..22
      Other External Drivers..26
      Identifying Your Internal Drivers...27

Political Climate.. 27
Who Is on Your Team?.. 29
The Enterprise's Business.. 31
Financial Environment... 33
Technical Environment.. 35
Industry 42
Assessment Checklist 46

2   Plan 55
Overview 55
Foundation Concepts.. 55
Critical Skills 56
Visioning 56
Strategic Planning.. 57
Negotiating... 57
Marketing 58
Talent Assessment 58
Critical Skills Summary 58
Critical Knowledge... 59
ISC² Common Body of Knowledge (CBK) 59
Other Security Industry Resources 60
Planning Methodology.. 62
Understanding Your Program's Mandate.................................... 63
Determining Your Program Mission 64
Mission Statements 64
Building Your Mission Statement... 66
Determining Your Program's Structure....................................... 68
Operational Versus Non-Operational.................................... 68
Size of Your Enterprise.. 74
Political Climate.. 74
Centralized Versus Decentralized... 75
Common Reasons for Choosing a Centralized Model 80
Common Reasons for Choosing a De-Centralized Model 80
Security Pipeline... 81
Architecture... 81
Maintenance.. 83
Inspection.. 84
Size of Your Program 85
Large Program Considerations 85
Small Program Considerations 88
Conclusion 91
Common Security Responsibilities.. 91
Information Security Program Structure Summary 92
Determining Your Program's Staffing.. 92
Define the Roles and Responsibilities of Your Team Members 93
Critical Attributes 93
Security Roles and Responsibilities....................................... 97

Influence on Staffing by the Information Security Program
Structure 101
Perform a Gap Analysis... 102
Evaluate Talent 103
Planning Summary 106
Planning Checklist... 106

3 Design...111
Overview 111
Foundation Concepts... 111
Critical Skills... 112
Analytical Skills.. 112
Discovery 112
Evaluation 112
Strategy.. 112
Formulation... 114
Organizational Skills... 114
Sales... 114
Financial Planning and Budgeting... 114
Critical Skills Summary 115
Critical Knowledge... 115
Opportunity Cost.. 115
Security Documents 115
Policies 116
Standards... 117
Procedures 117
Guidelines 118
Example 118
Risks, Threats, and Vulnerabilities ... Oh My!.......................... 118
Example 119
Types of Security Controls... 119
Preventive Controls 119
Detective Controls 121
Gap Analysis.. 121
SMART Statements.. 123
Types of Projects... 123
People Projects 123
Process Projects 124
Technology Projects 124
Methodology.. 124
Preview 124
Security Document Development... 125
Project Portfolio Development... 125
Communication Plan Development.. 125
Incorporating Your Enterprise Drivers 125
Constraints... 126
Laws and Regulations 127

Corporate Responsibility/Code of Conduct 127
Enablers... 127
Requirements 128
Business Requirements 129
Example 129
Example 130
Functional Requirement... 130
Example 131
Business Requirements of PCSC 131
Functional Requirement... 131
Analysis 132
Methods for Creating Functional Requirements 132
Requirements Summary 133
Gap Analysis.. 133
Building Security Policies, Standards, Procedures,
and Guidelines 135
The Theory of Security Policies... 135
Drafting Your Information Security Policies 136
Ratifying the Security Policies.. 138
Standards, Procedures, and Guidelines... 138
Build Security Documents Summary 139
Building the Security Project Portfolio... 140
Performing the Policy Gap Analysis.. 140
Example 142
Analysis 142
Defining Ambiguities 142
Evaluating Controls (Gap Analysis)... 143
Risk and Exposure Statements... 145
Risk Rating... 145
Risk Rating — High 146
Deriving the Security Projects.. 146
Quantitative Evaluation... 146
Qualitative Evaluation... 148
Cursory Project Scoping 151
Projects Versus Core.. 152
Scheduling (First Three Years).. 152
Capital Budgeting... 153
Approval of the Security Project Portfolio 155
Believe in Your Product 155
Ensure That Your Logic for Prioritization Is Understood 155
Know Your Product 155
Know What Others Are Buying... 156
Identify the Buyers and the Roadblocks... 156
Those Who Will Buy Your Offerings... 156
Those Who Will Not Buy Any of Your Offerings........................... 156
Those Who Can Apply Pressure to Individuals Who Won't Buy
Your Offerings 157

Sell through Momentum 157
Sell through Others 157
Ensure That It's Sold before You Attempt to Sell It 157
Always Present in Person 157
Summary 157
Annual Portfolio Review 158
Build the Communication Plan 158
Potential Channels for the Communication Plan 159
Chapter Summary 161
Design Checklist 161

4   Execute **165**
Overview 165
Foundation Concepts 166
Preview 166
Critical Skills 167
Executor 167
Commander 168
Communication 168
Tactician 168
Research 168
Analysis 169
Critical Skills Summary 169
Critical Knowledge 169
Overview of Project Management Methodologies 169
Benefits of a Project Mentality for Your Information Security
Program 170
The Project Management Triangle 172
Technical Control Layers 175
Summary 177
Methodology 178
Preview 178
Project Execution 178
Development Methodology Structure 178
Critical Success Factors for a Project 183
Business, Functional, and Technical Requirements 188
Marketing Metrics 193
Project Governance Model 196
Management Support — Sponsorship 196
Establish a Team 197
Shared Vision 197
Formalized Project Plan (Gantt Chart) 198
Identifying and Working through the Lull of Doom 199
Critical Success Factors Summary 200
Warning Signs for Projects 200
Train Wrecks 200
Project Types and Their Intricacies 204

Common Guidelines for All Projects 204
Common Guidelines for People Projects 205
Common Guidelines for Process Projects 206
Common Guidelines for Technology Projects 207
Project Type Summary 208
Incorporating Security into Projects 208
Tools for Adding Security into a Properly Structured Project 209
Deploy 213
Tools for Adding Security into a Project
with Missing Components 214
Vendor Evaluation/Selection 217
Preparing the Marketing Material 223
Chapter Summary 224

5 Report 225
Overview 225
Foundation Concepts 226
Critical Skills 227
Writer 227
Presenter 227
Critical Knowledge 227
Primary Principle of Reporting 227
Basic Reporting Components 228
Delivery Mechanisms 229
Marketing 229
Branding 230
Metrics 231
Damage Control 231
Summary 232
Methodology 232
Report Construction Process 233
Identifying the Need 234
Determine Intent 235
Desired Reaction 236
Determine Target Audience 238
Internal Audiences 238
Executive Management/Board of Directors 239
Technical Engineering Staff 245
Employees 247
Internal Audit/Regulatory Compliance Office 248
External Audiences 250
Government Agencies/Independent Auditors/Regulators 250
Stockholders and Owners 252
Customers and Clients 252
Target Audience Summary 253
Delivery Mechanisms 253
Administrative Reporting 254

Operational Reporting.. 261
Types of Delivery... 267
Follow up on the Message... 270
Close the Deal... 270
Chapter Summary.. 271

6   The Final Phase **273**
Overview 273
Back to the Beginning 275
Parting Thoughts... 276

Appendices

A   Design Chapter Worksheets **277**

B   Report Creation Process Worksheet............................**281**

C   Requirements Sample **285**

D   SDLC Checklist..**289**

E   Recommended Reading **313**

Index **315**

Foreword

Information security is hard. There ... I've said it!

It's harder than selling life or automobile insurance because almost everyone knows they need that type of insurance. In fact, in many instances, the law mandates insurance. But the need for information security and controls, even today, is a tough sell. Notwithstanding the Health Insurance Portability and Accountability Act (HIPAA), Gramm–Leach–Bliley (GLBa), Sarbanes Oxley 404, and the myriad of recently enacted state and federal regulations intended to protect consumer privacy, implementing an effective, robust information security program is an uphill battle.

Therefore, it takes a special individual to assume the mantle and push the security agenda. I am proud to know three such individuals — persons with passion, devotion, dedication, and the sort of stick-to-it-ness that we don't often see in the corporate world.

They are the authors of this book. I've been privileged to work alongside them and consider myself fortunate to watch as they demonstrate the levels of professionalism and dedication that are critical to the work we do. Through their efforts, they've acquired and nurtured business prowess and technical proficiency that translates into personal and professional credibility. Their co-workers trust them. This crucial ingredient has encouraged others consistently to ask them to be a part of the solution. Security practitioners know this is the only way to succeed.

Moreover, they have assumed a task that few undertake — documenting the practical, real world application of a security program so others can benefit from their experience. In a logical, well thought out way, they walk the reader through a series of thought processes that tutors the burgeoning security professional toward a successful endeavor.

I encourage you to consider seriously the lessons herein, and sincerely wish you the best with your own program.

Micki Krause

Acknowledgments

Team Acknowledgment

We would all like to thank Micki Krause for her mentorship, support, and guidance during this process. We never would have attempted this project without her encouragement.

Mike Gentile would like to thank the following people and organizations:

- My wife, Tiffany, for supporting and believing in me on this project in a way that no one else could duplicate. And on a lighter note, for only charging a pair of shoes to review each chapter.
- My parents, Mike and Lorraine, for never missing a game — you provided me with the foundation needed to take on any challenge.
- Marcus Ziemer, for teaching me how to work effectively on a team — it is amazing how the skills you taught me through sports have paid massive dividends in the world of business.
- Mike and Laine Nelson, for being some of the most giving people I have ever met

Ron Collette would like to thank the following people and organizations:

- My wife, Alice, for her support, council, and friendship during this project; she is the best partner anyone could ever ask for
- My family for giving me the confidence to believe that I could accomplish anything
- Mitchell Kay (high school English teacher) for insisting that I learn how to form a grammatically correct sentence

Tom August would like to thank the following people and organizations:

- My family and friends for their continued trust, support, and encouragement
- Bill Barrett and Cheryl Moerson from Ernst & Young for showing me the importance of seeing the big picture early on in my career
- Stan Watkins and Rich Milo from Deloitte & Touche for their unwavering support and encouragement
- John Dubiel and Victor Wheatman from Gartner, Inc., for their sound advice and encouragement

Book Reviewers We Would Like to Thank

- Alice Collette, PMP, LC
- Tiffany Gentile, CPA
- George McBride, CISSP, CISM
- Bruce Lobree, CISSP
- Franjo Majstor, CISSP, CCIE
- Bonnie Goins, CISSP, NSA IAM
- Ben Rothke, CISSP, CISM

Cover Art Designers We Would Like to Thank

- Alice Collete of Design Alley
- Owrey Photography

Organizations We Would Like to Thank

- Richard O'Hanley and everyone at Auerbach for giving us the opportunity to make this book happen.
- The manufacturers of Red Bull, Emergen-C, the coffee growers of Columbia, and Pepsi-Cola. You all made a very tight deadline possible.
- Indie 103.1 FM for being the first commercial radio station in Southern California to take a risk and play some real music for a change.

Introduction

If you read only one section of this book, please read this. Many years of experience went into the development of this material, and it's our sincerest goal to help you to succeed with the implementation of your security program — whether your company is an established Fortune 500 enterprise or a small start-up company. This section provides the big picture of a proven methodology, and our book is designed so you can use this to identify and focus on the areas that are most critical to you.

Overview

In ancient times, mapmakers were rumored to have marked unexplored areas or regions with pictures of sea monsters and the words, "Here Be Dragons," as a warning to sailors and explorers. It's not that these areas were particularly dangerous; they just hadn't been explored or mapped before. The educational material available to information security professionals today is in many ways similar to these early maps of the world.

Perusing the shelves of your local bookstore, you'll see two main types of reading materials for the security professional — technical hacker guides or ultra high-level theory and exam preparation books.

The first and most prevalent type of book is the hacker guide. These highly technical manuals show you, in excruciating detail, how to bypass the defenses of a given set of controls and security defenses. However, they don't give any real guidance for building and defining an effective and measurable information security program that will provide the outstanding return on investment a company requires. In addition, many of these books are often written from a single point of view, thus limiting their ability to properly address areas that the author may have little expertise in. Another problem with these books is they often have to make a number of assumptions that may have nothing in common with your environment. For example, many known vulnerabilities can only be exploited under a finite set of circumstances. While the authors of these books generally do a good job of explaining their assumptions, the fact that they have to make these assumptions cause them to be of little practical value for the practicing security professional. These books are fun, to be sure, but again they do not properly lay the groundwork necessary to build an information security program.

The second type of book falls into the category of theoretical reference textbooks and exam preparation guides. These books are essential for people wishing to learn the history of the information security industry, its key terms and concepts, and the various theoretical concepts that information security is built from. They are also very useful for preparing the various information security examinations available today. However, the material presented in them is often too generic or nebulous to be of any value to someone responsible for actually building or maintaining a security program. In addition, these books often make a number of assumptions that cause them to be of little or no practical value for the practicing security professional. For example, a common fault among these books is to assume you already have fully functioning processes in your company, such as an integrated Systems Development Life Cycle (SDLC). While that assumption may be fine for a theoretical discussion of how things should be, the reality of the situation is many companies simply don't have the robust control structure that would effectively support a full-fledged SDLC. Another real world example is when executive management insists that an application system be implemented within a truly non-optimal timeframe (i.e., yesterday, or sooner if possible). In the meantime, you are faced with a huge challenge — how can we still keep our company safe?

The goal of our book is simple: provide practical insight and guidance to those tasked with one or more aspects of implementing an effective and measurable information security program — one that provides true value to the stakeholders of a company. We feel this area remains a mystery to many security professionals — especially those ultimately responsible for its design and implementation. Our goal is to present several essential high-level concepts and then build a robust framework that you can use to map these concepts to your environment.

What this book is:

- A comprehensive roadmap for designing and implementing an effective information security program based on real-world scenarios
- A bridge between high-level theory and practical execution
- A set of actionable practices that security professionals can use in the course of their everyday jobs

- A look at information security from experienced professionals with different functional backgrounds providing the reader with a blended perspective
- An assessment tool to assist people in understanding all of the practical issues related to information security, including items often overlooked by theoretical books
- An integrated and modular resource that can either be read from cover to cover or straight to the applicable chapter
- A framework that can be expanded or contracted to accommodate your unique situation

What this book is not:

- A high-level theory or history book
- An exam prep guide
- A technical how-to hacker manual
- A product-specific technical guide

Chapter Structure

The following shows how each chapter is organized.

Overview

This section should be self-explanatory. If you have only a couple of minutes to read something, this is a good place to start.

Foundation Concepts

This section defines those essential concepts that we found to be critical success factors to understanding the material presented in each chapter. Failure to review and understand these items could impede your ability to fully understand or implement the ideas presented in the chapter. This book simply isn't large enough to provide in-depth training on each these concepts, but merely points them out and bring them to your attention. To be honest, most of these concepts have already been written about by people far more knowledgeable than we are in these areas. Our goal here is to point you to sources you might want to familiarize yourself with.

Methodology

This is the section where we identify and explain the steps necessary to achieve the goals of each chapter. This is explained in more detail in the following pages.

Chapter Checklist

Here we illustrate the key items that you should be able to document as you complete the material in each chapter. Each set of deliverables feeds into the successive chapter. For example, the deliverables from the chapter on Assess are inputs into the following chapter on Plan.

Examples and Scenarios

Many times, dry discussions about how to do something can best be explained with a simple example or case study. Here is where we'll show you some real-world examples of things we've seen over the years — from the outstanding to the supremely non-optimal. Where applicable, we will present how the situations may look from different points of view.

Methodology

The book is presented in chapters that follow a consistent methodology — assess, plan, design, execute, and report. Each chapter is related to the prior chapter in a dependent hierarchy, where the information gathered in one chapter provides the inputs for the next. Below, in Figure 1, we have illustrated the entire flow of the book and the corresponding relationships of each chapter.

Assess

In this chapter, we guide the reader through a process of identifying the various elements that drive the need for an information security program, such as regulatory requirements, competition, industry best practices, technology standards, geographic and political considerations, as well as physical and environmental constraints.

Some of the key deliverables that you should be able to complete after finishing this chapter include:

- An inventory of your stakeholders
- An analysis of your business or regulatory requirements
- An assessment of a number of other known drivers for an Information security program

Plan

In this chapter, we discuss how to build the foundation for your information security program. These elements include how to:

- Obtain an executive mandate for the program
- Develop a charter or mission for your program

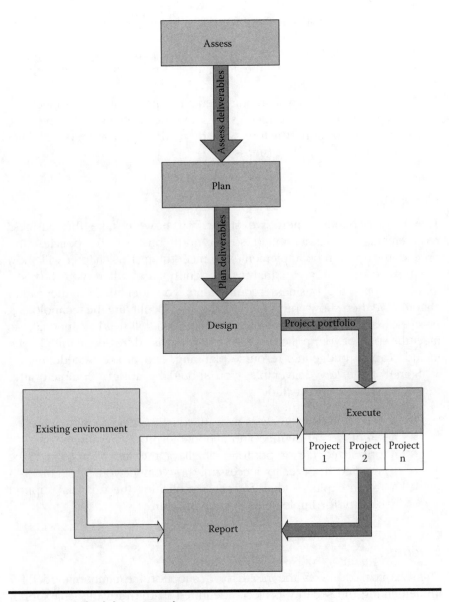

Figure 1 Methodology Overview

- Develop your overall program strategy
- Define the organization structure of your team
- Create job descriptions for your team members
- Identify key personality traits we've found to be critical for the different roles a program may have

Some of the key deliverables would include:

- Your program's charter or mission statement
- Executive support in the form of a formal policy statement or executive mandate
- A list of the business requirements the program should meet
- High-level reporting metrics to show the program's effectiveness
- An organization structure with defined roles and responsibilities that truly fits your business

Design

This is the chapter where we show you how to take the business requirements you've identified so far and construct the policies and procedures that can be implemented to meet them. This chapter will show you how to perform a gap analysis to identify areas where your business may not meet the business requirements you identified in the earlier chapter. We then show you a methodology for identifying the technologies, processes, and education/awareness projects you will need to undertake to meet the spirit of your policies. Other critical areas addressed in this chapter include capital budgeting, resource planning, and project scheduling.

Some of the key deliverables you should be able to complete after reviewing this chapter include:

- A completed gap analysis against your business requirements
- A set of clearly defined and actionable project requirements
- A prioritized list or portfolio of all of the major projects to be completed in order to successfully implement your program
- A rough capital budget for use in soliciting the financial support necessary for implementing your program

Execute

This chapter addresses the need for a successful execution model for implementing the security projects identified in the previous chapters. It has been our experience that having a consistent methodology for executing security projects is one of the most critical success factors in running a successful program. The overall goal of this chapter is to present some guidance on how to successfully execute your security projects given all of the various constraints you face everyday in your business.

This chapter focuses on the project management skills and execution tactics you will need to ensure that the projects you have won management's support for actually get accomplished to everyone's satisfaction.

This is absolutely critical in that your security program's credibility and ongoing success will depend on how well you identify and execute your projects and leverage your successes.

After discussing the elements of project management techniques, we will leverage that knowledge to aid you in the incorporation of security into every initiative within your organization; even if it isn't an initiative driven by the security office.

We also try to address some the known "gotchas" and realities that face many of us each day in our jobs. We discuss the most common types of project failures and how to prevent them, how to establish successful project teams, how to effectively define team roles and responsibilities, how to capture clear, and actionable project requirements, and how to develop clear, actionable, and measurable project goals that can be leveraged as you build your program.

The only deliverables to come from this chapter should be your ongoing portfolio of successfully implemented projects.

Report

This chapter focuses on the reporting process for both external and internal stakeholders of your program. We discuss the various types of audiences, their needs, successful strategies for reporting to them, the types of information they will be most interested in, and the best methods and formats for communicating this information to them.

Key deliverables from this chapter include an analysis of your various reporting audiences, a strategy for reporting to each audience type, and an assessment of the types of information you'll need to report and where to find it in your organization.

The Final Phase

This small book is packed with information, as well as repeatable proven processes and techniques to aid in developing your own information security program. Along each step of the way, we have attempted to distill each critical concept into a digestible and mechanical process that can be adapted to your unique circumstance. So, find a comfortable chair, pour yourself a drink, and hold on for the ride.

Chapter 1

Assess

Overview

The assess phase of the methodology is the process of determining information about the enterprise to support the planning of your information security program. This process involves the identification of the external and internal business drivers for your program, so your program can be built on a solid structure that meets the essential factors influencing your business.

In some organizations, this process is not undertaken in a formal, structured manner. This typically results in a band aid approach to building an information security program. If we view it in terms of purchasing a new car, it would be similar to purchasing a two-seat convertible to move a large family across the country. In this example, action was taken prior to understanding the specific requirements that needed to be met.

In the assess phase, we identify major categories and components that are common to every business, as well as their impact on the development of an information security program. Though we acknowledge that there are additional factors that can play a role in the assessment, we have attempted to distill the common high impact items.

Why do we start with assessing your environment? The initial evaluation of any environment is analogous to dating someone for the first time — you need to gather a lot of critical information as quickly and efficiently as possible. You're attempting to get the big picture, which will provide insight into the very reasons you need a program in the first place.

The goal of this chapter is to provide you with a consistent methodology for quickly and effectively gathering this critical information. Before moving on to the methodology, we will start with the foundation concepts needed to be successful.

Foundation Concepts

The objective of the foundation concepts for this chapter is to help identify critical skills and information you should possess to provide the necessary leverage to successfully implement your information security program. Critical skills are those soft skills that will help you get the most from your efforts, while critical knowledge applies to the essential information you will need to give you the appropriate perspective, or leverage, as you assess your environment.

Critical Skills

Consultative Sales Skills

Most people see security as a cost center, not a profit center. This perception almost automatically places you in the unenviable position of constantly having to sell the virtues and benefits of your program. Selling and marketing the initiatives and ideas associated with your information security program is easily one of the most important skills you can develop. This skill has helped us to no end in the implementation of the security projects and programs we build or maintain.

Your customers may be external companies who have hired your firm, or it might be someone from another department of your enterprise. By treating them all as valuable customers, you are effectively saying to them your success matters to me, and are setting yourself up for increased cooperation and improved participation in the development of your program.

Information security controls are sometimes seen as having a negative or adverse impact on enterprise culture, a high administrative price tag, and they are sometimes seen as hindering the enterprise's ability to profit. Because these controls do not directly add to market share or revenue, they often take a backseat to more visible revenue-generating activities. As a result, you will need to be able to market your program to show either (a) enabling new business opportunities, or (b) reducing business risk.

Enabling New Business Opportunities

This can best be explained through a quick example. With the advent of the Internet, many companies are attempting to deliver business solutions via the Web. As a result, they are implementing systems that are processing sensitive data over the Internet. This presents a new twist on an old business issue — getting potential customers to trust your business. Because of the many risks and threats associated with doing business over the Internet, one significant way to help market your information security program is to show how increased security controls can directly increase your potential customer's trust. By implementing controls such as firewalls, encryption, logging, strong authentication, and independent testing, you will most likely have a strong set of controls that will help your customers trust your business. By working with your public relations and marketing personnel, you might be able to leverage the existence of these controls into your enterprise's marketing plans. Consultative sales skills allow you to work with other people and teams, understand their needs, co-develop potential solutions, sell them to the powers that be, and ensure their successful implementation. Companies such as eBay, e*Trade, and Amazon.com are great examples of companies whose information security professionals have successfully enabled new Internet business through their strong consultative skills.

Reducing Business Risk

Another way to show the value of your information security program is to show a reduction in overall business risk. In a sense, this method is similar to selling insurance — you're trying to sell the benefits of a plan to minimize the impact of an unforeseen event to the enterprise. This is the most prevalent method we are seeing security professionals use today, and entire books have been written on how to best do this. Because a great deal of information on this subject already exists, we will not try to reinvent the wheel. However, we would like to share a few key ideas that have proven helpful in our careers:

- Take the time to learn about the needs and issues your customers are facing.
- Actively listen to your customers. Keep an open mind and try not to project your ideas into their statements.
- Identify the root cause of the problem the customer is trying to communicate to you — not just the symptoms.
- Co-develop solutions with your customers that you both can support.
- Co-present your solutions to management in a manner that is appropriate for the management level, educational background, temperament, and political motivations of your audience.
- Leverage your wins — as you help one customer, use them as a reference for other projects where feasible. Establish and maintain forward momentum in all your initiatives.

- Be flexible.
- Project confidence. Would you let a surgeon perform an operation on you if she seemed uncertain of the procedure?
- Don't second guess yourself. Collect enough information to make an informed decision and resist alterations.

Hopefully, we've whetted your interest on this topic, and have shown how these skills can help you in the implementation of your information security program. A number of excellent reference books that have helped us on this topic can be found in the Appendix.

Critical Knowledge

In this section, we will identify areas of information you will need to effectively perform an assessment of your environment. However, it is well beyond the scope of this book to provide comprehensive instructions on each topic. Where applicable, we will point you to a few reference materials we found to be of value in understanding these critical knowledge areas.

The several areas of critical knowledge we present are:

- Understanding your business
- Understanding risk
- Understanding your enterprise differentiators
- Understanding your legal and regulatory environment
- Understanding your organization
- Understanding your organizational dynamics
- Understanding your enterprise culture
- Understanding your enterprise's view of technology

In our opinion, these areas are critical in your ability to perform an assessment of your environment. If you feel you possess a deficiency in any of the material presented in the foundation concepts, we suggest you refer to the recommended reading Appendix for additional guidance. The concepts identified above will continue to be used and built on throughout the book.

Understanding Your Business

How does your enterprise make money? Exactly what products or services does your enterprise provide? Who are your largest clients or customers? Is your enterprise profitable? If you don't know the answers to these questions, then we strongly recommend that you start learning about your business immediately. If you are in a publicly held enterprise the answers to many of these questions can be found in your company's annual report. If you are in a charitable organization, smaller enterprise, or a government entity, you may need to ask around to get the answers to these questions. People you may want to talk to include your public relations staff, chief financial officer, and sales directors.

Here are just a few of the things all of the members of your information security program should know:

- How does your enterprise make money?
- Does your enterprise have any subsidiaries or minority interests in other companies? The other side is also a great question to ask — is your enterprise a subsidiary or minority interest of another company?
- Where does your enterprise usually spend most of its money?
- Is your enterprise profitable?
- Does your enterprise have a positive cash flow from operations?
- Is your enterprise publicly or privately funded?
- How does management decide what products or services your enterprise should provide?
- Exactly what products or services does your enterprise provide?
- Who are your largest clients or customers?

To understand how to best implement an information security program that adds the most value to your enterprise, you need to understand the role your information security program will play in the overall scheme of your business. There is usually a significant cost to implementing an information security program, and being able to balance the operational needs of your enterprise with the business risks your enterprise faces is a critical success factor. This concept is the whole point of the chapter. Throughout this chapter, we will guide you through the process of assessing the business drivers behind your need for an information security program, and how to determine the basic level of information security controls that should be implemented.

Knowing the various drivers of your information security program and their relationship with the business operations of your enterprise is a critical success factor in effectively implementing your program. For example, implementing too few information security controls, when your business drivers require otherwise, can lead to a number of problems for your enterprise. These may include such issues as regulatory non-compliance, numerous audit findings, theft/loss of data, lost revenues, inaccurate data, excessive costs, wasted time, inability to prosecute wrongdoers, and excessive system downtime. On the other hand, implementing too restrictive of a control environment without the requisite business drivers can actually hurt your enterprise. Lost revenues, excessive costs, wasted time, redundant processes, and crushed employee morale are just a few of the negative results that can come from an overzealous information security program.

Figure 1.1 helps to illustrate the costs associated with implementing too few or too many controls.

In addition to understanding general information about your enterprise's business operations, you should also have a strong understanding of its internal financial processes. Knowledge of your enterprise's financial budget cycle and approval process is a success factor that will directly impact your ability to get funding for the initiatives that you will want to put into operation as you build your enterprise's information security program.

Listed below are a few critical items you should know about your enterprise as you implement your information security program:

- How does management decide what internal projects your enterprise should invest in?
- What is our enterprise's budget cycle?
- Who is involved in the budgeting process and exactly what are they responsible for?
- What types of projects or which sponsors typically have the most success in being funded?
- How far in advance should you begin to start marketing your ideas to your key financial decision makers?
- What sort of research, analysis, or supporting documentation would be of most help in persuading these key financial decision makers to support your initiatives?

In determining the balance between business operations and security controls, the next portion of the equation is the concept of risk.

Understanding Risk

Risk comes from not knowing what you're doing.

—Warren Buffett

The concept of risk is often defined using many different examples, types, and forms. Some of the more well-known terms used to describe risks

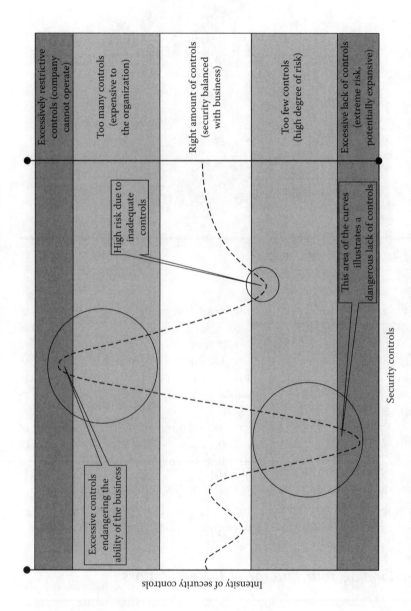

Figure 1.1 Control Result Chart

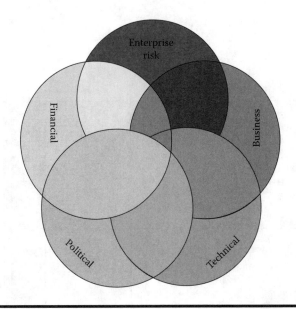

Figure 1.2   Enterprise Risk Factors

facing today's enterprises include business risk, financial risk, geo-political risk, and technology risk (see Figure 1.2). Understanding the various elements of risk that affect your enterprise can be a powerful tool for building support for your program. Understanding the nature of these risks and being able to communicate their potential impact to your business operations can be a valuable tool in getting some stakeholders to support your program.

A number of security vendors use an extreme form of this strategy in trying to sell you their products and services — they employ the use of FUD (fear, uncertainty, and doubt) to scare customers into buying their products. Although we certainly don't recommend ever playing the FUD card, we found that the ability to clearly understand and articulate the potential impact of the various risks facing your enterprise can sometimes help to convert even the most stubborn obstructionist to a champion.

Understanding Your Enterprise Differentiators

Enterprise differentiators are aspects of the business that cause an enterprise to succeed against its competitors, e.g., better product and service offerings, lower prices, faster delivery, better customer service. These are all things that make one enterprise stand out from another. Accordingly, these elements need to be protected because they are either directly or indirectly responsible for generating revenues.

The primary concept is that business requirements drive security programs...not vice versa. To effectively plan your information security program, identify your enterprise differentiators and watch out for information security controls that could have a negative impact on them. The following is a quick example to illustrate.

Scenario

SpamCo is in the business of direct mass e-mail marketing, and derives its revenue from the ability to design and execute direct marketing campaigns to individuals. SpamCo's most critical enterprise differentiator is how effectively it processes e-mail responses from its various direct marketing campaigns. Oblivious of this fact, SpamCo's new information security officer decides they need an e-mail filtering system to cut down on the volume of inbound spam its employees are receiving on their desktops. He researches the various options, chooses the most aggressive one available, and has the engineering staff route all incoming mail through it — including the e-mail responses from its direct marketing campaigns. By not understanding SpamCo's main enterprise differentiator, the information security officer managed to negatively impact a mission critical area of the business, and "won" a big CLM (career limiting move) award.

Analysis

This was an extreme example, but it is clear that the factors that were taken into consideration when determining the use of an inbound spam filter were incomplete. This error was compounded by the fact that it was introduced into an aspect of the enterprise's competitive advantage. Though the initiative reduced the risk, it sacrificed a major component of the business.

Understanding Your Legal and Regulatory Environment

For purposes of this book, we'll define your regulatory environment as being comprised of laws and regulations imposed on your enterprise by outside entities. It is essential that you obtain a solid understanding of the federal, state, and international laws that affect your business. In addition, industry groups, trade associations, and governmental entities often have regulatory requirements your company must follow to operate in a given industry. Laws and industry regulations are often mandatory, and are usually critical drivers for information security programs. As such, they can also be very effective tools that can be used to solicit support for your program. The best resource for obtaining information about the laws and regulations facing your enterprise is your company's legal counsel and executive officers. These requirements will become major factors in the development of your information security program.

Understanding Your Organizational Structure

The next step in your quest to understand your role is to obtain a copy of your enterprise's organization chart — not just for your immediate area, but for the entire enterprise. A quick review of your enterprise's organization chart can yield a large amount of information without much work on your part. What can you learn from your org chart? First, does your organization even have one? If not, that speaks volumes. An organization that has failed to document the roles and responsibilities of their management and staff may not have the control infrastructure necessary to support an effective information security program yet. This would be analogous to a soccer coach placing players on the field without assigning positions or informing the players of their roles. Second, how accurate and current is the org chart? An organization that fails to maintain a relatively current set of org charts may not strongly emphasize maintaining a strong set of internal controls, and may be a difficult place to build an effective information security program. Third, the org chart is an excellent reference for identifying the key players in the organization, their roles and responsibilities, and the areas they may exert some control or influence over. You always want to be prepared to speak to the level of the target audience; not find out who they are after you have misspoken. Finally, review the organization structure itself. Identify whether the following areas exist — operations, information technology (IT), sales and marketing areas, financial operations, internal audit, regulatory compliance, and public relations and their relation to the overall organization. Is this organization centralized or decentralized? The organization structure review is the most subjective aspect of your review, and will be referenced throughout our book.

The functional design of the organization is going to vary based on the business of the enterprise. We are not attempting to provide a lecture on organization dynamics. Our objective is merely to provide some basic techniques that will aid you in performing a cursory analysis.

The best place to start is to compare and contrast the structure to companies that you have been exposed to in the past. What worked? What didn't work? Obviously, this task will be made easier if you have worked at a similar type of enterprise. If not, apply what you think is best. You are attempting to identify potential opportunities or obstacles. You are looking for inconsistencies or lack of standard practices.

For example, after reviewing the organization chart for a commercial software development enterprise you realize that it doesn't have a separate quality assurance (QA)/testing department. Instead, you find that the QA/testing department reports directly to the manager of software development. Looking back on your own experience, you recall having worked in several software development environments and you realize that this organization structure isn't consistent with standard software development principles — there's an inherent conflict of interest. This conflict of interest could negatively impact your ability to effectively implement an information security program. Because of this organizational conflict, it could be that the QA/testing department might somehow be influenced to pass or certify software without adequate testing. The goal here is to identify potential areas within the organization that could impact your ability to implement an effective information security program.

Another thing to consider is where your information security program reports to. Do you and your program report to the head of IT, your risk management office, legal department, corporate security, or business administration? Although it makes business sense for information security offices to report to more senior levels of management, you may very well have a different situation.

Understanding Your Organizational Dynamics

Many people confuse organizational structures and organizational dynamics. An organization's structure is important, and can tell you a great deal about how much support you can expect to find for your program. As a result, you should take the time to review your organization chart and identify areas and people that can directly assist you in the development of your program. Areas you should consider include your legal department, risk management office, regulatory compliance office, internal audit, physical security, public relations, financial reporting and accounting, and IT department.

Organizational dynamics, on the other hand, includes those not-so-obvious things that can have a significant indirect impact on your information security program. After reviewing your organization chart, a great next step is to look outside of your existing organization structure and identify any other people who can indirectly help or hinder you. While your enterprise is the obvious first place to look for these people, you may want to consider external third parties, such as technology vendors, clients/customers, auditors, consultants, or governmental agencies; do not limit the evaluation solely to employees.

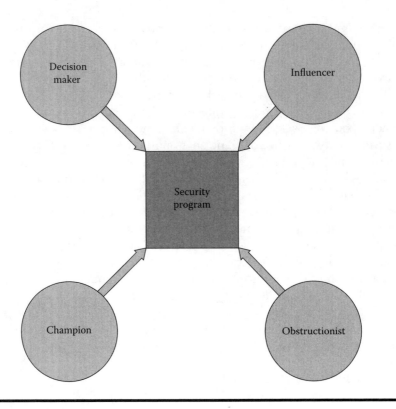

Figure 1.3 Types of People

There are three types of people that will play a significant role in the development of your program — decision makers, champions, and obstructionists (see Figure 1.3).

■ Decision makers: these are people who can directly support your program through their authority or responsibility. These people are typically found at the executive level, and can easily be found by reviewing your organization chart.

■ Influencers: sometimes, you may find individuals who may not necessarily be decision makers, but may have the ability to indirectly influence the outcome of your program — either through their support or through their resistance. These people can impact your program through their relationships with decision makers, subject matter expertise, control over resources, or industry reputation. There are two main types of influencers:

  – Champions: champions are often executive assistants, system architects, legal counsel, internal auditors, and accounting managers or anyone who could have a vested interest in the success of your program. Champions can assist you in implementing your program by allowing you access to the people, resources, and information you need, and can help to sell your ideas to key decision makers.

- Obstructionists: obstructionists, on the other hand, can typically be found where projects and initiatives are supposed to be happening but consistently aren't. We think of them as the defenders of the status quo. Obstructionists tend to possess a significant amount of professional or personal insecurity, a modicum of laziness, and are easily threatened by change. Because change of any kind presents a threat to obstructionists, they'll often do whatever they can to resist or obstruct the implementation of your information security program. Identify the obstructionists in your organization and avoid them at all cost.

Nothing is more rewarding than to watch someone who says it can't be done get interrupted by someone actually doing it.

—John M. Capozzi

The key here is to identify decision makers with the authority, influence, credibility, and responsibility to affect your program — both positively and negatively. Although much of this information can usually be found by looking on your enterprise's organization charts, you should also pay special attention to rare people outside the normal organization hierarchy who can potentially influence the outcome of your program. The most successful program leaders we've seen consistently identify and leverage their decision makers, champions, and obstructionists.

As you review your organization and begin to identify these individuals, there are several questions you should consider to help in identifying your decision makers, influencers, champions, and obstructionists.

- What role do these people play in making decisions in your enterprise?
- What role do these people play in influencing decisions in your enterprise?
- What role do these people play in getting things done?
- What is this person responsible for?
- What has this person accomplished in the past six months?
- Who does this person report to?
- What role does this person play in the budget approval process?
- What is this person's relationship with executive management?

If you're new to your organization, this process will require constant diligence until you fully understand the culture, politics, and personality of your enterprise. If you've been around for a while, then this may require you to take a fresh look at your organization.

Enterprise Culture

For the purposes of this discussion, we will define enterprise culture as the ideals, values, beliefs, attitudes, customs, organizational structure, policies, and processes that are consistently followed or maintained by an organization. It is the combination of multiple factors that create a specific atmosphere within an organization; it is more of a feeling than a tangible, definable element. There are many aspects of enterprise culture. Listed below are some common examples that can collectively contribute to the culture.

■ Work hours
■ Accepted employee interaction
■ Dress code
■ Emphasis on family and work/life balance
■ Décor and lighting
■ Industry mandates
■ Manner of speech
■ Preferred mechanisms of communication
■ Enterprise-specific nomenclature

Though the items listed are excellent clues to the culture of the enterprise, they do not possess the potency of the next four items. With this in mind, we shall elaborate on the definition and ramifications below:

■ How is training perceived within the enterprise? Training will most likely be a significant component of your information security program. It is the primary method by which you can increase the security awareness of the people within your organization. Does management believe in training? How much money will be set aside for training? Will the people be given time to attend the training? And will the people participate or merely attend? You are attempting to identify the usefulness of training as a tool.
■ How are rules, regulations, and policies communicated and enforced? The prime considerations for this factor involve the perception of employees toward the enforcement of existing policies. You need to determine whether the enterprise has consistently held people accountable for their actions. If so, you're in

good shape. This will generally reflect an enterprise's willingness to accept tighter controls. Therefore, it will be easier to predict enterprise acceptance of various initiatives and their related delivery and timing. For example: if you are working within an enterprise that is used to executive mandates, the timing and repetition for the delivery of a new mandate will be significantly less than in a more free-spirited environment.

■ What is the enterprise's attitude toward change? The flexibility of the people in the enterprise toward the introduction of anything new will determine the means, timing, and delivery of initiatives from your program. For example, an accounting firm where the majority of employees have been there for the past thirty years will be far more resistant to change than an Internet service provider (ISP) who has only been in business for the past two years. To most people, information security is a new concept that involves the development of new skills and procedures. The advantage of this, though, is that security is alluring to the average individual. Even if the specifics are dull, the imagery of corporate espionage or crime can seem very exciting.

■ What is the enterprise's attitude toward monitoring? Everyone is concerned with who is looking over their shoulders. A new information security program will introduce security controls that will increase employee scrutiny. Take the time to learn what measures are currently employed and the acceptance of those elements. For example, the employees of a defense contractor are more likely to accept additional security measures due to their conditioning toward monitoring and secrecy.

Understanding Your Enterprise's View of Technology

To the man who only has a hammer in the toolkit, every problem looks like a nail.

—Abraham H. Maslow

Newly minted information security professionals sometimes view technical solutions as the only tool to be used in an information security program. These well-intentioned individuals look for technical solutions to everything, not realizing that a manual procedure or training class may be all that's needed to effectively address a risk. On the other hand, some executives still believe that their trusty Internet firewall protects them from everything and are loath to purchase any new technical tools. For these people we offer the following advice: technology is merely one of several tools that should be used to implement your information security program.

The enterprise's support of technology (or lack thereof) will ultimately determine which technologies can be used within your existing environment. If you are in an enterprise that relies solely on Linux and Open Source software to support their business operations, for example, you probably won't be successful recommending a Microsoft Active Directory solution.

Assessment Methodology

In order for you to effectively implement any aspect of an information security program, it is essential to identify the various business drivers that need to be addressed. Our assessment methodology consists of identifying and understanding those internal and external factors driving the need for your information security program:

- Identifying your primary driver
  - Why are you here?
- Stakeholders
  - External stakeholders
  - Internal stakeholders
- Identifying your external drivers
  - Industry
  - Legal and regulatory environment
- Identifying your internal drivers
  - Political environment
  - Financial environment
  - Technology

By identifying and understanding these areas within your enterprise, you'll have a firm grasp of the drivers behind your information security program. This will provide the basis for the design of your program and the various initiatives you may want to implement in the future.

At the end of this chapter, we present a tool called the assessment checklist. In this checklist, we include an area for you to capture information to help you maintain perspective during this process. This tool will also serve to assist you in gathering the information required in Chapter 2, Plan.

On completing this book, we will direct you back to an assessment phase. Assessment is the first step in a never-ending cycle of continuous process improvement (CPI). Because many aspects of business (i.e., staffing, laws and regulations, technologies) are constantly changing, you must adapt your program to accommodate changing requirements. Because of this, the methodology presented in this book can effectively be used by anyone responsible for building a new information security program from scratch, as well as those who are already part of an existing program.

Identifying Your Program's Primary Driver

> Those who cannot remember the past are condemned to repeat it.
>
> **—George Santayana**

Why Are You Here?

If you're new to your position, or have recently been given new information security responsibilities as part of your job, this is the first question you should be asking. If you don't establish that from the beginning, you're going to be spending a great deal of time behind the proverbial eight ball.

So, exactly why were you hired?

Implementing an information security program is a non-trivial event for an enterprise, usually requiring a significant investment in resources, technologies, and training dollars. Usually, a specific event or trigger caused your enterprise to commit to establishing an information security program. It may be the passage of a new law or regulation, the recent theft or loss of sensitive data, or a costly business disruption from a major virus or worm outbreak. If there is a specific reason, we recommend you learn as much as you can about it. Your initial short-term success may be judged on how quickly and effectively you resolve that single problem. The following is a quick example.

Scenario

No-Down Corporation, a huge ISP, has hired you to establish a formal information security program as the result of a severe virus incident. This event completely halted business for ten days due to insufficient staffing and technical safeguards. The impact was not merely limited to the internal systems of No-Down; all of their customer's networks were also off-line. For an ISP, this is the stuff nightmares are made of. The result of this event was that No-Down had losses approaching $23 million for the quarter, and had lost several of their top customers to a rival ISP. The executives at No-Down haven't been able to determine the exact cause of the event, and aren't sure how to prevent a similar occurrence in the future. Of course, none of this information was made available to you during the hiring process.

Analysis

After reading the scenario above, what do you think is the very first problem your stakeholders want addressed? They're probably going to want you to put controls in place to prevent any future virus outbreaks. If during the first 90-120 days of employment you weren't aware of this and weren't working toward a solution, you're probably not going to get off to a good start with the various stakeholders of your program.

The scenario we presented illustrates a point. There are usually one or two main reasons why you got the job. Asking the question, "why am I here?" establishes your initial mission, sets expectations, and provides some historical and social context to your program.

Stakeholders

Stakeholders are those external and internal bodies who have a vested interest in the success of your program. The stakeholders of your information security program include all of the individuals, teams, departments, companies, regulatory bodies, and governmental agencies that either influence or are influenced by your information security program. Once they have been identified, they need to be categorized. Like any good sports team, you need to know the players and their relative roles and skills. Why do we need to know this?

Types of Stakeholders

Not all stakeholders will have the same effect on your program. There are several questions to consider as you identify the various stakeholders of your program:

- Who is the stakeholder?
- How could the stakeholder impact your program?
- How could your program impact the stakeholder?

These questions are important because they provide insight into the requirements that may need to be incorporated in the development of your information security program. Some of these stakeholders will have mandatory requirements, while other stakeholders may merely have requests. It all depends on your answers to the previous questions.

External stakeholders to consider:

- External clients/customers
- Government/regulatory agencies
- Industry associations
- Vendors and contractors
- Business partners
- Bankers/investors
- External auditors
- Ratings agencies

Internal stakeholders to consider:

- Board of directors/audit committee
- Internal clients/customers
- Executive management
- Middle management
- Technical management
- IT operational staff
- Law department/legal counsel
- Finance department
- Regulatory and compliance department
- Internal audit department

External and internal stakeholders will provide the requirements that you will use to build your information security program. These requirements will help you to establish your strategy, program deliverables, initiatives, and overall program priorities.

Some stakeholders, such as your board of directors/audit committee, executive management, and governmental and regulatory agencies have such a large amount of influence you should take the time to consider their motivations and drivers.

Stakeholder motivations can sometimes be derived through your review of the history surrounding your hiring. Who were the people who felt your position was necessary? What were the circumstances that led them to this conclusion? Is there a mandate from the board for an increased level of internal controls? Was there new legislation passed that made the board of directors want to support the creation of your information security program? What is the new legislation, and what government/regulatory agency is responsible for ensuring your business's compliance? Is there a group of stakeholders who don't feel that such a program is necessary? What do they have to lose by the creation of such a program? Who is most impacted by the creation of your program?

Interviewing the major players is a good next step whether you are building a new program from scratch, or playing a role in an already existing program. The reason is new responsibilities require a fresh evaluation from that new perspective. This is a good habit to establish because opinions change over time with politics, individual experience, and the development of professional relationships. All of these factors can be altered in the background without any apparent evidence.

Here are some additional questions you may want to consider as you meet with these various stakeholders:

- Why is this program important to them?
- What are their expectations for the program?
- What are their short-term goals for the program (12 months)?
- What are their long-term goals for the program (12–36 months)?
- What are the political realities that constrain them?
- What do they perceive as potential obstructions?
- What quick wins would help them sell the program?

These questions will provide a great deal of useful information whether they have been answered honestly or not. How do you determine whether your sponsors have been completely forthright with you during the interviews? Let us use the analogy of a detective to illustrate the point. We have reviewed the evidence, interviewed the witnesses, and now we need to corroborate the stories with the facts (see Figure 1.4).

The best way to proceed is to evaluate the various operations that are run by your stakeholders. Compare and contrast your first-hand inspection of the day-to-day operations, past projects, and staff interactions to that of your stakeholder interviews. Another valuable tool is chatter. What do the staff-level employees think about their boss? Inevitably, you will come across a common theme regarding the way that individual conducts himself within the organization.

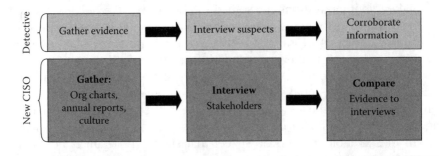

Figure 1.4 Detective Comparison

Let us illustrate the interview with an example. Once again, let us return to our friends at No-Down ISP.

Scenario

As the new information security officer, you will be reporting directly to the chief information officer. However, the chief financial officer (CFO) is very interested in the program. This interest has led to the establishment of the CFO as a primary stakeholder in the program. Below we have listed her answers from the interview.

- Why is this program important to you?
- "We lost a ton of money and prestige as result of the last virus incident. Not only that, it made me look bad to the Board of Directors when I had to restate our projected earnings by 35 percent. I went out on a limb to get this program created. Don't make me look bad…OK?"
- What are your expectations for the program?
- "Ideally, eliminate productivity loss. Realistically, reduce productivity loss to a predictable level."
- What are your short-term goals for the program (six months)?
- "Identify the costs associated with the program and provide a robust ability to audit the environment."
- What are your long-term goals for the program (12–18 months)?
- "Great question, I never really thought about the long-term objectives for the program. I was merely looking to solve some immediate problems."
- Are there any circumstances or issues that you feel I need to know about?
- "The VP of Sales comes from an enterprise that had such a strict security program that it limited the enterprise's ability to deliver product solutions for customers in a timely manner. He suffered massive attrition due to the complexities that were inflicted by the security office. He is not going to make things easy. Be especially sensitive when you work with the development teams, the messaging platforms, or any other element that can affect sales."
- What do you perceive as potential obstructions?
- "As I told you, I had to restate our profitability for this year. As a result, your budget is going to be tight. Make sure you have a strong business case and return on investment for all of your initiatives."
- What quick wins would help to sell the program?
- "Don't let another damn virus get in the door. I don't want to pay that bill again."

Analysis

Based on the interview she is a good short-term ally. However, you have a difficult task ahead. Though she has championed the inception of your program, she is reluctant to pay for it. Her primary expectation is for you to halt all viruses into the enterprise, which could possibly affect the bottom-line. This is a manageable objective that can be achieved over time; but not in the short term. An item such as the education of end-users is a massive component of an effective anti-virus initiative that would be difficult to administer in the short term. Another critical issue that was uncovered was her lack of long-term vision for what the security program can do for No-Down. As a result, it will be difficult to get future initiatives that have extended duration or vast scope approved, both of which are common to security. A little golden nugget from this conversation are the insights she provided regarding the VP of Sales. This is an important piece of information, which will require additional research, making the VP of Sales the next logical interview.

Identifying Your External Drivers

Our definition of external forces is anything originating outside the control of the corporation, which could potentially impact any aspect of the business (see Figure 1.5). These forces are important because they are inflicted on the enterprise; rarely are they self-imposed by the enterprise. As mentioned earlier, this is not necessarily a bad thing. Because these items are seldom negotiable, they represent the finest and purest form of leverage to your information security program. Let's take a closer look.

Regulatory/Audit Environment

Before you can address regulation compliance, you must first identify which regulations are applicable to your enterprise. So, how do you do this? The first step should be to talk to your legal counsel or law department (see Table 1.1). Their job is to identify and understand the various laws and regulations impacting your business and the business requirements you'll need to incorporate into your information security program.

The following list comprises just some of the laws and regulations that you should discuss with your legal counsel. After receiving their guidance, you will be in a much better position to identify how your information security program should address their requirements:

- ■ Sarbanes–Oxley Act. Sources for more information:
  - – http://www.aicpa.org/info/sarbanes_oxley_summary.htm
  - – http://www.aicpa.org/sarbanes/index.asp
  - – http://www.sarbanes-oxley.com/

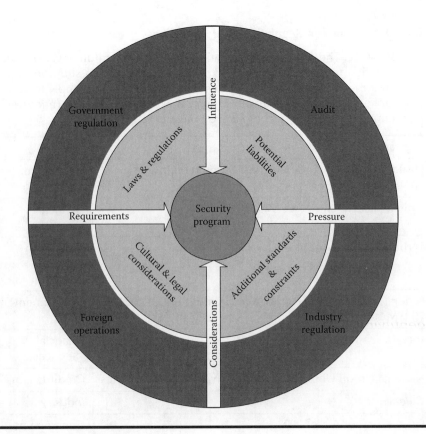

Figure 1.5   External Drivers

- Health Insurance Portability and Accountability Act of 1996 (HIPAA). Sources for more information:
  - http://www.hhs.gov/ocr/hipaa/
- The Financial Modernization Act of 1999 (also known as Gramm–Leach–Bliley Act). Sources for more information:
  - http://www.ftc.gov/bcp/conline/pubs/buspubs/glblong.htm
  - http://banking.senate.gov/conf/
- Office of the Comptroller of the Currency (OCC) Web Linking Guidelines. Sources for more information:
  - http://www.occ.treas.gov/ftp/bulletin/2003-15a.pdf
- National Credit Union Administration (NCUA) Guidelines. Sources for more information:
  - http://www.ncua.gov/IST/ISTrregs.html
- E-Government Act of 2002. Sources for more information:
  - http://www.ssa.gov/legislation/legis_bulletin_112202a.html

Table 1.1 Common Regulations and Guidelines

PLEASE NOTE: The following information does not constitute legal advice. It is provided to you for information purposes only, and to show you the sheer number of laws and regulations that may or may not apply to your enterprise. Your legal counsel should make the final determination regarding your regulatory compliance obligations.

Regulation	Industry
Health Insurance Portability and Accountability Act (HIPAA) of 1996	Healthcare, Insurance
Gramm–Leach–Bliley Act (GLB) 1999	Financial Services
Sarbanes–Oxley Act of 2002	All Publicly Traded Companies
Federal Information Security Management Act of 2002 (FISMA)	Government
sec 17a	Financial Services
National Credit Union Administration (NCUA) Guidelines	Credit Unions
Guidelines	Industry
E-Government Act of 2002	Government
ISO 17799	All Industries
Office of the Comptroller of Currency (OCC) Guidelines	Government
National Strategy to Secure Cyberspace 2003	All Industries

- Children's Online Privacy Protection Act (COPPA). Sources for more information:
  - http://www.ftc.gov/coppa/
- National Strategy to Secure Cyberspace. Sources for more information:
  - http://www.whitehouse.gov/pcipb/
  - http://www.us-cert.gov/reading_room/cyberspace_strategy.pdf
- EU Safe Harbor. Sources for more information:
  - http://www.export.gov/safeharbor/
- Disability Discrimination Act 1995 (DDA). Sources for more information:
  - http://www.w3.org/TR/WAI-WEBCONTENT/full-checklist.html

- Section 208: Privacy Compliance (EGOV) for Federal Agencies. Sources for more information:
  - http://www.whitehouse.gov/omb/memoranda/m03-22.html
- Section 508: Accessibility Compliance for Federal Agencies. Sources for more information:
  - http://www.access-board.gov/508.htm

Now that you've worked with your legal counsel to identify the various laws and regulations that your information security program may need to address, you should also work with them to understand their impact to your enterprise. During this process, you may be asked to provide technical input for your legal counsel, but the formal interpretation of these laws and regulations should come from only your legal counsel or law department. These interpretations may well become cornerstone elements of your information security program. Your role will be to interpret these business requirements into more technical controls that can be implemented to meet them.

Depending on the level of service your legal counsel or law department can provide you with, you may want to monitor industry news and information regarding possible federal, state, or municipal legislation that could be submitted to your legal counsel for a formal interpretation. Once you receive a formal interpretation of the law, the next step is to establish definitions for the more ambiguous elements of the law.

For example, in reviewing the impact of the HIPAA on your business, your legal counsel informs you that there is a requirement the company needs to meet that states, "No protected health information (PHI) can be transferred over open networks unencrypted."

For the above example of a business requirement, you may want to ask some additional questions to define the functional requirements your program needs to address:

- What is PHI?
- What constitutes an open network?
- Does our company currently send information over an open network?
- What is the minimal level of encryption required by this law (will I be able to utilize my vintage Captain Midnight decoder ring or do I need something slightly stronger)?

The good news is that you're not alone in attempting to quantify these nebulous statements. Many enterprises are struggling with the same issue. Your goal is to find the generally accepted definitions of applicable elements of the law that will provide adequate definition to enable the determination of a tangible solution. Laws and regulations tend to be broad, sweeping statements that tell businesses the types of things they need to be doing — but not necessarily how to do them.

Identifying upcoming laws/regulations before they are enforceable gives you a head start in locating the generally accepted definitions. This forecasting also allows for unhurried, thorough analysis, and planning that will be necessary for your security program.

There are a few other things you may want to consider doing as you begin to drill down to identify the specific things your information security pogram will need to address.

- Participate in the organizations or identify the participants who will be creating the generally accepted definitions. Because regulations generally align to a specific industry, the associated professional organizations will begin working toward specific definitions of a law once it is enacted. Another excellent source will be security-based organizations.
- Talk with your vendors. Vendors use any potential new law as a sales tool. They realize the power associated with identifying and participating in the establishment of the associated component definitions. Therefore, they will generally be on the forefront of the formulation to ensure that their products meet or exceed the elements of that definition. Even if they are not directly involved, they will know who is, and what the trends are prior to a general acceptance.
- Watch for companies that are quick to comply with the new laws. Their implementations will be used as case studies, and in many instances will become de-facto standards. This is not merely circumstantial; these companies will apply a great deal of energy, time, and money to ensure that their solutions meet every aspect of the new legislation.

Other External Drivers

Industry Self-Regulation

Not all external regulations will be mandated by law. Some will be the result of an industry that is attempting to self-regulate its constituency. Be aware of the potentiality and include this in your assessment of your specific industry.

Foreign Operations

Given the global economy, more companies have begun to conduct business outside of the United States. This adds an additional element of complexity due to the introduction of the laws, customs, and practices of that specific country. Obviously, the complexity level increases with each additional country in which the enterprise operates. It also raises additional concerns regarding U.S. laws, specifically in the area of technology exports. Examples would include encryption technologies and specific software packages.

Identifying Your Internal Drivers

Internal drivers are the aspects of the enterprise with which you must contend and understand (see Figure 1.6). These are the factors that must be addressed before we can begin planning the program.

Political Climate

> Politics (definition 4): "Intrigue or maneuvering within a political unit or group in order to gain control or power."
>
> **—*The American Heritage® Dictionary of the English Language*, Fourth Edition**

The word, "politics," is frequently used and has come to have a negative connotation. However, it may very well be a driver behind your information security program. To aid in this discussion we have included a paraphrased definition from *The American Heritage® Dictionary* above. It sounds complex, but not any more complex than the daily interactions that occur within your enterprise. We would like to present the concept of corporate politics using a metaphor. It will ease assimilation of the dependencies between the various elements. Our analogy is a professional sports contest between two teams (choose your sport...anyone will do).

Scenario

Here's the line-up.

Stakeholders represent the players on the field. The team for which they play is determined by their professional agendas. Where agendas coincide, there will be the formation of a team. These players do not

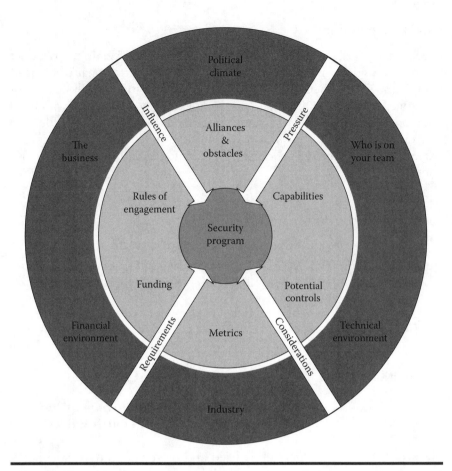

Figure 1.6 Internal Drivers

wear uniforms, have numbers, and are not listed in a program; this is the challenge.

Teams only last the duration of the current game. Further, there are multiple games being played concurrently. Translation: individuals are on multiple teams simultaneously; don't get confused as to which game you are participating in.

The field of play is the enterprise culture. It will define the rules of sportsmanship, length of play, and the manner in which the contest will be officiated. Just as in any sport, the enterprise culture will determine the atmosphere of play; at a Buffalo Bills game, you expect it to be sold out, −10 degrees, and still people will arrive five hours before the game to tailgate.

The audience for this event consists of all the individuals who will be impacted by the outcome of the game. After all, every game has a winner and a loser. The spectators are there because they have a vested interest in the outcome. The audience is not merely comprised of local fans. There are people from other cities: investors, regulatory agencies, and munici-palities. There are scouts for other teams in the league attending the game: industry competitors. Lastly, there are reporters at the game: trade journals and newspapers…they really are reporters.

Every sports team has players on the bench waiting to enter the game. You, as the new information security officer, are warming up to enter the field of play. If you don't warm up properly, you will get injured. The following are the basic elements that you will need to address for a proper warm-up:

- Always pay attention during practice. Practice, for the sake of our example, is the individual stakeholder interviews. These provide the necessary information to determine what games are in progress and which ones are on the schedule. Additionally, you can find who is assigned to each team's roster for each game. Don't forget during your warm-up to pay attention to the crowd in the stadium.
- The fans are watching every play diligently in anticipation of a victory. Not every fan is watching every game. Try to identify the season ticket holders. They attend every game and are obsessed with the outcome. Think of a fantasy football participant. Fans are also important because they provide critiques regarding past games and predictions on future match-ups. Don't be shy about interacting with the fans. After all, they are experts in elements of the game.

After you've warmed-up it's time to enter the game. The time and place for your initial participation is up to you. How you play is also up to you. If your timing is good and plan is sound, you'll score. If you select your teammates and match-ups carefully, you'll win more than you'll lose. Lastly, the more you win, the easier it is to recruit the best players for the next game; everyone wants to play with a winner.

Who Is on Your Team?

> Associate with men of good quality if you esteem your own reputation; for it is better to be alone than in bad company.
>
> **—George Washington**

In a perfect world, everyone is looking out for the well-being of the enterprise. Everyone has the same objectives, perspectives, and principles.

We have never worked at this enterprise; please notify us when they are hiring. The reality is that not everyone is going to support your mission.

Security tends to have a polarizing effect on management. It doesn't bring in revenue. It can create massive operational inefficiencies. It increases the complexity of all tasks. It adds the big brother effect. It applies the concept of ramifications for actions taken. It is difficult to quantify the benefits. With all of this taken into account, you will definitely have people who are not on your team.

Because this is the assessment section, guess what we want to do with these individuals? That's right, identify them. Keep in mind that later on we will be analyzing them to determine their motivations and ambitions. For now, just identify them. We will toy with them later. The best way to perform this task initially is to evaluate the impact of your drivers on the different functional areas within the business.

Scenario

Congratulations, you are the new information security officer for No-Down Corp., the former premier ISP. You have identified why you were hired (see earlier No-Down example). Based on this information you know that you will be heavily impacting the server management department. The server management department is managed effectively, but is understaffed. The manager is a team player who is ultimately concerned with the continued success of No-Down. The other area that will feel the greatest impact from your initiatives is the network management department. They are adequately staffed and trained, but have no control over the events that are adversely impacting their efforts.

Analysis

Based on the scenario, who is on your team? The network management department will most likely be on your team. They have everything to gain without costing them any resource, time, or money. This is the case because the servers provide the primary vector for a virus to spread within the enterprise. As this happens, the network department is adversely affected through the increase in work due to virus propagation and bandwidth consumption. In contrast, your efforts are going to create more work for the server management department who is already overburdened. Though the server department would like to do the right thing for the enterprise, they simply don't have the capacity. Initially, chances are the server management department will not be on your team. We will discuss how to change that later in the book.

The Enterprise's Business

> Never underestimate the importance of money…it's how business people keep score.

—Mark H. McCormack

News flash! The enterprise is in business to make money. Therefore, start at the end. How does the enterprise convert its goods or services into money? The best place to start is by asking co-workers to explain the business processes of the enterprise. Begin with anyone with the goal of identifying specific subject matter experts. You don't need to become an expert; merely identify and establish a relationship with those who are. Your objective is to identify the business-sensitive processes that are unique to every enterprise. A business-sensitive process is defined as anything that can affect the cost, timing, quality, or volume of sales. Further, you need a complete picture of the various phases that encompass the sales process (see Figure 1.7). This lifecycle is the important factor, not the minutia of operational detail. Select only details that lead to the discovery of business-sensitive processes. Additional resources, aside from the experts, that will aid in the discovery process include product brochures, the corporate annual report, Internet articles, and conferences. We will illustrate this concept with an example.

Scenario

ABC Shoe Corp., a U.S.-based enterprise, is a chain of discount retail shoe stores. They make their money by selling inexpensive, designer knock-off shoes. This is a low margin, high volume business; ABC is a slave to its supply chain management. The enterprise's business lifecycle can be distilled into five distinct phases.

1. Buy designer knock-off shoes from Taiwanese wholesaler.
2. Ship the shoes to the West Coast distribution centers.
3. Transport merchandise to stores.
4. Stock shelves with new inventory.
5. Sell shoes to customers.

Analysis

The level of detail in the example is purposely rudimentary. Your evaluation should be just as simplified. As stated, keep it simple and avoid

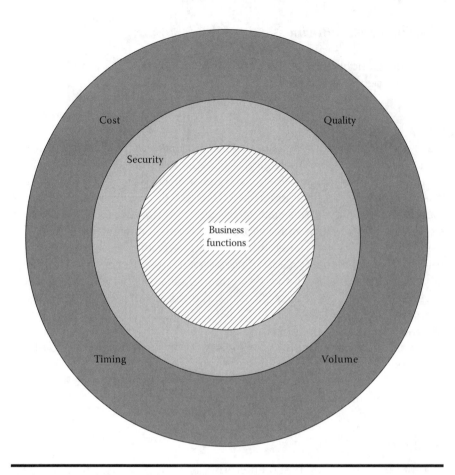

Figure 1.7   Business-Sensitive Processes

getting tied up in the details; remember you're looking for the process flow and the associated dependencies. Based on the scenario we can begin to determine the areas of potential business sensitivity. For example, anything that could potentially impact the consistent stream of inventory to the stores would negatively impact the business.

A disruption to the shipping mechanism could present a catastrophic event to the enterprise if working capital is tight. This is especially important because it is early in the lifecycle, presenting the potential impact to all downstream phases; this could halt the business entirely. In this particular example, you would affect approximately 80 percent of the remaining business processes with any changes to the procurement/shipping phase. These would be considered initial processes because they begin the entire lifecycle for the business. Always note that initial processes that have dependencies will generally possess a higher profile with upper management due to the cascading nature of the disruptions. A prime example would be affecting the sales organization of an enterprise. How many times have you heard a salesman state, "Without me, none of you would have a job."? There is validity to this statement. Moral of the story: be careful when dealing with initiating processes.

Timely transportation to the stores is a necessity for the business. Too much inventory represents idle capital although too little inventory affects the volume of sales. Therefore, any alteration to transportation-related services could impact the profitability of the enterprise. Lastly, we need to discuss the in-store elements of ABC.

A critical component enabling the sales of shoes to customers is the point-of-sales system within each store. This system does not require the associates to authenticate and is integrated into the inventory control for each store. Any alteration to this system can adversely affect the supply chain for the enterprise; once again, impacting the available inventory. Though, this looks like an easily identified risk with an easy solution, it could have a negative effect on the rate of customer closure for the sales associates. We are not suggesting that this issue go unaddressed. What we are stating is you need to exercise extreme caution when altering a business-sensitive process.

This example illustrates that business-sensitive processes can be either macro or micro in nature. Never assume that because something appears to be technically insignificant, its impact will not be highly significant to the business; this can be positive or negative. In closing, let's recap the critical steps derived from this example:

- Identify the major business phases of the enterprise.
- Start at the end and follow the money.
- Identify process inter-relationships.
- Select the business-sensitive elements of the lifecycle — anything that can affect the timing, quality, or volume of sales.

Financial Environment

How are you going to fund your program? There are several factors that will drive your ability to sell and fund your emerging information security program. The lead question is regarding the current financial position of the enterprise. Businesses aren't any different than individuals: if you're a starving student, you'll spend money much differently than if you've just won the lottery. So, what is the state of the enterprise? Is it living off investment money? Is it profitable? What are the profit margins? Is the enterprise privately held or publicly traded? Each of these questions relate to the mentality of the enterprise toward investing in your program. It's not enough for the enterprise to have the means, though that is important; they must also have the will. Let us lead you through the analysis of this monumental series of questions.

Is There Any Money Accessible?

This relates directly to the questions of corporate liquidity. Why liquidity and not profitably? History shows, via the dot-com era, that investment money is just as accessible as money from a profitable corporation. We are merely looking at accessibility to funds. Just because an enterprise has money, doesn't mean that you can get any of it.

There are many factors that can influence your ability to access funds such as the program's primary driver, industry, enterprise culture, stakeholders, and political climate. Although we have already addressed how to assess each of these elements, this additional dimension needs to be included. You've now identified if there is any money and the factors that can influence your acquisition of it. Now we need to address how you get the money.

Fortunately, this information is not difficult to ascertain; it is the enterprise budgeting process. Every manager in the corporation needs access to funds and most companies have a formal or informal mechanism for addressing this need. Because all companies revolve around money, the controls associated with the distribution of money are usually very tightly controlled and well defined even if the process is informal. After you understand the budgeting processes, you need to learn the timing for various events within the fiscal year.

There are many milestone events that occur during a fiscal year that will determine your access to funds. An associated aspect of access to funds is the timing when you require money and when you can get it. The milestones that you'll want to consider are:

■ The beginning of the annual budgeting process
■ The duration of the annual budgeting process
■ Annual budget approval
■ Delegation of financial authority — what is the amount that you are authorized to spend on a single purchase?
■ Corporate spending controls — for example, a budget of $1,000,000 cannot be spent all at once. You may be limited to $250,000 per quarter.
■ Self-determined versus inflicted budgets — will you be formulating your own budget or will it be determined for you?

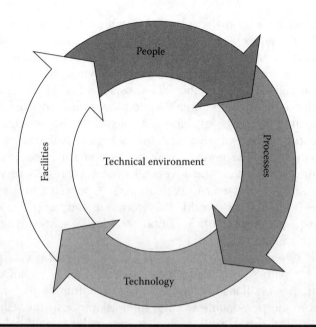

Figure 1.8   Elements of the Technical Environment

The thorough understanding of this process is not optional. If any of the elements listed above seem foreign, then you have some work to do to catch up.

Technical Environment

The assessment of the technical environment is probably the most widely misunderstood area of this methodology. Most individuals view the technical environment merely as the hardware, software, and just about anything that gets plugged into the wall. We would like to propose a broader holistic view of an enterprise's technical environment (see Figure 1.8). Our definition would be the people, processes, facilities, and technologies that are utilized by the enterprise for communications, data processing, imaging, or any other non-human aid that enables the business. This definition broadens the assessment of our environment from a simple hardware inventory to an anthropological safari.

Technology Culture

When discussing people within a technical environment, we need to view it from the perspective of a culture. Though an enterprise possesses an overall culture, there are many sub-cultures within it. The technology culture is derived by the types of individuals, equipment, practices, and beliefs that make up the IT area of the enterprise. Just as it is important to understand the culture of a foreign country in which you would like to do business, the technical culture presents the same obstacles and challenges.

For example, it would be unadvisable to enter a computer department that is populated by a tribe of zealous Apple Macintosh pundits and begin to espouse the virtues of Microsoft technologies. Not only would your message be completely ignored, you may irreparably close that channel of communication forever; Mac lovers take their computers very seriously. This may seem like an over-exaggeration, but people in technical fields tend to live in an on/off world. It is common for people from outside the culture to get turned off and not even know it. So, what types of individuals populate this culture?

Because different technologies tend to be very specific, they often attract people with similar characteristics. Within an IT organization, you may find the personalities that constitute the mainframe tribe are distinctly different from the personalities of the Intel operations tribe. Hiring trends within a technical organization will also impact the overall culture. These trends are influenced by the way the enterprise's business uses technology. This is best illustrated with a few examples:

■ Scenario 1: an online brokerage is dependent on technology for its day-to-day operation. It provides the enterprise's products, distribution channels, and storefront. As a result, all of the products that are developed require technology for the enterprise to generate revenue. Therefore, the hiring practices for the IT department tend to focus on speed, stamina, and the ability to adapt. Because our brokerage is highly profitable, they tend to hire experienced, proven, talented professionals in the prime of their careers; they can afford it.

■ Scenario 2: a different online brokerage that is also dependent on technology for its day-to-day operation. The difference is they are new and currently operating on investment money. The pace for IT is much faster than the first scenario because the enterprise is not profitable yet. Further, they are producing new products at a very high rate to compete with other companies already operating in the space. The resulting hiring practices have produced a trend of acquiring young, hungry, cheap engineers with no social lives. These people are capable and willing to work 16 hours per day.

These examples are generalities used to illustrate the influence the business exerts on the technical culture. Identifying the hiring trends and types of individuals that populate the culture will have a massive effect on deciding the best means of communicating your information security program to the various technology tribes within the enterprise.

Technologies and Facilities

After evaluating the people, we move to the facilities and technologies that make up the technical environment. We started with the people because they will provide the insight and access into the technology. The primary objective is to determine technical trends and additional clues into the personalities of the people who built the environment. The technical trends are the easiest to identify.

Technical trends encompass the consistency, quality, and general condition of the equipment that has been deployed. Every piece of equipment has a reason for existing within the environment and a motivation that placed it there. These trends will be used in formulating execution strategies later in the program. Even the smallest detail can sometimes provide tremendous insights; however, these insights generally come with experience. For example, does the enterprise use leading brands? Is the environment homogenous or best-of-breed? Is the cabling properly dressed and color-coded? Does the cable map include telco and data? Is it current? What is the state and quality of the documentation? Is all the equipment rack mounted? If so, is the equipment racked properly? These are merely examples, but they begin to form a story that we will dissect in the following paragraph.

As you can see, there are a number of technical aspects to implementing an effective information security program. If you do not feel the questions listed above could tell you anything about the technical culture of the enterprise, then you probably do not know enough about technology and the people who operate it. You will want to find someone who you can rely on to help you understand the impact of technology on your information security program. As we stated before, technology is merely a tool of your program. But, your inability to utilize this tool can be devastating. Let's review the questions again and see what types of clues the answers could provide:

■ Does the enterprise use leading brands? Walking into the data center, you notice all of the equipment is new, top quality, brand-name devices. This demonstrates recognition by the enterprise that technology is of value to the business. They're willing to spend large sums of money. This is good news for your program.

■ Is the environment best-of-breed or homogenous? This provides insight into the philosophy of the individuals who evaluate and decide on technology. Generally, companies that subscribe to a best-of-breed concept rely more heavily on information provided by outside sources for decision making, whereas companies that employ a homogenous technical environment are usually driven by the premise of improved product synergies. We are not stating that either philosophy is correct, merely that they provide additional information in putting together the puzzle. The over-arching concept given here is that it will affect the process by which you will introduce new technology into the environment. For example, if the enterprise is solely populated with Cisco equipment, do not expect to implement a checkpoint firewall without a great deal of pain and effort.

■ Is the cabling properly dressed and color-coded? This little tidbit of information can yield a great deal of valuable information. It is an indicator of the quality of work the company is capable of performing and willing to perform. It addresses the issues surrounding time availability to perform quality work. Lastly, it is a direct reflection of management and their due diligence and care of the technical environment.

■ Does the cable map include telco and data? Is it current? This addresses the issue of tunnel vision; how does this organization view technology? Many enterprises' perspective on technology only includes data processing and networking; big mistake. The cable maps will provide insight into that belief. The currency of the maps gets back to the idea of diligence and care of the environment.

■ What is the state and quality of the documentation? This is a big one. Assuming any documentation even exists, which in and of itself says a great deal, the quality of the documentation attests to the time allotted to roll out the implementation. It also provides evidence of the level of engineering, as well as the attitude toward the formal processes used to deploy new technologies. In the future, documentation will become a critical part of your information security program.

■ Is all the equipment rack mounted? Whether the equipment is racked or not tells you the level of planning this enterprise undertakes. It is also another visible display of the perceived value of technology by the enterprise. If the equipment is completely racked, cabled, and fully clean; is there any additional space in the racks? What is the capacity for expansion? Once again, this item addresses the issue of strategic planning. It's like a person's garage at home. If you walk into a garage that is full of junk, what is your immediate evaluation of that individual? In the technical world this should raise some additional questions.

- How would they know if something is missing?
- How would they know if something has been changed?
- How would they know if something is no longer needed?

Technology Processes

Now you know where to look for clues regarding the people, technology, and facilities, we will address the processes used throughout the lifecycle of technology within a given environment (see Figure 1.9). This will break down into four distinct phases: design, implementation, maintenance/ change, and de-commissioning. These processes will have a profound effect on determining your ability to use technology as a tool for your information security program as well as the ability to secure the enterprise. The design and evaluation process is the beginning.

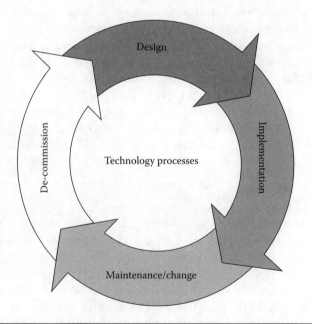

Figure 1.9   Technology Lifecycle

- Design Processes: design is the quantification and qualification of any new technology implemented to satisfy a requirement of your organization. What is the process the enterprise employs for the design, evaluation, and testing of new technologies? You will struggle with the rest of your program if you don't fully understand this process. It may be extremely informal or a full systems development lifecycle (SDLC). Whichever it may be, learn it in detail; it's the gateway to a very important tool set for your program.

- Implementation Processes: implementation is the introduction of new technology where the design is solidified and tested. What are the processes that the enterprise employs for change-control? Is it a full-blown change management system or is it a plug-it-in-and-pray mentality. If it is the latter, find a means of politically insulating your program.

- Maintenance/Change Processes: the maintenance processes addresses the state of your environment and how it is changed. The technical environment is at a specific state or security profile at any given point; think of it as a snapshot. The methods employed to ensure the snapshot matches the accepted risk for a specific point is the primary concern. Remember that a minor change to the environment can lead to a major change in the risk profile.

- De-Commissioning Processes: the risk exposure for an enterprise increases with the existence of additional equipment to the technical environment. You need to ensure, if a device is no longer necessary, that it is removed from the technical environment. Additionally, ensure that there is a method for reporting the equipment removal for your information security program. Subtracting equipment represents the same issue as adding equipment; they both indicate a change that could affect the enterprise's risk profile.

Existing Security Posture

The final concept that we would like to discuss in assessing the technical environment is the current view that is held toward information security. As with any assessment performed in the area of technology, break it down into the people, technology/facilities, and processes. Begin by making a determination of what is the general state of knowledge regarding basic security concepts. This will provide a starting point for your program, specifically the education and awareness elements. It will also aid in forecasting the degree of effort required to create a successful program.

Next, evaluate the skill-sets of the individuals to implement the afore-mentioned security concepts. Just because someone understands the concept, doesn't necessarily mean he knows how to implement an affiliated control. For example, your network manager may understand the need for complex passwords (e.g., passwords with a minimum of seven alpha-numeric characters that have not been used in the past six months), however this does not mean that he understands what technologies would enable the policy nor the means to configure them.

Moving from the people, we'll review the technology. Once again, we start with the people because they provide the clues as to where to begin. Start with an inventory of the security tools that are currently available. Next, review the quality of the implementation. For example, though the enterprise has a state-of-the-art firewall, it only has one rule — allow all traffic. This is certainly not a very effective use of the tool. After investigating the security-specific tools, move to the general computing environment for an inspection of security practices. Examples would include logging practices, authentication mechanisms, and access control. We are referring to common elements of most technical devices; focus on items that relate to confidentiality, availability, and integrity. Keep the assessment simple. Do not attempt to perform a full gap analysis of the current technical environment (this will be covered later in the book). After reviewing the technology, move on to the supporting processes.

The objective of the evaluation of processes is to determine which existing processes will aid your program, which ones will present obstacles, and which ones are missing. Once again, this is not a full gap analysis; only enough information should be collected to aid in the planning of your information security program. An example would be the processes surrounding the departure of an existing employee.

The ABC Enterprise currently has no formal process for managing the access of a departing employee. The event outlined above should trigger a number of processes regarding access and data integrity. What is the process for disabling the account? What is the process for disabling remote access? What is the process for limiting physical access to the building? What is the process for ensuring the integrity of the work performed to date? Identify the key events and review the resulting processes, then compare them to best practices. Moving on to the bigger picture, what have you learned regarding the general state of processes within the organization? Are they thorough? Are there major gaps? Are they misguided? Do they hamper the business? This is going to determine how much work is needed to establish a minimum level of risk prevention. If it is determined that critical processes don't exist, this deficiency must be addressed and incorporated into your program during the plan phase.

Industry

> If you think education is expensive, wait till you see what ignorance costs you.

—Mark H. McCormack

A comprehensive knowledge of your industry will be a recurring and ongoing requirement if you are to achieve a pertinent and effective program. A large portion of your program will be influenced by the industry and its constituent members. Therefore, it becomes a priority to require research in the assess phase. Before moving into full-blown research mode, ask yourself what is your current level of knowledge regarding your associated industry.

The objective of this section is to present a different approach to industry assessment. Even if you have been working in the same industry for some time, we hope to present this information from various perspectives; taking information that was previously regarded as meaningless and exposing the value. This new realization will be added to your ever-expanding toolbox: industry information is an important tool from this point forward. This tool will be used to garner political and financial support for your program. For example, once you have established industry metrics for a particular element within your program, it can be used whether the metric has been met, exceeded, or is sub-standard.

Scenario

You are attempting to justify staff additions for the coming year. On researching your industry, you ascertain that competitors of the same size and complexity have a substantially larger staff.

Analysis

This information now becomes a leverage point for justifying future staff additions; basing your request on industry-established metrics for the size and complexity. If you compare your enterprise to other similarly sized enterprises in your industry, and you find that they have, say, 40 percent more staff than yours, you have the basis for a business case supporting an addition to staff.

If for some reason you are unable to obtain your requested staff additions, this information can become rationale for explaining why your program is not able to achieve the industry average of performance in a specific category. However, if you find that your staff are meeting or exceeding industry averages with less staff than your competitors, you now have a completely different type of leverage — success.

There are many places to gather this sort of information. The first and easiest place is your industry's trade publications.

Trade Publications

This material generally addresses trends and issues that affect large segments of the industry. The key is it enables you to customize your research, studying the items that impact your immediate concerns. Not only will these journals provide interesting and valuable editorials, they are also full of advertisements for vendors you can leverage for additional information. The advertisements provide you with a virtual rolodex of vendors, associations, and conferences related to the specified trade. Conferences are the next most accessible tool, not to mention an easy place to gather a lot of information quickly.

Conferences

Conferences provide a safe environment where some ignorance of the information security industry topic is expected. They provide direct access to industry experts, peers, and vendors.

- Industry experts are an excellent source for presenting macro concepts and the associated debate. They usually focus on emerging trends in a given industry, thus providing an inexpensive forecasting tool. The other area where industry experts are valuable is in identifying the current major issues. They spend most of their professional time identifying and attempting to resolve common problems and issues that affect the majority of the industry. Find one who's an expert in a topic you want to learn about, and try to have a conversation.
- Peers are individuals who share the same roles, responsibilities, and may possess a similar level of authority as you. There's a lot of value in identifying and establishing relationships with your peers — they can provide a nice sanity check by allowing you both to compare your professional skills and your information security program. Most peers are anxious to exchange war stories and lessons learned. Listen carefully; there isn't any reason why you need to duplicate an avoidable mistake that one of your peers is willing to share. They provide a sounding board for the presentation of ideas and concepts, thus aiding in the solidification of your own ideas.

■ Vendors are individuals who are attempting to sell services, products, and information. They are the most powerful tool because of the inherent vested interest they possess for displaying their value; they are eager and hungry to prove their worth to make a sale. As a result, the larger the potential sale the greater the effort the vendor will produce. This translates into mountains of useful data. The other element of vendors that is important is they are identifying and solving problems; if their product or service doesn't address a need then they won't stay in business very long. This makes them an eager and willing ongoing source of information. This information is enhanced by their knowledge of your competitors. Because they would like to have the broadest pool of available customers, they will inevitably pitch or sell to your competitors. As a result, they will possess an intimate knowledge of industry trends for addressing common issues.

Industry Organizations

The next most valuable means of attaining information is the industry-specific organizations. These organizations sometimes manifest themselves as professional associations and working groups.

Professional associations, technical working groups, and industry organizations can help you make contact with information security professionals in the same relative position as you (see Peers above). There are a number of organizations that information security professionals can join. The following is a short list of the many associations that are available:

■ American Accounting Association
■ American College of Forensic Examiners International (ACFEI)
■ American Institute of Certified Public Accountants (AICPA)
■ American Society for Industrial Security (ASIS)
■ Applied Computer Security Associates (ACSE)
■ Association of Certified Fraud Specialists (ACFS)
■ The Canadian Society for Industrial Security, Inc.
■ Computer Security Institute (CSI)
■ Computing Technology Industry Association (CompTIA)
■ Electronic Freedom Foundation (EFF)
■ Forum of Incident Response and Security Teams (FIRST)
■ High Technology Crime Investigation Association (HTCIA)
■ Information Systems Audit and Control Association (ISACA)
■ Information Systems Security Association, Inc. (ISSA)
■ Institute of Internal Auditors (IIA)
■ International Association for Computer Systems Security, Inc. (IACSS)

- International Information Systems Security Certification Consortium (ISC2)
- International Society for Professionals in E-Commerce (iSPEC)
- Internet SOCiety (ISOC)
- National Security Institute
- National White Collar Crime Center
- Network Security Framework Forum (NSFF)
- PKI Forum
- Professional Information Security Association (PISA)
- SANS Institute

Industry Stereotype

What comes to mind when you think of specific industries? Industrial manufacturing is always located in an old, dirty part of town. High tech companies are agile and cool (well, they were much cooler in the late 1990s). Regardless of your industry, it has some sort of reputation or general stereotype. Not being the sort of people who would let a perfectly good stereotype go to waste, we recommend that you discover your industry's reputation and determine how closely your enterprise fits the stereotype.

A recurring theme we present in this book is, where possible, you should always look for potentially advantageous situations and leverage them as much as possible. Industry reputations can be used in just this manner, either by positioning yourself as conforming to the stereotype or as working against it. We gave two example statements at the beginning of this section: high-tech companies and industrial manufacturing.

High-tech companies are often associated with the utilization of cutting-edge technologies within their business. As a result, one generalization you can make about the industry is that people in it typically work hard at fulfilling that very reputation — they're known to use the latest and greatest technologies at every opportunity. This helps to support the enterprise's culture of freely accepting new and different ideas. We say: take advantage of this situation! Where appropriate, you could highlight the use of leading-edge technologies, new concepts, and cutting-edge vendors in your information security program — you might find your ideas may be highly supported by the enterprise's self-image as a cutting-edge enterprise.

The other extreme can also be leveraged. For example, one stereotype regarding the industrial manufacturing industry is they never invest in cutting-edge technologies — instead they rely on older, more proven ideas and vendors. If we were to describe an industry that is the exact opposite of our high-tech nirvana, this would be it. To use this stereotype to our advantage, we could highlight using very stable, mature technologies and vendor solutions to match the enterprise's self-image. This is just the sort of information you will want to consider as we move into the next chapter of the book, Plan.

Assessment Checklist

> The dictionary is the only place that success comes before work. Hard work is the price we must pay for success. I think you can accomplish anything if you're willing to pay the price.
>
> **—Vince Lombardi**

The assessment checklist (see Table 1.2) is a bridge between the chapter on Assess and the chapter on Plan. The information furnished in this checklist will be needed to make decisions in the next chapter. Not completing this questionnaire will reduce the value of future chapters, because they will rely on the gathered information. The answers do not have to be lengthy, just enough to remind you of the thought process that went into the formulation of the answer. To help you, we have limited the responses to one or two sentences. Take the time to complete this exercise.

Table 1.2   Assessment Checklist

Foundation Concepts

Personal Assessment	Sufficient Skill (Y/N)	Book Review	Affected Methodology Phase
Critical Skills			
Consultative Sales Skills			Assess, Plan, Design, Execute, Report
Critical Knowledge			
An Understanding of Business			Assess, Plan
An Understanding of Risk			Plan, Design, Execute
An Understanding of Company Differentiators			Assess, Plan, Design
An Understanding of the Legal and Regulatory Environment			Assess, Plan, Design
An Understanding of Your Organization			Assess, Plan, Report
An Understanding of Your Organizational Dynamics			Assess
An Understanding of Your Enterprise Culture			Plan, Design, Execute, Report
Knowledge of Technology			Assess, Plan, Design, Execute

Table 1.2 (continued)   Assessment Checklist

Assessment Methodology	
Why Are You Here?	**Affected Elements of Planning**
Describe in a single paragraph the primary driver of the security program.	Mission
	Mandate of the program Hi-level strategy Key success indicators
Understanding Your Company	**Affected Elements of Planning**
Industry	**Centralized Versus Decentralized**
What is your industry?	
	Measurement techniques Key success indicators
Describe the stereotype(s) associated with your industry. Complete the following sentence: My industry is generally characterized as...	
	Key success indicators
Organizational Structure	**Centralized Versus Decentralized**
Does your company have a current organization chart? Do roles correspond to responsibilities?	
	Operational versus non-operational

Table 1.2 (continued)   Assessment Checklist

Stakeholders	Program Mandate and Mission
List your stakeholders.	
Political Climate	**Centralized Versus Decentralized**
Describe the political climate at your company.	
	Operational versus non-operational
Who Is On Your Team?	**Centralized Versus Decentralized**
Identify all the people who may be your champions.	
	Operational versus non-operational

Table 1.2 (continued)   Assessment Checklist

Identify all the people who may be road-blocks.	
	Operational versus non-operational
Understanding Company's Business	**Affected Elements of Planning**
Identify the major lifecycle components of your company's business.	
	Mission mandate
Identify the main business-sensitive processes.	
	Mission Mandate Staffing

Table 1.2 (continued) Assessment Checklist

Financial Environment	Mission
Is there money available?	
	Mandate Program size
Are you familiar with all the related financial processes to acquire money?	

Technical Environment	Operational Versus Non-Operational
Describe the technical culture at your company.	
	Operational versus non-operational Skills needed for team Centralized versus decentralized
Do you have the ability to identify technical trends.	Operational versus non-operational
	Operational versus non-operational
List identified technical trends.	Skills needed for team
	Skills needed for team
Evaluate your personal knowledge of the following:	Operational versus non-operational

Table 1.2 (continued)   Assessment Checklist

Design processes	Skills needed for team
Implementation processes	
Maintenance processes	
De-commissioning processes	
In a sentence, identify your company's current view and attitude of Information security.	Operational versus non-operational
	Skills needed for team
Understanding External Forces	**Affected Elements of Planning**
Regulations	**Mission**
List applicable regulations.	
	Mandate Program size Centralized versus decentralized program
Industry Self-Regulation	**Mission**
Identify applicable industry specific regulations.	
	Mandate Program size Centralized versus decentralized program

Table 1.2 (continued)   Assessment Checklist

Foreign Operations	Program Size
Does your company do business outside of the United States? Which ones?	
	Centralized versus decentralized Staffing level
List all of the known customs or formalities of working with those foreign governments.	
	Centralized versus decentralized Staffing level

Chapter 2

Plan

Overview

The plan phase of the methodology is the process of analyzing the information attained in the assess phase and combining it with various options to create a customized information security program for your organization. These options will be presented throughout the plan methodology with the end goal of providing insights into which type of information security program structure is right for you. This methodology can be applied to both new and existing information security programs.

Because every organization is constantly evolving, there will be times when an existing information security program structure must be changed to meet the new needs of the enterprise. Because of this, the information presented in this chapter is designed to be applicable whether you are working within an established program, or creating one from scratch.

To facilitate this process, we will begin as we did in the assess phase, with the foundation concepts that will be utilized during the discussion later in the chapter. The concepts will be broken down into the critical skills and knowledge necessary to attain the maximum benefit from the methodology portion of planning.

Foundation Concepts

As discussed in the first chapter, every section of this book will be preceded with foundation concepts. This section should provide you with why you need to know it, as well as a brief description of each idea.

The information we will cover in the foundation concepts for the planning phase includes the following critical skills:

- Visioning
- Strategic planning
- Negotiating
- Marketing
- Talent assessment

We will also define the knowledge required to successfully complete the planning phase. There will only be two main areas covered, but they are extensive and represent a solid foundation on the topic of information security. It should be noted that a comprehensive discussion of these materials is beyond the scope of this book; a full understanding of this material will require additional study. These main areas include:

- ISC² common body of knowledge
- Industry resources for developing information security programs

Critical Skills

Visioning

Vision is the art of seeing what is invisible to others.

—Jonathan Swift

Visioning is the ability to foresee the completed state of your information security program prior to taking any action to build it. It also includes the ability to know the sort of changes you may need to make in an environment to achieve your envisioned end-state.

Just as a ship's captain needs to be able to envision the destination and plot a course prior to departure, a Chief Information Security Officer (CISO) will need to set a safe course for their information security program. Visioning encompasses evaluating your circumstances, setting a destination, and making adjustments along the way to ensure the correct destination will be reached. There may be clear skies and calm seas one minute, typhoon conditions the next, and your goal will be to steer your ship to your destination. Only under the harshest conditions will the destination be altered.

Your vision is the product that you will be selling to your stakeholders. The more completely you can describe your vision, the more tangible your product will appear to others. This will help you to be effective in helping you sell your vision to your stakeholders. This vision needs to be as complete as possible, defensible, attractive, and meet the current requirements of the business. This is the tangible result of the efforts put forward in the assess phase where you identified the drivers of your information security program.

Strategic Planning

We are going to continue our sailing analogy for discussing strategic planning. Strategic planning is the plotting of an initial course. A sailor would not leave the harbor without a destination and the course required to arrive there safely. The course would take into account the portion of the world that would be traversed, the skill of the crew, the time of the year, whirlpools, storm conditions, the dread pirate Roberts, or anything that could deter the ship from arriving at the desired destination as quickly and painlessly as possible.

You are about to embark on a journey of your own. The destination is the successful completion and implementation of your information security program as defined by your vision. Strategic planning is the ability to plot a high-level course to enable the arrival at the destination in the smoothest and most advantageous way.

Negotiating

For the purposes of the plan phase, negotiating skills are defined as the ability to obtain the necessary components for establishing the foundation of the program. This foundation will include all of the elements required to execute the vision during the life of the program, and includes such items as staffing, roles and responsibilities, level of authority, processes for executing projects, and any required tools. You will probably have to negotiate for one or more of these things, so the skill of negotiation will be a critical success factor in the development of your information security program. To continue with our sailing analogy, you are the captain of a ship and you have a clear destination in mind. However, you don't quite have your ship, a crew, or the necessary supplies yet.

Your ability to get the best ship, the best crew, and the best supplies will rely entirely on your ability to sell your vision to your stakeholders and negotiate with them to support your acquisition of a ship, crew, and supplies. Successful negotiations are best built on momentum of previous negotiations — it's always easier to negotiate for the best crew if you have already managed to acquire a great ship and have the necessary funding to go to a great destination.

Marketing

> Braggin' is advertisin'.
>
> **--Jef I. Richards**

For the purposes of this book, marketing skills are defined as the ability to identify components that are of worth and the mechanisms that will be utilized to publicize them. After all, your program will only be as successful as it is understood and perceived by others. Your efforts to reduce your organization's risk won't be as visible to others as you might hope. Therefore, your efforts can go unnoticed unless it is effectively communicated and marketed to others. Your ability to communicate the positive accomplishments of the program to others is a critical success factor in maintaining the ongoing confidence and support from the various stakeholders of your organization.

Talent Assessment

> The first method for estimating the intelligence of a ruler is to look at the men he has around him.
>
> **—Niccolo Machiavelli**

Scouting talent is matching the needs of the information security program with the available pools of resources capable of meeting those same needs. Having a brilliant vision and an impeccable strategic plan for attaining the vision are virtually useless without the talent to consistently execute it. Your ability to locate, hire, and develop the best professionals for your team is another critical success factor in the development of your program.

Critical Skills Summary

Though there may be other critical skills that may ultimately be needed during the plan phase, we have attempted to highlight the most relevant ones. Once again they are visioning, strategic planning, negotiating, marketing, and assessing talent. Now let's move on to the required knowledge needed to get through the Plan chapter.

Critical Knowledge

There is a lot of knowledge you will need to have before you can effectively implement an entire information security program. Luckily, there are a number of great resources available to assist you during the process. Rather than attempt to list all of these resources, we will focus on what we found to be the most relevant and timely resources you should consider during the development of your program.

ISC² Common Body of Knowledge (CBK)

The first place we recommend starting is the International Information Systems Security Certification Consortium, Inc. (ISC)². The following information can be found from their Web site (www.isc2.org):

"(ISC)² is a global, not-for-profit organization dedicated to:

- Maintaining a Common Body of Knowledge for Information Security [IS]
- Certifying industry professionals and practitioners in an international IS standard
- Administering training and certification examinations
- Ensuring credentials are maintained, primarily through continuing education"

International Information Systems Security Certification Consortium, Inc. (ISC)² defines the Common Body of Knowledge (CBK) as:

> "A compilation and distillation of all security information collected internationally of relevance to Information Security [IS] professionals. With no industry standards for such knowledge, (ISC)² was formed, in part, to aggregate, standardize and maintain such information."

The CBK consists of ten distinct domains of security. They are:

1. Security management practices
2. Security architecture and models
3. Access control systems and methodology
4. Application development security
5. Operations security
6. Physical security
7. Cryptography
8. Telecommunications, network, and Internet security

9. Business continuity planning
10. Law, investigations, and ethics

The CBK is an excellent reference point for ensuring the completeness of design of the various aspects of your information security program. However, it can be seen more as a framework of concepts, not a how-to guide for information security professionals. As with any general resource, it is intended to apply to a broad audience allowing for specific customization. It is an index of major concepts and topics that should be considered in your design. The CBK is a great resource that allows you to determine if the most significant elements of security are addressed in your program.

Other Security Industry Resources

Recently, a countless number of potential resources became available for information security professionals, covering everything from the most technical of implementation challenges to the highest-level theoretical discussions. To illustrate, at the time of this writing a simple Google search for the words, "Information Security Resources," returned over 9,700,000 results. We recommend you check out as many of these resources as you have time for, and pick several that you feel the most comfortable with. Aside from our own site at www.cisohandbook.com, some other resources we recommend are:

- SANS: SysAdmin-Audit-Network-Security Institute (www.sans.org) — the following is an excerpt from SANS's excellent Web site:

   SANS is the most trusted and by far the largest source for information security training and certification in the world. It also develops, maintains, and makes available at no cost, the largest collection of research documents about various aspects of information security, and it operates the Internet's early warning system–Internet Storm Center. The SANS (SysAdmin, Audit, Network, Security) Institute was established in 1989 as a cooperative research and education organization. Its programs now reach more than 165,000 security professionals, auditors, system administrators, network administrators, chief information security officers, and CIOs who share the lessons they are learning and jointly find solutions to the challenges they face. At the heart of SANS are the many security practitioners in government agencies, corporations, and universities around the world who invest hundreds of hours each year in research and teaching to help the entire information security community.

■ The Computer Security Resource Center maintained by the National Institute of Standards and Technology (http://csrc.nist.gov/) — the following is an excerpt from NIST's excellent website:

The Computer Security Division (CSD) — (893) is one of eight divisions within NIST's Information Technology Laboratory. The mission of NIST's Computer Security Division is to improve information systems security by:

Raising awareness of information technology (IT) risks, vulnerabilities and protection requirements, particularly for new and emerging technologies

Researching, studying, and advising agencies of IT vulnerabilities and devising techniques for the cost-effective security and privacy of sensitive Federal systems

Developing standards, metrics, tests and validation programs

To promote, measure, and validate security in systems and services

To educate consumers

To establish minimum security requirements for Federal systems

Developing guidance to increase secure IT planning, implementation, management, and operation

■ SecurityFocus (www.securityfocus.com) — the following is an excerpt from the SecurityFocus Web site:

SecurityFocus is the most comprehensive and trusted source of security information on the Internet. SecurityFocus is a vendor-neutral site that provides objective, timely and comprehensive security information to all members of the security community, from end users, security hobbyists and network administrators to security consultants, IT Managers, CIOs and CSOs. With over 18 million page views a month and 2.5 million

unique users annually, SecurityFocus is the preferred information source for security professionals around the world.
We provide the security community with access to comprehensive, timely, and accurate security information at no
charge.

As we mentioned above, there are countless resources available as
you develop your information security program. We recommend you
regularly check your local bookstores, attend information security-related
conferences, and search the Internet for new resources. However, there
are a couple of considerations you should keep in mind as you look over
these resources.

■ Because there are a large number of resources, we recommend
  you speak with your friends and industry contacts to see what
  they recommend as appropriate for your organization.
■ Because there are so many resources, they all look at the world
  of information security from different points of view, and sometimes have different definitions to commonly used terms and
  concepts. This can cause confusion when you're trying to understand some of the concepts they present and the way they use
  certain words. We recommend you try to understand their definitions of the concepts and words they use, as they can sometimes
  be misleading.
■ The motivations of these groups vary. Some are truly altruistic;
  some will try to sell you something. When you're looking at a new
  resource, we recommend looking at their motive to determine the
  validity or spin of the information they are presenting.
■ When researching a given topic, we recommend using multiple,
  independent resources to validate any information you will be
  relying on.

Planning Methodology

In the assess phase, we suggested you look at your enterprise from a
very high level. In the plan phase, we present a number of more specific
concepts that will contribute directly to the development of the information
security program. This will be accomplished by combining the choices in
this chapter with the information that was gathered in the assess phase,
the assessment checklist. Where appropriate, we will be referring to the
assessment checklist we presented in the last chapter, because it provides
the input necessary for rendering decisions for your unique circumstance.

These concepts include:

- Understanding your program's mandate
- Understanding your program's mission
- Determining your program's structure
- Determining your program's staffing

Understanding Your Program's Mandate

> Mandate (definitions 1 and 2): 1. "An authoritative Command or instruction"; 2. "A command or an authorization given by a political electorate to its representative."
>
> **—The American Heritage® Dictionary of the English Language—Fourth Edition**

One of the single most critical things to identify in your information security program is an executive mandate. This, in turn, provides the power and authority necessary to implement your program throughout your enterprise. This mandate may come in many forms, including a formal memo, a public statement by the CEO, or the creation of a department that directly reports to an executive. It is much easier to get things done if you're on a mission directly reporting to the company's audit committee or board of directors than if you're reporting to the manager of network operations. This power will be the primary consideration during planning because it will determine the authority and responsibility for your information security program.

The first place to look when establishing the mandate is in the assessment question: why are you here. The answer provides insight to who created your position, it's funding, and the political momentum to establish an information security program. The who can sometimes be more important than the why, and helps to answer the question of where the program derives its mandate and power.

The greater the reason for establishing the position, the greater the involvement of executive management. For example, if the reason your position was created is that the network management team is looking for an excuse to play with some cool security technologies, chances are the mandate is insufficient to have a meaningful enterprisewide information security program. The primary indication of the strength of the program mandate is reflected in the organizational alignment of your position.

Organizational alignment refers to your relative position within the company. At what level is your position on the org chart? Your title and position are generally something you have little power to change. However, you must understand your place and the associated power that is available when defining your mission. Your level of authority and responsibility will be a recurring theme that will influence the design elements of the program. After identifying your mandate, the next step is to determine how to best use this power. This is your program mission.

Determining Your Program Mission

The program mission is a definable, achievable end-state that reflects the vision that you establish for the program. It is generally a long-term plan and is broad in its definition. It should adequately describe the ultimate state of the program and the desired objectives. Other characteristics of the program mission include:

- It supports the overall mission of your enterprise.
- It's widely communicated and publicized.
- It provides a broad, sweeping, and compelling vision.
- It should address relevant responsibilities of your program, such as information security and business continuity.
- It should provide the guiding principles for the program.

When defining your program mission, be sure the mandate driving your program is sufficient to support it. Do not set the program mission objectives beyond your ability to meet them. The next topic will be the description of the program mission. This is best encapsulated using a mission statement (see Figure 2.1).

Mission Statements

A mission statement is the written declaration of the intent, principles, and objectives of the information security program mission (see Figure 2.2). Mission statements can provide clarity and direction. When developing this statement, we recommend you keep it as short, succinct, and relevant as possible. Additional things to consider when building your mission statement include:

- It should address the needs of your stakeholders.
- It should describe the program's overall purpose.
- Avoid the use of company-specific nomenclature or phrases.
- It should be broad enough so that all initiatives should align and support it.
- It should last for several years before it is revised.

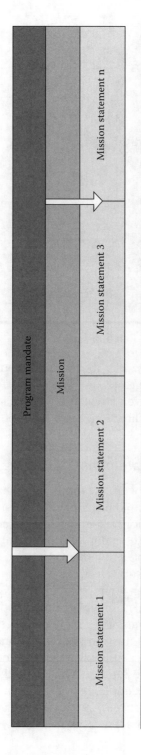

Figure 2.1 Mandate Flow

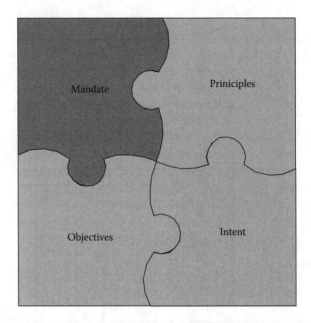

Figure 2.2 Mission Statement Relationship

You must decide what works the best for your personal style. The broader the definition, the greater freedom it will provide for executing the specific initiatives. However, it will also provide less political protection due to its lack of concrete direction; it's a trade-off.

Building Your Mission Statement

Now we have furnished the overview for the program mission, let's discuss some ideas to consider in building your mission statement. Many of the concepts driving your mission statement are based on the information you gathered from the assessment checklist. Table 2.1 illustrates the interrelationships between the assessment checklist, the mission statement, and the initiatives that will support it.

Before you begin writing your own mission statement, we need to address a simple measurement criterion cause and effect. Based on the assessment checklist, you must determine which factors will aid in the completion of your program mission and which ones will hinder it. After identifying the category for each applicable element, you must determine how the program will address them. You can either accept these items or try to change them. For example, if your program has inadequate funds to achieve the desired end-state, you can either adjust the end-state, or work to get more money to achieve your original objectives.

Table 2.1   Mission Statement Translation

Element from Assessment Checklist	Mission Statement Explanation	Impact to Initiative(s) Explanation
Why am I here?	Because "why am I here" is your main driver for having a program, your mission statement should be focused around it. Remember that this is the main expectation of your superiors.	This will only affect your initiatives if there was an event that led to why you were hired. In this case, your initial initiatives will focus on resolving this issue and will then decrease in influence as that factor diminishes.
Stakeholders	Must address the concerns of the stakeholders to ensure their future support.	Your initiatives must align to the support of your stakeholders. Without their support you will never get any initiatives done.
Political climate	The political climate will determine assertiveness that can be incorporated into the mission. Because the information security program represents a change-agent for the organization, it will inevitably alter the existing power structure. Your mission must be sensitive to the tolerance of the political climate.	N/A
Company's business	The mission statement must always align positively to the business objectives of the organization. These items are of paramount importance when describing the protections that you hope to afford the company.	Your initiatives must focus on protecting the integrity and capability of the business. Anything else will be perceived as a failure.
Financial environment	This item speaks directly to the overall capability of the program. It is the fuel that	You can only execute items that are within your budget. Therefore, the financial

(continued)

Table 2.1 (continued)   Mission Statement Translation

Element from Assessment Checklist	Mission Statement Explanation	Impact to Initiative(s) Explanation
	will empower your ability to achieve the overall objective. Keep the mission statement within the budget allotted for the program.	environment affects the overall scope of initiatives and the timing for their execution.
Technical environment	N/A	Each mission will affect one or more of the elements of the technical environment: people, process, technology, and facilities.

It's time for you to start writing your mission statement. Even if it is a rough draft, defining the general tone and direction of your program will aid in some of the decisions that will be required later in this chapter.

Determining Your Program's Structure

Following the sailing analogy, you could think of your program's mission as the destination and your program's structure as the ship you are building to get you there. What are the factors that need to be considered when building your ship? (See Figure 2.3.)

The items we will address and will influence the structure of your information security program are:

■ Operational versus non-operational
■ Centralized versus de-centralized
■ Security pipeline
■ Size of your program

Operational Versus Non-Operational

The first structural issue to consider is the degree of involvement the program will have in business operations. For the purpose of this conversation, operations will be defined as the ongoing support and maintenance of a production IT environment. When an information security program is operational, it is directly interrelated and responsible for those ongoing operations. In a non-operational model, the information security

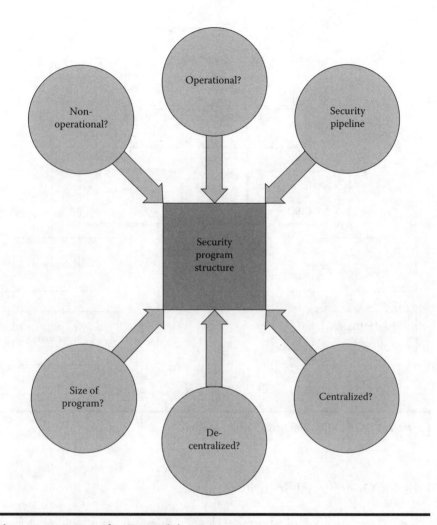

Figure 2.3 Factors for Determining Structure

office is aligned next to the operational teams with no support responsibilities. Let's look a bit closer at each type of security office structure.

As identified above, an operational information security office is generally responsible for both establishing security policies and supporting various operational functions of the overall IT environment. As a result, this can be a very effective means to meet your overall security mission because both operational and security resources are on the same team. (See Figure 2.4.) With no conflicting agendas between the team members, it can be easier for people to work together, ensuring that security is incorporated into the overall IT environment. Let's look at other pros and cons of building an operational information security program.

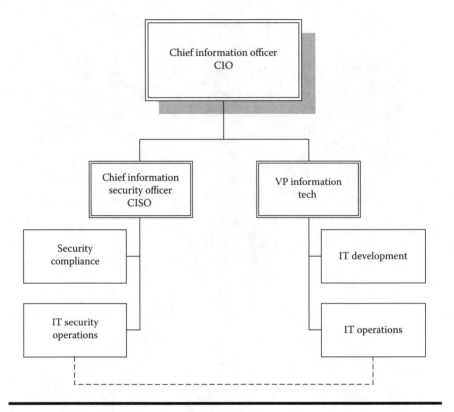

Figure 2.4   Operation Security Office Model

Pros for Operational Security Office

- There are no conflicting agendas and there isn't any selling involved ensuring that processes are incorporated, followed, and improved by the staff.
- The lack of conflicting agendas combined with full access to the resources provides a comprehensive perspective from which to design solutions.
- Generally, enables control of security-related devices and infrastructure. Just as control of the operational staff provides greater continuity between security practices and operational procedures, control of the devices that enforce the company's operational infrastructure supplies similar benefits.
  - The first is an ability to obtain a comprehensive view of the environment; allowing for tighter integration and integrity of security practices into those devices.

- It ensures that security-related initiatives consider business, operational, and security impacts.
- It allows for the quick reaction to security incidents.

Cons for Operational Security Office

Are you sold? Do you think the operational model is the way to go? Hold your horses, it's not all roses. Let us describe some of the potential negative aspects of an operational office.

- If you're running a 24/7 operations environment, you may need to support a 24-hour a day work staff and will need to be ready for that 2:00 a.m. page.
- The mission and objectives of information security and business operations can conflict at times. Typically, operations will be interested in getting things done quickly, cheaply, and effectively. Information security is more concerned with the concepts of confidentiality, integrity, and availability.
- Customer support. The customer's expectation for many elements of operations is 99.999 percent availability. Anything short of that can result in unsatisfied customers. This also ties into the previous topic of conflicting goals.
- The buck stops at your desk. You are now 100 percent accountable for the design, development, test, deployment, and management of any security initiative. If something goes wrong, you're entirely to blame.
- Building your team will be far more complicated due to the increased complexity and interaction of skill-sets required.

A non-operational security office is one that does not possess any authority or responsibility for the continued support and maintenance of the production IT environment (see Figure 2.5). This can result in a security office that functions as a policy, standards, and audit organization, pure risk mitigation as a mission. The goal will generally be to identify risk and to recommend solutions to reduce or mitigate those risks. In this model, the solutions the information security office identifies, will be implemented by resources from outside your information security program by the operational teams. Below we will address some of the pros and cons for a non-operational security office.

Pros for Non-Operational Security Office

- Enables your team to focus on pure concepts and design, instead of operational support. The lack of distractions presented by

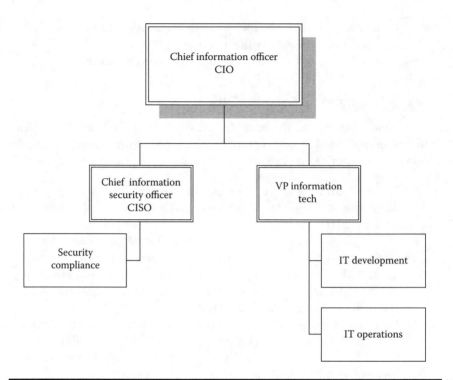

Figure 2.5 Non-Operational Security Office Model

supporting your business's ongoing operations, allows the security team to dedicate their time and energy purely on security-related issues.

■ The skill sets required for a non-operational team is narrower compared to a more operational security office. Because the responsibilities of the office are highly reduced in this model, the staffing requirements will be reduced as well. This will allow you to focus on obtaining only the skills required for the information security program.

■ A greater ability to set the pace of your program. The deliverables do not impact the day-to-day aspects of the business allowing for longer lead times for initiatives.

■ Initial program success is easier to achieve because the security deliverables are not convoluted by the expectations associated with operations.

■ Lower perceived cost of security. This concept is tied directly to the size of staff and the scope of the program's mission. A non-operational information security program will generally have a smaller staff and a reduced cost of mitigation; the costs will be shared across the operational teams.

■ Provides a built-in scapegoat, shifting the blame of failed implementation to the operational teams. We admit this can seem a bit harsh, but it's a reality in some companies.

Cons for Non-Operational Security Office

The negative aspects of a non-operational security office are primarily associated to the lack of control over critical areas that directly affect the program. This is analogous to the batting coach for a major league baseball team. You can teach the players how to hit a home run, but ultimately the batter needs to execute your instructions; this can be monumentally frustrating based on the talent and accountability of the team. So let's outline some of the other issues that detract from a non-operational security office.

■ Lack of ability to schedule and prioritize execution. Because the priority of operations is the maintenance and support of the IT environment, security will generally take second place in any contest. The agendas of the separate managers can conflict, thus affecting the priority of tasks.

■ Availability of resources. Resources are a fixed commodity. Just because you have the blue print for the ultimate security widget, doesn't mean that the resources are available to implement it.

■ Quality of resources. Just as all of your security initiatives are not the same, not all IT professionals possess the same skill, aptitudes, and work ethic. You are dependent on someone else in the operational areas to staff, manage, and execute your plan. Make sure the people responsible for executing your initiatives are on your team (refer to your assessment checklist) or you can be confident that you'll receive inconsistent results.

■ You own the risk, but not the ability to mitigate it. For example, if you identify a risk and present the operational teams with the mitigation plans, failure to prevent an occurrence of the risk is often still your responsibility.

■ Requires strong planning to be effective.

■ Higher real cost of security. The reason for this is the increased bureaucracy and complexity of communication that will enviably result from working through proxies.

■ Ensuring continued security integrity is difficult once a solution is deployed to the operational teams.

Obviously, the pros and cons we have listed above are generalizations, and will vary based on the intricacies of your company, including the size and political climate of your enterprise. Fortunately, you have already gathered the information that you need to feed this decision the assessment checklist. Remember no single issue will answer this question; the answer will come from a combination of factors. Listed below are some of the major components to consider in the decision.

Size of Your Enterprise

The size of the company will affect your decision solely based on the quantity of resources available to accomplish IT functions. A small company generally will not have the ability to support separate organizations for information security and operations, and may require that they are combined. Therefore, it is imperative that you clearly define the roles and responsibilities, along with the corresponding authority, for each.

Political Climate

Hell hath no fury like a bureaucrat scorned.

—Milton Friedman

The political climate addresses two very important questions for determining the operational status of the information security program.

1. Do the operational teams support your enterprise's information security program?
2. What is the operational team's capacity for impeding or hindering your initiatives?

Do the Operational Teams Support Your Enterprise's Information Security Program?

A non-operational model relies solely on the operational teams to execute the designs and strategies of the information security program. If the operational teams support your program, you will most likely not need to design an operational aspect in your information security program. However, if the information security program does not enjoy a large degree of support from the operational teams, you may want to consider implementing an operational security office. It may be the only way to effectively implement one or more of the initiatives of your information security program. If this is the case, the following is the next logical question.

What is the Operational Team's Capacity for Impeding or Hindering Your Initiatives?

As stated above, if your information security program is non-operational and the operational teams do not support the objectives of your program, what are the alternatives?

Try the following:

- Communicate the various drivers of your program, including the laws, regulations, risks, and other business drivers that caused the information security program to be created in the first place. Keep doing this and you'll eventually develop a few champions for your program. These champions can help you in getting additional support of operational management.
- Communicate the mandate behind your information security program and the people supporting it.
- Tailor your information security requirements to the operational teams, and clearly document the operational aspects of your program.
- Co-develop your operational information security processes and initiatives with your champions. Co-present these processes and initiatives to management with their help.
- If you have an internal audit department, they can also help you to get through political hurdles like this. They can help you in communicating your program's mandate to any unsupportive operational managers.

Centralized Versus Decentralized

The next issue that we would like to address is the decision of whether your information security program should use a centralized or de-centralized authority model. These authority models refer to the accountability, responsibility, and control for the enactment and enforcement of the information security program. Before proceeding, we would like to note that this decision might not be yours; it may have been pre-determined by executive management. If it has been, the information below will help you manage within that structure or aid in your ability to change to the desired structure. If the decision is yours, this information should help you determine the best course of action for your information security program. Let's begin with the definitions of the two choices.

A centralized security office is wholly responsible for the security function of the entire company. In contrast, a decentralized information security office has multiple offices or divisions located throughout the company that are individually responsible for the security function. So how do you choose between the two authority models? As we stated above, there is only one question that needs to be answered to make the determination between a centralized and a de-centralized security office model, which is:

■ What is the degree of autonomy of each business unit?

This question is pertinent as it relates to your ability to apply the information security program to the enterprise. This is due to the amount of authority that will be at your disposal to enact and enforce the program. For example, if the business units are independent and autonomous, such as in the case of independent subsidiaries, you simply lack enough authority to influence their decisions. This is the result of the mandate and mission of the information security program. Your program's mission speaks to your responsibility for the execution of the information security program, although your program's mandate can be a source of authority for accomplishing the mission. Although many people tend to focus on the acquisition of authority, ownership of the responsibility is the issue that needs to be addressed; this raises a key, recurring concept: authority must be at least equal to responsibility.

If these two elements are not equal, your chances of success decrease. Think of a police officer who is responsible for stopping crime, but lacks the authority to make an arrest. It just doesn't work. Therefore, you should identify the necessary level of authority needed to successfully meet the responsibilities specified in the mission. Next, you must communicate your need for this authority clearly and concisely to executive management. Don't expect management to understand the level of authority that is needed for the mission to be met. If you are unable to obtain the authority required to complete the mission, then renegotiate either the responsibilities or the authority. The means by which you can accomplish the renegotiation is the authority model. The model that you choose will allow for the distribution of responsibility to other entities, lowering your responsibility to match your level of authority. This model can manifest itself into three variations:

■ Centralized model with exclusive ownership of the responsibility (see Figure 2.6).
■ De-centralized model with exclusive ownership of the responsibility residing in a single office (see Figure 2.7).
■ De-centralized model with ownership of the responsibility distributed among a number of offices (see Figure 2.8).

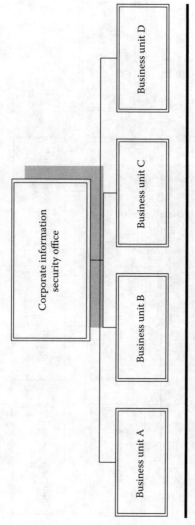

Figure 2.6 Centralized Authority Model

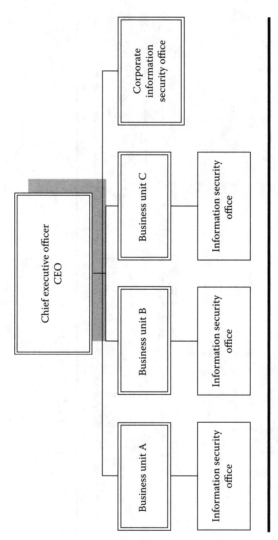

Figure 2.7 De-Centralized Authority Model

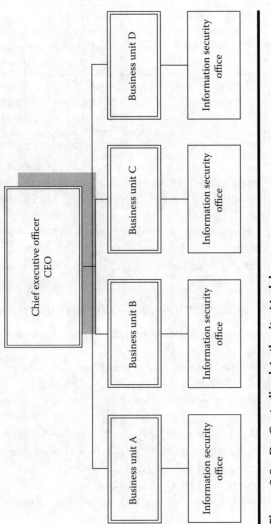

Figure 2.8 De-Centralized Authority Model

Table 2.2   Authority Model Comparison

Authority Model	Authority/Responsibility Equation	Explanation
Centralized model	Authority = responsibility	This is a good model when the two are equal.
Decentralized model with exclusive ownership	Raise authority to = responsibility	The exclusive ownership of responsibility in a decentralized model borrows the authority from the other business units.
Decentralized model with distributed ownership	Lower responsibility to = authority	Lack of centralized ownership distributes the responsibility thus reducing it to your individual program.

Table 2.2 illustrates a comparison of the different models.

Obviously, a single point of ownership is preferable, allowing for a higher degree of continuity between security initiatives. However, it is better to forgo this design than to pursue it without the proper balance of authority and responsibility. Now that you understand the interrelationship of the mission, responsibility, authority, and the authority model, we'll discuss some additional reasons for selecting one model over the other.

Common Reasons for Choosing a Centralized Model

■ A company that participates within a single industry with a single product line
■ If the company is highly risk sensitive [i.e., Central Intelligence Agency (CIA), National Security Agency (NSA)]
■ If the information security program is not resource constrained (i.e., people and budget)
■ If other areas of the company do not possess the requisite skills to perform aspects of the information security program
■ If the individuals that will be responsible for the distributed portions of the program are not on your team
■ If your information security program is operational

Common Reasons for Choosing a De-Centralized Model

■ A company that has multiple divisions engaging in different industries
■ If your information security program is not operational
■ The information security program is resource constrained (i.e., people and budget)

- If the individuals who will be responsible for the distributed portions of the program are on your team
- If other areas of the company possess the requisite skills to perform aspects of the information security program
- If the information security program has strong security policies

As you can see, this complex issue may require you to consider relevant empirical data, as well as your intuition. Either model may work in any type of environment; the trick is to select the one that provides the greatest balance between your explicit authority and responsibility. Some elements you will not be able to control, others will be determined through politics, others will need your direct involvement to ensure the desired outcome.

We hope we have given you a different perspective on evaluating your specific situation. As we said before, there is no single solution for every organization. No matter what the situation, the success or failure of the program will always return to the authority/responsibility equation.

Security Pipeline

The security pipeline represents the concept of the creation, implementation, and measurement of the initiatives you have identified as part of your information security program. It enables the infusion of security elements into the many aspects of IT in your enterprise. The reason we discuss the pipeline in the planning chapter is to illustrate how your information security program will participate. Participation in every phase of the pipeline is mandatory. The manner in which they are addressed will aid in the structure of the information security program. The pipeline uses a construction analogy to describe its major sections: architecture, maintenance, and inspection (see Figure 2.9).

Architecture

Architecture is the technical design that is incorporated into a product, process, procedure, or facility. To fulfill this role, there must be a mechanism by which the security requirements are built into the requirements. This is best illustrated by the following scenario.

Scenario

Your company has decided to build a new Web-based sales portal to enable customers to purchase widgets over the Internet. Listed below are some of the functional requirements that are included.

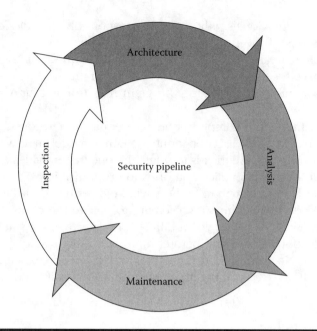

Figure 2.9 Security Pipeline

Operational requirements:

- Customers need to be able to view and purchase their widgets.
- Customers need to be able to pay for their purchases via credit card.
- The application will be Web-based.
- The application must be able to support 1,000 simultaneous customers.
- The application must be available 24/7.

Security requirements:

- The system must prevent unauthorized access (confidentiality).
- The system must prevent unauthorized disclosure (confidentiality).
- The personal and financial data collected from customers is protected (confidentiality).
- The system must be highly available (availability).
- The data delivered to customers is accurate (integrity).

Analysis

The goals of the operational requirements are substantially different from those of the information security program. The operational requirements address the issue of providing the customers with a mechanism for purchasing widgets over the Internet. The security requirements speak to the issue of reducing risk to the enterprise by addressing the confidentiality, integrity, and authorization of the customer's purchases. This results in the incorporation of security without providing a single technical solution to the development teams. The moral of the story is he or she who controls the requirements, controls the project. This is the distinction for the architectural area of the pipeline; it is solely concerned with the incorporation of security elements into new work. Keep in mind that this is the single most important area to control when considering the introduction of security into any new endeavor. If security isn't included at this point, it will often never be fully incorporated into the solution.

The incorporation of security requirements is mandatory for the success of your program; therefore, we have furnished the following to aid in accomplishing this task.

- Include the security office on the project planning teams.
- Provide tools to the development teams providing the knowledge for building in the security requirements [i.e., checklists, training, Systems Development Life Cycle (SDLC)].
- Ensure that the security office is part of the final approval process for the design requirements. This is another example that authority must be greater than or equal to responsibility.

Please note we do not address the actual construction. As long as your requirements are part of the plan, they should be included in the final product. If your requirements are not fully implemented, this will be detected during the inspection portion of the pipeline. Moving on, the next portion of the pipeline that we would like to discuss is the maintenance section.

Maintenance

The incorporation of security principals into the daily operational activities of the IT organization is the definition of the maintenance phase of the pipeline. In this phase, we are specifically interested in the change control process of on-going operational systems.

Systems originally architected with security requirements can mutate into unsecured elements for the environment. Every change to the environment holds the potential of exposing a new risk to the organization. This defines an area that requires security integration. Below are some of the options for achieving this task.

■ Create a formal change control process if none exists.
■ Ensure that the security office participates in the change control process.
■ Establish the ability for the security office to veto changes that pose a high risk to the organization. This is another example that authority must be greater than or equal to responsibility.

Lastly, we'll discuss the inspection phase of the pipeline.

Inspection

Inspection is the means by which all existing processes, tools, and procedures are measured and graded. It is where the company's true risk profile is determined. The reason this area is entitled inspection, instead of audit, is because it can refer to daily tasks to provide insight into the security profile of the company instead of relying exclusively on formal point-in-time audits. An example of this type of duty would be the daily review of server logs or automated reports. Though this is a type of audit function, the resulting data is far too detailed to be included into a more general IT audit. This portion of the pipeline is a critical area of participation for the security office because it catches any potential risk that was not addressed in architecture, construction, or maintenance.

The level of participation will be determined by whether an internal audit function exists within the company. Because the level of participation is dependent on the existence of an internal audit function, we have separated the requirements of incorporation into different lists.

An organization without an internal audit function:

■ Establish a formal audit of computer controls.
■ Establish reporting systems and metrics for sensitive functions (this area is covered extensively in the reporting chapter).
■ Incorporate findings from previous audits into the architecture of new initiatives.
■ Enforce the remediation of any findings from audits.

An organization with an internal audit function:

■ Establish a common nomenclature with the internal audit department.
■ Establish a single set of security requirements acceptable to both audit and your information security program.

- Ensure that the leader of the audit function is on your team.
- Negotiate findings with audit before they are published.
- Establish the level of responsibility for the remediation of findings.
- Incorporate any audit findings into the architecture of new initiatives.

In closing, even if your authority to direct the architecture and maintenance is minimal, a formal inspection process can sometimes compensate for these deficiencies. However, relying exclusively on the inspection process can create windows of opportunity for a risk to emerge and to be exploited. Conversely, the participation in the architectural and maintenance phases of the pipeline practically guarantees that any identified risks are addressed quickly; limiting any window of opportunity for further risk. A well-balanced program will participate in each section of the pipeline.

Size of Your Program

The next component of the information security program structure is the size of the program. When discussing the size, we are referring to the quantity of the staff. Up to this point all of the factors we have discussed (operational versus non-operational, centralized versus de-centralized, and participation within the security pipeline) all contribute to the determination of the staff size of the program.

The size of the program is a relative term. Several factors contribute to this determination. The first factor is the proportional size of the company population. For example, if the company has 50 people, a large information security program could be defined by as few as five employees or 10 percent of the staff. Another method for judging the relative size of the program is by using industry-based metrics for companies of similar size, complexity, and industry.

Size is also influenced by the relative size of other entities within the company. For example, if the audit department has fifty people and the network operations department has fifty people, then the group of three people who comprise the security office will be viewed as small. Only you will know what is correct for your specific situation. We merely would like to discuss the issues associated with each choice.

Large Program Considerations

See Figure 2.10 for information on considering a large program.

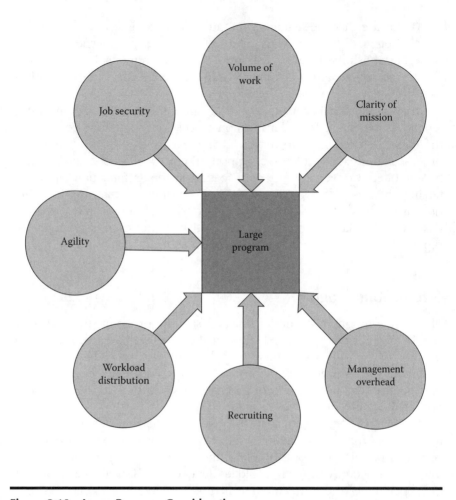

Figure 2.10 Large Program Considerations

Volume of Work

The most obvious consideration of a large information security program is the amount of work it can complete. A large staff can be spread to a myriad of initiatives providing the program with quantum leaps in it's progression of the mission.

Workload Distribution

A seldom-discussed benefit of a large team is the ability to distribute the workload effectively for a given set of circumstances. This achieves three objectives:

1. It allows resources to be redirected toward key initiatives while maintaining other initiatives at sufficient levels.
2. It allows cross training of critical functions, protecting the organization from disaster or attrition.
3. It establishes the separation of power through checks and balances.

Job Security

An esoteric benefit of a large information security program is the inherent job security that can be attributed to any large organization. Generally, once a large program has been established within a company, it becomes very difficult to remove it completely. The program may shrink or change missions, but the chances of it being completely dissolved are much less when compared to a small, specialized information security program.

Agility

The larger the security organization the harder it becomes to alter course. This speaks directly to the issue of changing focus, direction, and priorities for the organization. The primary reason revolves around the ability to clearly and accurately share the vision of the new direction. Everyone will receive the information within the context of their daily jobs; interpreting the new direction differently. The more people within the organization, the greater the variation of views toward the new vision resulting in conflict and confusion. The size of the staff is a direct influence on the agility of your organization.

Staff size is generally a reflection of the degree of responsibility entrusted to the information security program; the greater the variation in the responsibilities, the larger the staff. As the responsibilities begin to vary for the program, the amount of integration with other areas of the company will increase. This dependency will complicate the ability of your program to modify its direction. It's just like a tree; the larger and more deeply rooted the tree, the harder it is to relocate. Another consideration that we would like to discuss is the degree of visibility associated with a large program.

The problem and the blessing with large information security programs is they attract a great deal of attention. This increase in visibility makes any change more difficult due to the amount of opinions that will be offered regarding the change. This increases the amount of sales preparation that must be completed prior to any alteration.

Management Overhead

Large security organizations have a higher degree of bureaucracy associated with them. Management overhead will manifest itself as additional levels of management structure, reviews, authorizations, meetings, HR issues, and everything else that's fun about being a manager. The increase in the intricacies is not linear: one additional employee does not equate to one additional degree of overhead. It more closely represents an exponential curve because one issue will generate multiple associated issues. As the number of difficulties increases, the amount of time allotted to address each individual issue is reduced further, compounding the situation.

Clarity of Mission

As the program increases in size, the mission begins to become diluted. This is due to the increased scope and level of responsibilities associated with a large program. Companies do not generally like a large staff for a single mission. There will always be an attempt to fully utilize the staff, resulting in the assignment of additional responsibilities that can convolute the original mission. For example, a security organization responsible for risk management for the entire company is given operational responsibility for software development. These two areas have separate missions that often do not support one another. The result is the two missions will be blended to achieve operational efficiencies, obscuring the original direction that was purely security based.

Recruiting

Recruiting is the lifeblood of your program. Recruiting is a difficult skill to master and recruiting for security is down-right hard, even for a seasoned pro. The reason is modern IT security is a relatively new field. As if it wasn't hard enough, let's add an additional level of complexity — statistical probability.

The bell-shaped curve applies to IT security professionals just as it does for every other discipline. Statistically, the majority of candidates available for any given position will be of average or below average skill. This leads us to the following conclusion: the larger the information security program, the more difficult it will be to staff it with quality professionals.

Small Program Considerations

See Figure 2.11 for information on considering a small program.

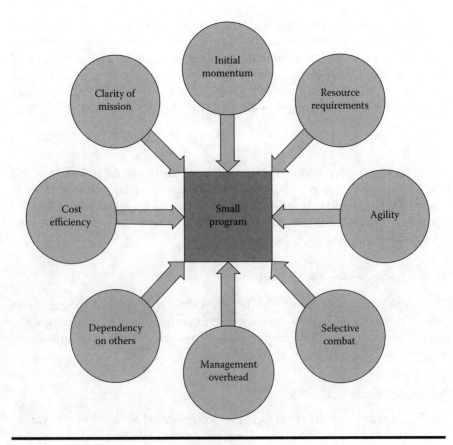

Figure 2.11 Small Program Considerations

Initial Momentum

A small information security program has a distinct advantage during the initial development of the program. A smaller team will generally have fewer responsibilities allowing a concentrated effort on critical aspects of the program. This equates to a rapid, focused delivery of quality components early in the program's life. The resulting perception to executive management is that the security office is running a lean, effective, well-managed team of security professionals; this reflects well on their choice of chief information security officer (CISO).

Clarity of Mission

The aspect of focus was briefly mentioned during the discussion on initial momentum. Every organization must face this ongoing issue. The small information security program will have an easier time maintaining its focus due to the limited capacity of the team. Simply stated, the team will not have the bandwidth to accommodate issues that could alter the focus of the program. Because there are fewer initiatives executing at any given time, the amount of attention that can be directed toward individual issues is much greater. This usually will result in a higher quality deliverable.

Agility

It is a generally accepted principle that small teams are capable of altering their direction far more quickly and efficiently than large teams. This is due to the simplified nature of communication and coordination for smaller groups. The smaller the team, the easier it will be to reconfigure them to accommodate the change in mission.

Less Management Overhead

This item speaks for itself. The fewer people that require management attention, the lower your management overhead will be. This greatly simplifies the initial efforts for a new information security program, allowing you to concentrate on issues of high value.

Resource Requirements

Staffing a small security team becomes complicated because of the varied skills that will be needed regardless of the size of the team. There are certain skills that the team must have in order for the program to succeed. A small team will demand a higher diversity in skills for each member. You will need players who can play multiple positions. This will make staffing a far more challenging exercise. These types of people are difficult to locate and are generally more expensive. Additionally, because the team is small, there isn't any room for errors in staff selection; each position is more valuable. We will address the specifics of staffing in the next section of this chapter.

Cost Efficient

The small information security program will consistently be viewed as less expensive by upper management because of the small overhead component of the program. This does not mean the program is truly less expensive; it is only perceived to be less expensive. The reason for this is the work and costs are shifted to other groups within the IT structure. The work still needs to be completed, but the cost of the work is spread through more than one budget.

For example, a small information security office that utilizes the network team to enforce perimeter security for the organization. The implementation of security policy is transferred to the operational team, thus transferring the cost associated with performing that function. This creates the illusion of reducing the expense of the security office. The moral of the story is if you choose a small information security program, the ability to use the resources of other teams is mandatory.

Dependency on Others

As stated above, the limited capacity of the information security program will increase its dependency on other departments within the company. To accomplish the initiatives of the program, the resources to complete the work are beyond your direct control.

For example, a small, non-operational program will require the operational teams to execute all of the physical implementation. This dependency will often create friction between the security office and the operational teams that will only increase over time. The increase is a result of the security office moving from strategic planning to tactical execution. We will address the shift in focus in Chapter 4, Execute.

Selective Combat

The lack of capacity combined with the dependency on others will force the security office to be selective about the initiatives to undertake. Security has a tendency to increase the complexity of everything, resulting in reluctance on the participants. All of these elements equate to the need to select the right place and time to exercise the limited energy and political influence of the program.

Conclusion

The ideas above are not meant to discourage or encourage an information security program of either size; they are merely considerations that must be acknowledged for proper planning of the program. For every decision, try to mind the ramifications that will result for the overall program.

Common Security Responsibilities

During the discussion on program structure, we addressed eight of the ten domains of information security. The final two aspects, Business Continuity Planning (BCP) and physical security, have been placed in this section together due to the variable nature of their placement within organizations. If your company plans to assign BCP and physical security management to the security office, they will need to be considered in the structure of the program. Some companies do not place either of these items within the security office, scattering them to departments such as plant management, compliance, and operations.

Information Security Program Structure Summary

There are quite a few considerations when planning the structure of your information security program. Though we have discussed many concepts and permutations, we have attempted to distill the core elements that need to be considered and balanced against the overall mission of the information security program. In closing, we would like to re-focus on the core decisions.

- Operational versus non-operational
- Centralized versus de-centralized
- The security pipeline
- Size of your program
- Common security responsibilities

Once you have evaluated your company and answered these questions, you are now ready to move on to the acquisition of the talent necessary to meet the mission of the program.

Determining Your Program's Staffing

> People who work together will win, whether it be against complex football defenses, or the problems of modern society.
>
> **—Vince Lombardi**

Staffing refers to the process of defining and obtaining professionals with the skills necessary to achieve the objectives of the information security program. This is analogous to drafting new players for your professional sports team. As the owner of the team, you need to ensure the new players who are drafted possess the skills and attributes that are lacking on the team. Additionally, you must ensure that you are drafting the right positions. For example, if your football team needs a good quarterback, drafting the best available linebacker in the league does very little to fulfill the need of the team. To successfully bring in a good quarterback, five things need to occur:

1. Define the roles and responsibilities for your team members.
2. Perform a gap analysis of the current team (if you already have one).
3. Identify all of the potential sources for available talent.
4. Evaluate the candidate to confirm their skills, attitude, and general fit for the position on the team.
5. Hire the best candidate for the job.

Define the Roles and Responsibilities of Your Team Members

The requirements for staffing provide the benchmark for evaluating potential candidates. Many elements can help you define the roles and responsibilities of the team you may be putting together for your information security program. If you are a member of an already existing team, these elements may help to refine the individual roles and responsibilities of existing team members.

The first of these elements is an understanding of certain attributes that help the information security professional to succeed in the various roles they may be responsible for. Once you have identified the various attributes you'll want to match with your defined roles, you will need to address the application of the roles within a given program structure, as outlined in the previous section of this chapter. Let's begin by discussing the critical attributes that will help your team to succeed in the various roles typically found within an information security program.

Critical Attributes

Critical attributes are those skills, aptitudes, experiences, educational backgrounds, and personality traits that can be leveraged in performing the roles that are common to information security programs. You will use this information to aid in the design of your staffing plan. During that process, you want to ensure these roles have been addressed in the job descriptions for your program. Keep in mind that one individual can possess multiple required attributes and fulfill multiple generic roles. First, let's define the attributes.

Visionary

The visionary attribute refers to the ability to see how aspects of your completed program will look before they are completed. This attribute allows someone to extrapolate current events, trends, and other information to formulate useful strategies to be incorporated into future elements of the program. This can include the entire program direction, individual initiatives, or projects. Returning to our ship analogy, this individual determines the destination and the initial course for the journey.

Commander

The commander attribute refers to the ability to inspire, motivate, and lead others. It requires an air of calm, thoughtfulness, and executive presence that others can look to for direction and have confidence to follow. An additional quality of this attribute is a certain degree of empathy to understand and comprehend the issues faced by subordinates.

Writer

The writer must be capable of communicating thoughts and concepts in an orderly, structured written form such as policies, procedures, and guidelines. This skill is invaluable to an information security professional because written documents will represent the majority of your sales, marketing, and education tools.

Presenter

The presenter must be capable of communicating thoughts and concepts in an orderly, structured verbal form such as initiatives, training, meetings, and sales presentations.

Architect

The architect must understand the technical environment from both a macro and micro perspective. This attribute provides the ability to view the enterprise environment in its entirety and dive into specific technical issues as necessary. Further, there must be a comprehension of the inter-relationships and dependencies between these differing views of the organization.

Consultant

The consultant has the ability to enter new environments, work on a wide variety of projects and initiatives, research various topics, co-develop potential solutions, and present them to their clients.

Technical Guru

The technical guru is usually more knowledgeable than most of your technical operational staff. The technical guru can be used as a tool to win battles where most of the discussion is over technical issues. This role requires knowledge of a wide array of subjects, including operating systems, networking, application coding, databases, and information security concepts. Although the technical guru doesn't necessarily need deep expertise in every subject, they should have a thorough understanding of inter-relationship and dependencies of various technologies. This person needs to know what they know, know what they don't, and find the answers to the things they don't.

Educator

End-user education of security concepts is one of the least expensive and potentially most effective controls you can implement. Your program should definitely have somebody with a passion for teaching and presenting information. This is someone who can take complex concepts and relay them to non-technical personnel in a manner that average people can understand.

Talent Scout

A good talent scout always keeps his eyes open for people and resources that can aid him in his goals. Because hiring qualified and talented information security professionals can be a challenging task, this attribute can come in handy during the recruiting process.

Salesperson

The salesperson has to be able to market and sell the products and services that your office is producing. These products are typically going to be the various ideas, concepts, and initiatives your program is responsible for, while the services may include any consulting, education, and awareness building your program may be involved in. This individual should have strong consultative sales skills, and should be able to identify and leverage the successes your program has provided for your enterprise. Typically, these will be any desirable, tangible results your program has already enjoyed, and can include any operational efficiency your program may have enabled, threats successfully reduced or avoided, and any improved end-user experiences your program may have enabled.

Planner

The planner attribute allows someone to prioritize actions and initiatives, coordinate the logistics required to execute successfully, and identify the resources necessary for execution.

Negotiator

As we have stated before, not everyone will be supportive of each initiative that comes from the information security program. The negotiator is the individual who works with your clients, stakeholders, and operational teams to gain support for the security aspects of any given project. This attribute includes having strong debate skills and a keen eye for identifying win/win situations for everyone.

Executor

The executor makes things happen for the program by understanding how to get things done in your environment, and by maneuvering through the various political, operational, and other hurdles that crop up from time to time. This includes being able to use all of the formally accepted processes, as well as any back-channel mechanisms available for accomplishing the program's goals.

Researcher

The researcher is responsible for keeping current on security practices, industry trends, issues, and other knowledge areas required by your program. They accomplish this goal by monitoring a variety of internal and external information sources.

Auditor

The auditor provides the information security program with the ability to measure the current state of security within the company as well as evaluate its progress. This is accomplished using standard audit techniques and tools such as audit log reviews, interviews, and the establishment of metrics. Some of the intricacies of this attribute will be further defined in the chapter on reporting.

Detailer

The detailer is the detail-oriented and possibly somewhat obsessive-compulsive individual who can help to create structure where none exists, or refine existing structures to meet his own high personal standards. This attribute is not something that is easily learned; either the individual has it or doesn't.

Organizer

The organizer has the amazing ability to gather, arrange, schedule, and coordinate large amounts of information and resources and organize them into a sensible, searchable, and logical way. This attribute is critical because your program may occasionally receive large amounts of information that may need to be readily available on a moment's notice.

Additional Considerations for Required Common Attributes

In closing, we would like to reiterate some considerations when applying these various attributes to your staffing plan.

- Each person may have multiple attributes.
- The size of the company and type of security office (large, small, operational, and non-operational) will change the emphasis of which attributes are the most important.
- Any amount of these attributes can help your team members in completing their roles and responsibilities. The more they have, the better, but they don't have to be perfect.
- There may be other attributes we didn't include above that may be of help to your team members. The idea is to identify those attributes that can be leveraged to help build your program.

Security Roles and Responsibilities

Now that we have described some critical attributes, the next step is to create the roles for your security team. To aid in this process we have created some generic roles that incorporate the attributes described in the previous section and are common to information security programs. The roles we describe are generic and meant only as an example of matching attributes in a potential model. In the last section of this chapter, we will present a matrix mapping these attributes to the typical roles required by an information security program.

Chief Information Security Officer (CISO)

This can be a complicated role to fill. If you have purchased this book, chances are that you're the one to fill it. The CISO position requires the broadest mix of attributes including commander, visionary, writer, salesperson, planner, negotiator, organizer, and presenter. If you feel you are lacking in any of these attributes, you might want to consider finding someone on your team to help you in your development of your program. For example, if you are strong in all of the above attributes except for sales and negotiation, you may want to leverage someone with a strong background in consultative sales to help you prepare for your more important presentations and meetings.

Security Architect

The security architect role works to identify and mitigate risks associated with technical projects and initiatives. However, just because someone has functioned in an architectural capacity does not necessarily qualify him or her for the security architect role. Some common attributes that the security architect should have include architect, commander, educator, salesperson, consultant, negotiator, technical guru, and presenter. Because of the various levels of technical skills and attributes necessary for this role to be successful, you may need to have several people perform different aspects of it.

Security Consultant

The security consultant role differs from that of the security architect in that the consultant is primarily concerned with solving existing problems while the architect is addressing future designs. The consultant will work primarily with operations to ensure the program's objectives are met through risk mitigation, policy compliance, and implementating the technologies, procedures, and processes. The attributes that are usually associated with a security consultant include consultant, salesperson, presenter, executor, technical guru, writer, educator, and negotiator.

Security Analyst

The primary function of the security analyst is to perform operational tasks on behalf of the information security program. Depending on the design of your program, he may also be called upon to research trends, issues, risks, threats, and vulnerabilities from an industry perspective. Additionally, this role is sometimes tasked with the implementation of the security policies, standards, procedures, and guidelines. This role sometimes performs certain planning functions for the program, taking the policies and standards and designing initiatives to move the company toward an increased security profile. The attributes that are most commonly associated with this role include researcher, writer, consultant, organizer, and presenter.

Training Specialist

The training specialist is a role that creates the materials, conducts the presentations, works with outside training agencies, and plans events aimed at increasing security knowledge and awareness across the enterprise. The attributes of this role include educator, writer, salesperson, presenter, planner, and executor.

Operations Manager (Optional)

The operations manager is an optional role that is based on the information security program structure. The assumption for this role is that you have an information security program with operational responsibilities. The operations manager is a dual role combining the ability to run the daily IT operations of the company while possessing a fundamental knowledge of security practices. The reason for the lack of emphasis on security is that the other members of the security team will often act as a resource to this role. The attributes associated with this role include executor, commander, negotiator, auditor, organizer, and detailer.

Business Continuity / Disaster Recovery Manager

This role is responsible for working with the operational teams to design, develop, and test business recovery plans for the enterprise. Business recovery plans for the purposes of this conversation include the four major categories: people, processes, technology, facilities. The required attributes for this role include: planner, detailer, commander, writer, salesperson, executor, presenter, and consultant.

Physical Security Specialist

The role of physical security specialist addresses the issues surrounding plant operations and the implementation of relevant physical security and environmental controls systems. Common responsibilities might include: data room access, facility security integrity, capacity planning, environmental planning, and asset management. The attributes associated to this role include: planner, executor, detailer, auditor, and architect.

Table 2.3 illustrates the various roles we have discussed with their associated attributes.

Table 2.3 Roles and Associate Attributes

	CISO	Security Architect	Security Consultant	Security Analyst	Training Specialist	Security Operations Mgr	BCP Mgr	Physical Security Specialist
Visionary	✓							
Commander	✓	✓				✓	✓	
Writer	✓		✓	✓	✓		✓	
Presenter	✓	✓	✓	✓	✓		✓	
Architect								✓
Consultant		✓	✓	✓			✓	
Technical Guru		✓	✓					
Educator		✓	✓		✓			
Talent Scout	✓							
Salesperson	✓	✓	✓		✓		✓	
Planner	✓				✓		✓	
Negotiator	✓	✓	✓			✓		
Executor					✓	✓	✓	✓
Researcher				✓				
Auditor						✓		✓
Detailer						✓	✓	✓
Organizer	✓			✓	✓			

Summation of Roles

We have defined the basic requirements that form the foundation of the information security program staffing plan. By having a clear understanding of these requirements and how they interrelate, the chances of successfully hiring, training, and promoting your team members as they help in the implementation of your program is much greater. We are not stating this is an easy task. Quite the contrary, each of the roles that have been outlined above are very complex.

Influence on Staffing by the Information Security Program Structure

As you make decisions about your program structure, it will influence both the types of roles and the relative strength and priority of the affiliated attributes each role will need to possess. The factors that will affect the quantity and selection of roles and attributes are:

- Operational versus non-operational
- Centralized versus de-centralized
- Organizational alignment
- Program size
- Common security responsibilities

Regardless of the decisions surrounding these factors, staffing will only be affected in the following manner.

Variety of Roles Required

The variety of roles that the information security program will need is determined by the scope of the responsibilities. The greater the responsibilities owned by the program, the larger the number of roles will be required. For example, an operational security office will have the additional responsibilities for the ongoing health and well-being of the technical environment, increasing the types of roles when compared to a non-operational program.

Concentration of Attributes per Employee

The size of the staff is impacted by every decision you make regarding organizational structure, but is most directly determined by the size of the company and the organizational alignment of the information security program. The size of the staff can affect the concentration of attributes among your team members. A large team may result in a lower concentration of attributes per person allowing for specialists, where a small team will require higher concentrations resulting in generalists.

Conclusion

In this section, we discussed the required attributes and incorporated them into a generic set of roles for an information security program. Then we illustrated the impact of the decisions regarding the information security program structure on the determination of roles. The next step in the process is yours:

- Identify the roles that are applicable to your organization based on the mission and structure of the information security program.
- Apply the generic roles to the available positions on your team.

Once you have completed this exercise, we are ready to move on to determine the sources for obtaining talent.

Perform a Gap Analysis

A gap analysis is a differential comparison between a desired state and the existing state. For the purposes of staffing, your gap analysis should evaluate the attributes and roles of your current staff and compare it to the desired staff you just created in the prior section. This differential between the two teams is where we will focus our attention: acquiring the missing elements.

Identify Sources

Now we have established a baseline understanding of the requirements for the new positions within the information security program. It's time to determine where to locate candidates. There are a number of good places to search for prospective additions to your team. We will examine the major categories with some insights on each of them.

Internal Recruiting

Internal recruiting is the process of locating employees that currently work in other areas or positions within your enterprise. With existing employees, there will be less uncertainty regarding the candidate's talent, history, and accomplishments. From the candidate's perspective, this may represent an exciting new opportunity. You may find this is the least expensive option for you because the amount of overhead necessary to obtain a qualified individual will be reduced in terms of time, effort, and money. They may require additional training or professional development to meet your exact needs, but it's a great place to start looking for talent.

External Recruiting

External recruiting is the process of locating qualified professionals outside your enterprise. The different methods available for external recruiting can range in cost from free to very expensive. Regardless of the method (or methods) you choose, the concept you need to remember is the more specific and detailed your requirements are, the higher the chances of eventually getting the right candidate. It may take longer because you're looking for a more specific skill set, but when a potential candidate arrives there's a better chance he will have the skills and attributes you're looking for. With that in mind, here are some of the more well-known places for locating talent:

- Recruiting agencies
- Temporary agencies
- Consultancies
- Vendors
- Professional organizations
- Professional network
- Schools

Evaluate Talent

The idea that we believe is often overlooked when evaluating talent is the concept of "skills displayed within a given context." This means a person who appears to be a superstar at one company may not have all of the attributes necessary to be a superstar at a different company. The reason this error occurs is that most positions are filled without considering all of the applicable requirements of a successful candidate. Hiring managers sometimes focus solely on technical certifications, professional licenses, technical prowess, and experience of the applicant — but not all of the requirements necessary for this person to succeed. Don't get overly impressed by candidates with 20+ certifications and licenses. Instead, focus more on the total package — evaluate their professional experience, their skills, and their personal attributes that you believe will best fit the specific position you're hiring for.

In the event that you can't find the perfect candidate, you may need to hire the best person available and make some small adjustments to your team. However, you now have a clear picture of any attributes you may need to have them focus on developing. Because you'll be adding people to your team, we would like to recommend a couple of tips and tricks used during the resume reviewing process.

Resumes

Looking critically over a resume for the following can reveal a number of potential things about the attributes of your candidates. While some may be somewhat obvious, others may require a little more thought. Examine any resumes you receive very closely, and you might be able to learn a little more about your candidate, as shown in Table 2.4.

With a little practice, you might be able to identify a number of your candidate's attributes before they even step through your doors. After

Table 2.4 Resume Review Tips

What you see:	*What it might mean:*
Typographical errors Grammatical errors	Lack of attention to detail Lack of personal pride Lack of professionalism Poor written and communication skills
Unexplained employment gaps	Inability to commit Lack of focus and direction in life Inability to do the job at hand Lack of dependability
Filler content—irrelevant facts included to add volume	Lack of experience Lack of judgment Untrustworthy Poor salespersonship Lack of focus and direction
Emphasizing areas of irrelevance (e.g., majoring in the minors)	Lack of experience Lack of judgment Poor salespersonship
Poor formatting	Lack of presentation skills Lack of attention to detail Lack of professionalism Poor salespersonship Poor written and communication skills

going through the resumes, you'll need to interview them and discuss the position, what you're looking for, their experience, background and skills. If you have a number of candidates, you may want to conduct a quick phone interview before meeting them. Afterward, you should definitely meet them and spend some time getting to know them before deciding whether they are a fit or not.

Interviewing

The main purpose of your initial interview is to determine the potential fit of the candidate into the organization. This is a personality evaluation where you are attempting to determine both their attitude and their aptitude. This personality evaluation will tell if this person will meet your attribute requirements for the position, or if they have the attitude and aptitude to acquire the attributes they may be lacking. Your next interview, or series of interviews, should determine how closely the candidate matches the skill and experience requirements of the position you are trying to fill.

The best way to verify claims of expertise is to test the candidate. There are various ways of accomplishing this including:

- Administer an objective verbal test.
- Quiz the candidate with real-life scenarios.
- Administer a hands-on practical exam.

After verifying a candidate's skills and experience, you may want to introduce him to the members of your team and have your team interview him as well. Allowing your team to meet the candidate provides an opportunity to evaluate their interaction firsthand, get feedback from your team, and identify areas where you may want to learn more about the candidate.

Close the Deal

> When dealing with people, remember you are not dealing with creatures of logic, but creatures of emotion.
>
> **—Dale Carnegie**

After you've done all the hard work of identifying the various roles, responsibilities, and positions you want in your program, identifying and interviewing candidates, your final step is to hire the candidate. Although your HR staff may perform the technical details of this, there is one definite thing you should focus on during this process: co-developing performance expectations to ensure a true win-win situation for both you and the candidate.

A difficult and often overlooked aspect of hiring is expectations. Sometimes HR personnel can over-hype a position to acquire a desired candidate. This can occur when there is a high demand for and a low supply of truly qualified candidates in fields such as information security. Though it may seem natural to operate in this mode, specifically if you've identified a job requirement that's hard to fill, we still suggest resisting this temptation. We recommend being direct and spin-free about the good and the bad surrounding a particular position. By spin-free, we mean not turning every negative aspect of the job into a positive (i.e., spinning). Your goal should be to create a win-win situation; fitting the right person with a job he can like. The win for the company is placing a highly qualified candidate with a great attitude in your team. The win for the new employee is a great job that allows him to leverage his skills and experience in a position that motivates him.

Planning Summary

In this chapter, we presented you with a number of topics and concepts that will aid in planning your information security program. The methodology begins with identifying the mandate of the program and translating that into a mission statement, program design, staffing requirements, and organizational alignment. Each of the areas in this chapter will aid you in completing the security planning checklist at the end of the chapter. This checklist, like the one from Chapter 1, Assess, will provide necessary information for Chapter 3, Design.

Planning Checklist

> The dictionary is the only place that success comes before work. Hard work is the price we must pay for success. I think you can accomplish anything if you're willing to pay the price.
>
> **—Vince Lombardi**

The assessment checklist is a bridge between Chapter 2, Plan, and Chapter 3, Design. The information completed in this checklist will be needed to make decisions in the next chapter. Not completing this questionnaire will reduce the value of future chapters, because they will rely on the gathered information. The answers do not have to be lengthy, just enough to remind you of the thought process that went into the formulation of the answer. To aid you in this process, we have limited the responses to one or two sentences. Take the time and complete this exercise (see Table 2.5).

Table 2.5   Planning Checklist

FOUNDATION CONCEPTS			
Personal Assessment	*Sufficient Skill (Y/N)*	*Book Review*	*Affected Methodology Phase*
Critical Skills			
Visioning			Plan, Design
Strategic Planning			Plan, Design, Execute
Negotiating			Plan, Design, Execute
Marketing			Plan, Design, Execute, Report
Talent Assessment			Plan, Design, Execute
Critical Knowledge			
ISC²			Plan, Design, Execute, Report
Security Industry Resources			Plan, Design, Execute, Report
PLANNING METHODOLOGY			
Program Mandate		*Affected Elements of Design*	
Describe in a single paragraph the source of your information security program's mandate.			
		Security Policies Project Queue	

Table 2.5 (continued)   Planning Checklist

Write the mission statement for your information security program.	
	Security Policies Project Queue
Information Security Program Structure	*Affected Elements of Design*
Will your information security program be operational or non-operational? Provide your answer and the reasons for the decision in a brief paragraph.	
	Project Queue
Will your information security program be centralized or de-centralized? Provide your answer and the reasons for the decision in a brief paragraph.	
	Project Queue
SECURITY PIPELINE	
Describe how your information security program shall participate in the architectural portion of the pipeline.	
	Project Queue

Table 2.5 (continued)   Planning Checklist

Describe how your information security program shall participate in the maintenance portion of the pipeline.	
	Project Queue

Describe how your information security program shall participate in the inspection portion of the pipeline.	
	Project Queue

SIZE OF YOUR PROGRAM	
How many people will be reporting directly to you?	
List the roles that you have identified as necessary for your information security program.	List the associated attributes for each role.

Chapter 3

Design

Overview

The design phase is the process of aligning your business with the various drivers of your information security program. This process includes the following key steps:

- Defining a comprehensive set of information security policies that aligns your organization with any requirements coming from the various drivers of your information security program.
- Performing a gap analysis to identify areas of compliance and non-compliance with your information security policies.
- Prioritizing any areas of non-compliance and putting together a strategy to address them. This strategy will take the form of a prioritized portfolio of projects.
- Developing an effective communication plan to let others know the relevant information about your information security program.

This chapter represents a major transition from our previous chapters because the more vague concepts of risk and business drivers will be translated into more concrete deliverables and actions.

Foundation Concepts

The foundation concepts we will be discussing in this section consist of a number of critical skills and critical knowledge areas. However, a comprehensive discussion of these materials is beyond the scope of this book. Where applicable, we will provide a list of recommended resources for additional information.

Critical Skills

The critical skills we will discuss are:

- Analytical skills
- Organizational skills
- Sales skills
- Financial planning and budgeting skills

Analytical Skills

Our definition of analytical skills is the ability to discover, evaluate, strategize, and formulate cohesive and actionable plans based on available information as shown in Figure 3.1. Whew…that's a mouthful. What does all that mean? Let's take it one piece at a time.

Discovery

Discovery has many facets associated with it. The first is the ability to understand the available sources and uses of information. Information is not limited to books, magazines, and other written material. It can also apply to interpersonal communication, politics, or any other item that will aid in the development of an educated decision.

Evaluation

Evaluation is the process of taking the information that was gained in discovery and determining its value to the decision process. We affectionately refer to this area as the bozo filter. The key to evaluation is finding the balance between useful knowledge and superfluous information. This is similar to the concept we addressed in Chapter 1, Assess.

Strategy

Now that you have attained the necessary information, how should it be used? Strategizing is the process of taking the acquired information and determining a course of action.

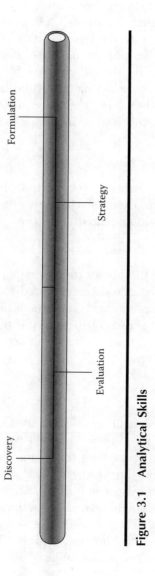

Figure 3.1 Analytical Skills

Formulation

Formulation is the process of determining the details that allow you to execute your tactical plan. This enables you to achieve an objective that conforms to the overall strategy. Keep in mind there may be many tactical plans to achieve a single strategic objective.

Now that have provided a common definition for the analytical skill, let's discuss its importance to the design phase of the methodology.

The degree of detail needed to make decisions will be much higher for the design phase than when compared to Chapter 1, Assess and Chapter 2, Plan. Due to the exact nature of the deliverables, the level of complexity will increase as we attempt to assemble the useful information from the multitude of details into a project portfolio.

Organizational Skills

> Just as the constant increase of entropy is the basic law of the universe, so it is the basic law of life to be ever more highly structured and to struggle against entropy.
>
> **—Vaclav Havel**

Organizational skills are the ability to arrange, schedule, and coordinate all of the information and resources gathered to this point. This skill is necessary because of the extremely large amounts of data that require compiling and organizing, usually in a very short period of time. Aside from the data, you'll need to coordinate the activities of your new team to aid in the design process.

Sales

In the design phase you will move into the realm of spending large amounts of the company's money. This will occur because of the information security program requesting funds and resources while defining, scheduling, and budgeting the projects that will represent your overall mission. Executive management will not just open their wallets and give you whatever you want; you'll have to sell them on a concept. This leads us to the irreplaceable skill: sales. The sales skill is the ability to gain the support and commitment from anyone who may be impacted by, or have resources needed, to achieve an initiative.

Financial Planning and Budgeting

Money is the lifeblood of your program; no blood...no life! You must master the skills of financial planning and budgeting to enable the various projects and initiatives you will design in this chapter to become reality. In Chapter 1, Assess, you determined the mechanisms and tools used by the company to acquire funding. Your ability to use these processes and tools are the aspects of planning and budgeting to which we are referring. These are the skills that need to be mastered because there will be competition for the same money.

Critical Skills Summary

Though there are other skills that will ultimately be required during the design phase, we have attempted to highlight the most relevant factors. Once again, they are analytical, organizational, sales, and financial planning/budgeting.

Critical Knowledge

The critical knowledge areas for the design phase include understanding:

- Opportunity cost
- Information security frameworks
- Policies, standards, procedures, and guidelines
- Risks, threats, and vulnerabilities
- Internal controls
- Gap analysis
- SMART statements
- Project types

Opportunity Cost

In the design phase, you will be faced with decisions regarding the use of a finite set of resources and funds. For every course selected, there will be another course forsaken. This is the heart of opportunity cost. This isn't a new or innovative concept; it's something we face every day. Should I go to work or stay home and channel surf? Should I pay my mortgage or buy the new Ferrari?

Security Documents

The security documents are comprised of policies, standards, procedures, and guidelines. To begin this topic, we are going to provide the definitions of the various documents and discuss their uses. We will not attempt to reiterate the details of these documents because there are many fine reference books available on this topic; we will merely furnish a basic overview needed to complete this phase of the methodology. Don't misinterpret our brevity for lack of importance to either your information security program or the methodology. These documents will represent the cornerstone of your information security program. Before we go into detail regarding the need for these documents, we'll move on to the definitions.

Policies

Policies are a series of documents that cover how you will secure various areas of your organization. They commonly break down into three distinct types (see Figure 3.2):

1. Organizational
2. Issue centric
3. System centric

Within a policy document, there is what is commonly referred to as the policy statement. Policy statements are strategic declarations that set the direction for a given domain of security practices. They are broad statements providing an outline that covers the primary categories of security. They are statements of concept and philosophy, not detailed

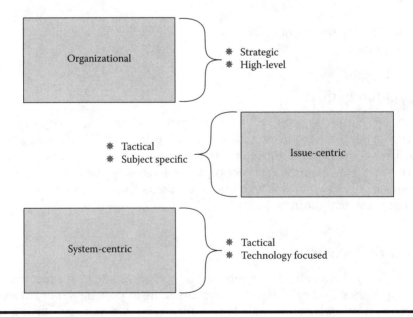

Figure 3.2   Policy Types

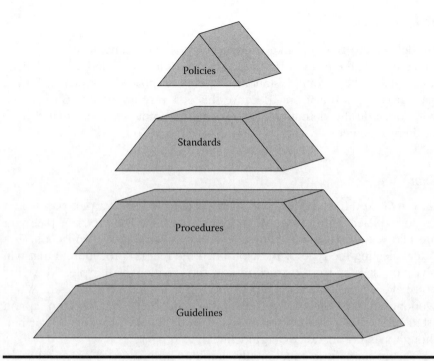

Figure 3.3   Document Hierarchy

statements or operational practices. The detail for each policy is furnished by the standards, procedures, and guidelines (see Figure 3.3). Now here is the confusing part. The word, "policy," is often used interchangeably between the two definitions of policy and policy statement. For the purposes of our book, any reference to policy is a reference to the policy statements.

Standards

Standards are the institutionalized means of conducting business; they are mandatory. This can apply to people, processes, technology, and facilities. An example of a standard would be the requirement that all desktop computers must run on Linux RedHat v7.0. In this case, Linux is a standard for the workstation's operating system.

Procedures

If policy statements are the strategic declarations, procedures represent their tactical execution. These statements are the step-by-step details on performing the exact security practices referenced in the policies.

Guidelines

Guidelines are typically like standards, but aren't mandatory. They tend to manifest in the form of best practices, and tribal knowledge. Guidelines are usually the adopted standard operating procedures when formal standards are non-existent. Because this is a very important concept, we will conclude the definitions section with a simple example that ties all of them together.

Example

If you worked for a bakery and were assigned to bake a pie, you would begin by selecting the type of pie you will bake. The types of pies you are allowed to bake are defined in the company's pie menu (policies). After selecting the type of pie, you need the recipe (procedures) that will give you step-by-step instructions on the creation of the pie. Now that you have all the information you need, you move to the kitchen. While working in the kitchen, you must wear a chef's hat and an apron (standards). It is common for the chefs in the kitchen to wear a hair net, though it is not mandatory (guidelines).

This example was intentionally simple to emphasize the concept without adding any unnecessary complications.

The single most important aspect of these documents is they represent the law; they are the distillation of everything your information security program will attempt to accomplish. This is the set of rules you will teach and publish to the population of your organization. They are important to the methodology because they furnish the reason and the authority for the projects that will be derived from each set of policies. Later in the methodology we will discuss how to build relevant, useful polices.

Risks, Threats, and Vulnerabilities ... Oh My!

Everything you do as the new chief information security officer (CISO) should be tailored to reduce risk. This is the underlying principle driving your office. Before we move on to our definition, it should be noted there are countless definitions for both the concept of risk and related functions such as risk management. From NIST SP 800:30 to the definitions found on the SysAdmin-Audit-Network-Security (SANS) Web site everyone has a slightly different approach, based on either their particular environment or unique methodology. This book is no different. Our definition of risk and the means by which we incorporate its identification, management, and reduction take many of the ideas found in the other sources and customizes them to best integrate them into our methodology. We highly recommend you review the available information sources on both risk and risk management to understand any tweaks you will need to make for your organization. For your convenience, we have listed many of these additional sources in the recommended reading appendix of this book. That being said, let's move on to our definition.

Risk is the probability of a threat exposing a vulnerability in your organization. That's right! Risk is a probability. It represents the chance of an event occurring as a result of an identified threat and vulnerability.

- A threat is a potential event that could adversely affect your organization (i.e., virus, burglar, hurricane, hacker).
- A vulnerability is the susceptibility of your organization to a threat or series of threats (i.e., unlocked doors, weak passwords, unpatched systems).

Example

Your company is located in beautiful, sunny Southern California, specifically within a 2-mile radius of a major geological fault. This region of the country faces the threat of a massive earthquake on a daily basis. The vulnerability in this case is the company's location in California, as well as its proximity to a fault line. The risk is the probability of a massive earthquake occurring. The magnitude and potential damage of the earthquake is a major component when determining the probability. The probability of a small quake that only rattles the windows is vastly higher than a massive one that turns Los Angeles into an island.

Remember when you begin to design your program, these elements must be included in each of your projects. Every project you design must focus on a threat that can potentially exploit a vulnerability; this is your guide for developing your project portfolio. The manner in which these issues are addressed is with security controls.

Types of Security Controls

Security controls are the tools that will be employed to reduce or mitigate an identified risk. They can be broken down according to the time frame in which they operate; before, during, or after an event (see Figure 3.4).

Preventive Controls

The primary objective of a preventive control is to reduce the risk of a security threat expoiting a vulnerability to an acceptable level for the organization. They can operate prior to, or during, the occurrence of a

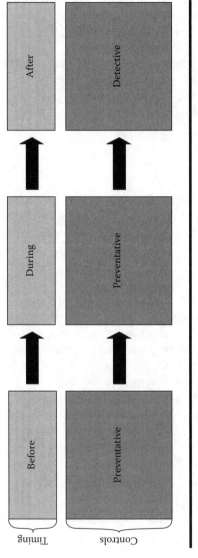

Figure 3.4 Control Timing

security event. An example of a preventive control would be an Internet firewall. It functions prior to an event as a deterrent and risk mitigation tool, but it can also function during an event as a means of eliminating the specific threat by denying traffic on a specific port or protocol.

Detective Controls

Detective controls are also primarily concerned with reducing the risk of a security threat or vulnerability; however, they accomplish this task after an event has occurred. This is accomplished by analyzing the evidence left by the event to determine the manner, means, and mechanisms that produced it. These types of tools are concerned with furnishing information for the prevention of a similar future risk or vulnerability. Forensic tools also fall into this category, but focus on the collection of data to determine the magnitude of the exposure and clues for determining the perpetrator. For this section, we will be focusing on risk-related uses of detective controls. Some examples of detective controls would include: log reviews, intrusion detection, and video tape.

Understanding the various types of controls and knowing when to use them will help in completing the design phase of the methodology. In the beginning of design, we coach you in the process of identifying the risk profile of your organization. Using these various controls will reduce the risk to the organization. The controls will be integrated into the projects that are deliverables at the end of this chapter.

Gap Analysis

A gap analysis is a differential process where the desired end-state is compared to the existing state; the difference between the two is the gap (see Figure 3.5). You will use this technique again and again until you retire from the information security field...then it will probably be used again. Get the idea?

In design, we will help you develop security policies, standards, procedures, and guidelines that will represent the desired end-state for your organization. The gap analysis will be used as a re-occurring tool to evaluate the current state and compare it against the desired end-state. This is essential for a few reasons:

■ Identifies the areas you need to focus on with your program.
■ Provides a true picture of your environment.
■ Can be used to measure progress.
■ The results of a gap analysis are where the majority of your risks will be identified.

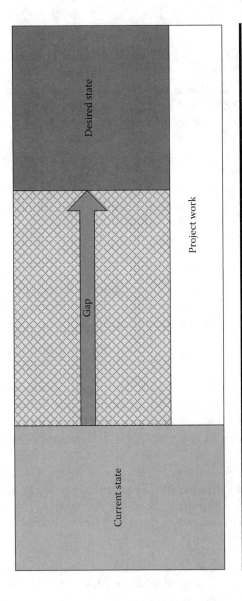

Figure 3.5   Gap Analysis

Though we discuss end-states, it is merely an illusion. As long as the risks facing an organization are constantly changing, there will be no end-states in security, only brief rest periods before we start the process again.

SMART Statements

A SMART statement is one that is specific, measurable, achievable, relevant, and timely. It's a means of describing the traits that should be considered when translating your policies into actionable projects. They act as a bridge between the high-level statements of your security policies and the actions that will be taken to enforce them. These statements will manifest themselves in your project scope statements and the supporting requirements of each project. Below is the decomposition of the acronym SMART with the associated explanation for each of its attributes:

■ Specific — each statement should be exact in the material that is referenced, as well as the action planned from it.
■ Measurable — each statement must possess the ability to be evaluated for success or failure.
■ Achievable — though it can be great sport to present an unachievable objective, it does little to further the mission of your program. Therefore, ensure each statement is within the realm of possibility.
■ Relevant — each statement should be supportive of the overall mission objective, and the policy from which it is derived.
■ Timely — each statement should have an expiration date. Open-ended statements are impossible to complete and ultimately measure. This is great if you never want to see the project end (ask Dilbert about those types of projects).

Types of Projects

A project is the aggregation and classification of requirements that describe a desired end-state. This exercise quantifies the energy and resources that will be required, as well as the schedule under which the effort shall be executed. For the purposes of this book, projects will fall into three types: people, processes, or technology.

People Projects

People projects refer to initiatives that affect or influence the manner in which individuals perform their daily tasks. It could be as simple as a security fair meant to raise awareness or as complicated as a companywide training initiative on the proper classification of data. In either case, the desired end-state involves an alteration to the level of knowledge that people employ to perform their functions within the organization.

Process Projects

Process projects deal with the manner in which individuals perform their function within the organization. Though this can involve the introduction of new tools, the focus remains on the alteration of an existing or future process. Examples of this type of project would include creating a new hiring process or the process of adding a new user to a system.

Technology Projects

Technology projects specifically deal with the addition, subtraction, or alteration to any technology component within the organization. Once again, this may involve people and processes, but the distinction is that technology is the driving force behind the project. Examples would include the installation of a new phone system, replacing an antiquated security system, or changing the standard desktop operating system.

By the end of this chapter, you will have stratified all of your projects along these three types. The reason for the classification is the types of resources that you'll need to accomplish them successfully. A people project will require a different blend of talent from your team than a technology project. It will also aid in determining the priority of a project and the balance of the active projects. We'll expand on the concept of project balance later in the design methodology.

Methodology

Preview

In order for you to complete the deliverables for this chapter, we will lead you through a structured, serialized exercise. Because of this approach, each section must be completed in order. This will require a substantial effort that will be time consuming. However, like most design processes, the more energy you exert at the beginning, the better the long-term results. The difference between a concerted effort at this point and one that is lackluster will be truly amazing. The tangible results of your efforts will be a thoughtful, defendable, and marketable course for your information security program that ties directly to the business needs of the company.

Listed below are the steps we will walk through to develop the deliverables for this phase. These steps break down along the lines of each deliverable: security documents, project portfolio, and communication plan.

Security Document Development

- Incorporating your enterprise drivers
- Transferring your drivers to business requirements
- Refining your business requirements into functional requirements
- Translating your business requirements into policy statements
- Performing a gap analysis against your functional requirements (policy requirements) and your existing policies and controls
- Mapping your existing policies against an existing framework (ISO 17799, CobIT)
- Drafting your information security policies
- Submitting them for review with legal, compliance, and audit
- Ratifying and implementing your information security policies

Project Portfolio Development

- Prioritize the results of your gap analysis against risk.
- Identify future initiatives and projects based on your gap analysis.
- Develop rough scopes and budgets for your projects.
- Prioritize and schedule your project portfolio.

Communication Plan Development

- Determine your communication channels and how to best use them.

There are a great number of steps in this process, but it's worth the work. After successfully completing the deliverables associated with this section, you will have a clear vision of the gaps, and will be able to identify your program's strengths and weaknesses. This will allow you to prioritize the various initiatives you will want to undertake as your program grows.

Incorporating Your Enterprise Drivers

Throughout this book, we have been instructing you to look for various things driving your information security program. In this chapter, they will be used to drive the requirements for the policy statements that will become the basis of your program.

In Chapter 1, Assess, you identified the critical business processes and the regulations applicable to your business. Enterprise drivers fall into two primary categories:

1. Enablers
2. Constraints

We recommend that constraints and enablers be reflected in your security policies to ensure their relevancy to the enterprise. By the end of this chapter, you will be able to develop a prioritized queue of security projects based on your policies. If your policies don't directly correlate to your drivers (and your business), any projects you identify might not be directly relevant to your business.

Enablers are aspects of the entity that contribute to the profitability or success of the business. Let's discuss why these factors should be considered in the development of the security policies.

We've heard of companies that implemented a series of information security policies based on generic templates without taking the time to learn about their business drivers. As a result, the policies supporting their information security program don't account for the unique constraints and enablers of their enterprise. Therefore, they may not be compliant with the laws and regulations facing their enterprise, and may have implemented a series of expensive controls that don't fit their business model.

When evaluating the constraints and enablers on your business, one of the first things to understand is which ones are mandatory and which ones are not. For each category of driver, we will provide some guidance for determining the degree to which each of your drivers may drive the formation of your policies.

Constraints

Constraints are those laws, rules, customs, moral directions, religious beliefs, or industry regulations that have the potential of restricting the manner in which your enterprise operates. These constraints are usually addressed by businesses, non-profit organizations, and other enterprises by implementing a set of internal controls, such as audit committees, internal audit programs, legal and regulatory compliance programs, or some sort of corporate responsibility or code of conduct program. Each of these areas will most likely be drivers of your information security program, and should already have been identified during the assess process. That said, we'd like to discuss a couple of these items in more detail to illustrate how these constraints can affect your information security program, and ultimately your enterprise.

Laws and Regulations

All of the legal and regulatory items you identified in Chapter 1, Assess, are mandatory requirements that will need to be addressed in your policies. Your legal department or legal counsel has supplied you with information as to the laws and regulations your organization must comply with. With their assistance, you determine that one of the legal requirements you must comply with is that all users must be individually authenticated on login to a given computer system. This legal requirement, along with a couple of similar items, can then be incorporated into a policy statement that reads: "All users must be uniquely authenticated and authorized prior to being granted access to our computer systems."

Corporate Responsibility/Code of Conduct

This item pertains to the responsibility and accountability of all members of your organization (or employees of your company) to follow all laws, regulations, and company policies while they are actively serving in some capacity within your enterprise. If you already have a corporate responsibility or code of conduct program in place at your organization, then you simply need to work with the people leading that effort to determine the best way your program can support their efforts, and vice versa. If you don't have a program in place, then we recommend you work with your executive management and legal counsel to identify the level of control they believe should be implemented here. Assuming you already have a code of conduct program, and legal and regulatory compliance office in place, here's how a sample policy statement might look:

"In the event an employee becomes aware of illegal activities being performed by a co-worker, the employee must report this to the compliance office for further investigation."

Enablers

Enablers address the enterprise's ability to successfully continue its operations. This will include the protection of such items as trade secrets, contract negotiations, intellectual property, critical business processes, or anything that if exposed or damaged could negatively impact the current operation of the organization. You will need to consider the business sensitive processes and differentiators you identified in Chapter 1, Assess, to ensure your policies, standards, and guidelines protect them, but do not negatively impact them. Once you've determined the relative value of your drivers in policy development, we will transfer them to the appropriate category of requirements to facilitate the creation of your security documents.

Requirements

Your program's requirements fall into three major categories (see Figure 3.6):

1. Business requirements
2. Functional requirements
3. Technical requirements

Each category of requirement is related to another in a hierarchical model (see Figure 3.6). Like most hierarchies, a pyramid best represents the requirements model denoting the degree of detail required by each level. Moving down from the top of the pyramid, the degree of detail necessary to fulfill each requirement increases. At the top of the pyramid are the business requirements, followed by functional requirements, and finally by technical requirements.

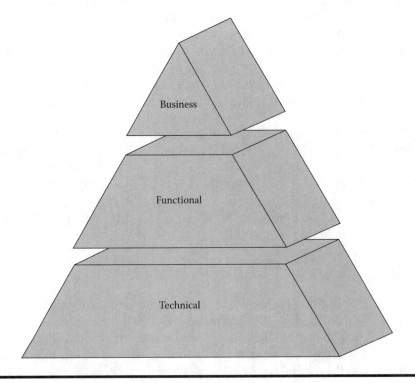

Figure 3.6 Requirement Types

Business Requirements

The objective of the business requirements is to take all of the drivers and organize them in a manner that will allow for the creation of functional requirements. We'll discuss functional requirements next, but for now all you need to understand is that business requirements are the mandatory inputs for the generation of the functional requirements.

Business requirements are the high-level statements that should capture the essence of what will be achieved for the business by your program. Because your program exists to support the business, any action taken by the program should map directly to a high-level business driver.

Below we have created some general rules for creating your business requirement statements:

- They should be broad and comprehensive.
- They must map directly to a business driver.
- They should be succinct enough to be captured in one or two sentences.
- Where possible, similar business requirements should be combined.
- There should only be a few statements broad enough to cover the necessary drivers. Let's apply these guidelines in a rudimentary example.

Example

The law firm of Dewey, Cheatum, and Howe, LLP, is determined to be constrained by regulations outlined in HIPAA and Gramm–Leach–Bliley. Therefore, during the creation of their information security program they developed the following business statement:

"Dewey, Cheatum, and Howe, LLP, is committed to maintaining a program of internal controls to provide reasonable assurance that all applicable legal and regulatory obligations are met."

That's all there is to it. Note that we did not make the statement specific to HIPAA or Gramm–Leach–Bliley; instead, we covered both of these by a single statement regarding regulatory compliance. Identifying your business requirements accomplishes the following objectives:

- They act as a contract with executive management setting the expectation for the overall objective of the information security program.
- They provide a discussion point that is easily understood and related to by everyone within the company.
- They provide a documented reminder of management's intentions.
- They provide a high-level framework to ensure that the things most important to your business are addressed first. This includes

providing assurance that your completed projects are based in the highest needs of your enterprise.

Now that we have provided you with an overview of what business requirements are, and their importance, we'll examine how to derive the requirements for the different types of drivers.

Enablers are a vague category of drivers that are generally subject to your interpretation. Your knowledge of the business combined with the business sensitive processes, which was discovered during the assessment, will provide you with ample information for this category. This is best illustrated with another example.

Example

You work for the Make-Fast Automobile Corporation. Make-Fast employs proprietary production and manufacturing techniques that allow them to build cars faster than their nearest competitor. If this information were to fall into the wrong hands, they would lose this competitive advantage. The business requirement for this driver might be: "Make-Fast Automobile Corporation must protect its proprietary production and manufacturing techniques."

Obviously, there is a large quantity of enablers in every organization. The key is to capture them at a level that includes as many as possible in one statement. The idea is to provide a broad enough scope to the statements so they do not need to be rewritten every year, merely interpreted. This is your cheat sheet to ensure all of the initiatives within the information security program map back to the business drivers.

Once you have your business requirements, it's time to get dirty and build your functional requirements. The functional requirements are the next level of the pyramid, providing an additional level of detail with which we will form the foundation for the security documents.

Functional Requirement

Functional requirements are the characteristics that describe the solution that meets the business requirements. They describe how something must function to meet the business requirement. In this process, we're not designing any of your policies, only the description of the functions that these policies must be able to address. This will provide your program with the flexibility to adapt changing technologies, changes in the culture of your enterprise, and new processes and operating procedures. The goal here isn't to rewrite your enterprise's functional requirements every year, merely to interpret them. Below are some criteria for creating your functional requirement statements:

- They describe what and when the solution must function like to meet the business requirement.
- They do not define how to do it (that's what technical requirements are for).
- They generally address one of the ten domains of the Common Body of Knowledge (CBK) for the information security industry.
- They must map back to all of the business requirements.

Let's take these criteria, write an example of a functional requirement, and discuss the various components.

Example

You are the new CISO for PeoplePop Cryogenic Service, Inc. (PCSI), the premier provider of cryogenic suspension services. PeoplePop has developed a unique concept of hotels that allow for the accommodation of their tenants. To enable this feature, they have developed a number of proprietary technologies and processes that are heavily dependent on the continuous flow of rare gases and inert materials, making them highly dependent on their procurement process. Lastly, because PCSI is considered a medical provider, it is constrained by the regulations outlined in HIPAA.

Business Requirements of PCSI

- The company must address all applicable security regulations.
- The company must practice due diligence and due care in protecting it's intellectual property.
- The company must protect the anonymity of the customers.
- The procurement process must not be hindered.

Functional Requirement

Any connection to a network that crosses organizational boundaries for the purposes of transmitting trade secret information must be encrypted and requires the incorporation of restrictive access controls.

Analysis

The statement meets all four of the criteria for functional requirements.

1. It communicates what needs to be done and under what circumstances.
2. It describes the characteristics of the solution, but does not provide the actual technical detail for accomplishing the task.
3. It addresses three of the ten security domains: network security, access control, and cryptography.
4. The statement can be successfully applied to each of the business requirements that were outlined in the example.

There is one additional caveat, which is the need for additional research when addressing compliance with law and regulations. It's one thing to identify the need to comply with specific regulations. However, it is a completely different matter to interpret the regulations and determine the specific level of control necessary to comply.

Now that we have defined and described the functional requirements, we will provide some strategies for creating them for your company.

Methods for Creating Functional Requirements

Information security affects, and is affected by, every aspect of an organization. The comprehensive nature of security can be daunting to some, which has led to a number of different approaches for developing functional requirements.

Below are the three common approaches for developing the functional requirements:

1. Establish your own set of custom functional requirements. This method can work, but is extremely time intensive and subject to flaws due to the potential for omission of critical areas.
2. Implement an industry standard template without customization. This method is fast to implement and comprehensive. However, the downside is that the lack of customization will result in the application of security controls that are inappropriate for the organization. The result will be the inevitable (and very costly) customization of your policies after the implementation of these templates. Retrofitting your security documents to your business drivers can cause a high-level of discomfort for the entire organization.
3. Utilize an industry standard template for developing a custom set of functional requirements. We saved this one for last because this

is the method we advocate. It is a hybrid of items one and two providing a high-level of customization with the comprehensive nature of an industry standard framework such as ISO/IEC 17799 (see Figure 3.7).

Requirements Summary

We've covered a number of concepts regarding what the types of requirements are, why you need them, and how to create them. It's now up to you. You can choose to breeze through this portion of creating your information security program, but our experience tells us it will likely come back to haunt you. The requirements are the foundation of your policies, which will become the laws for your company; skimp on the requirements and you will spend your time trying to implement policies that aren't customized for your enterprise.

Gap Analysis

The next step in the methodology is to build your security policies from the newly created functional requirements. To accomplish this task, you must have a complete and full set of documented business and functional requirements. We advocate mapping your functional requirements to an industry-accepted framework such as International Organization for Standardization (ISO)-International Electrotechnical Commission (IEC) 17799 or CobIT. This will ensure that your information security program has the flexibility and comprehensiveness to meet any changes to your enterprise drivers.

Before you work to draft a series of information security policies from scratch, you should check to see whether any of your enterprise's existing policies could be leveraged. There's no need to reinvent the wheel if you have existing policies that meet the functional requirements you've defined above. This should prove to be an interesting exercise because it will expose the degree of alignment that your current policies have with the business. During the reconciliation of your existing polices you may choose to categorize them into groups for your gap analysis, such as:

- Acceptable policies — policies that do not require any modification to support your information security program.
- Salvageable policies — policies that require minor modification to effectively support your information security program.
- Missing policies — policies that are missing from what has been identified as needed to support your information security program.

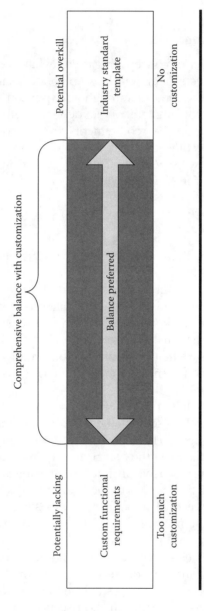

Figure 3.7 Requirements for Policy

Use of a known security standards template will make these types of policies easier to identify.

■ Questionable policies — policies that may have been implemented in your enterprise without a real business or functional requirement for them. This can happen when well-intentioned people don't go through the process of identifying their program's drivers like you are doing, instead of implementing policies without thinking them through.

After categorizing your existing policies there are two potential actions you may decide to take. You can either review the policies that you have determined to be salvageable in their entirety and change them, or you can start completely from scratch. If it's going to take more time to amend an existing policy in your enterprise then to create a completely new one, then you might want to start fresh if that's possible.

Building Security Policies, Standards, Procedures, and Guidelines

There are many fine books and guides for the creation of security documents. It certainly is not our intent to try to provide extensive detail in this area. However, some criteria needs to be addressed for this methodology to be successful. Let's begin at the beginning...policies.

The Theory of Security Policies

Policies are the foundation for all the documents your information security program will require. It is virtually impossible to develop appropriate security procedures, standards, or guidelines without the policies representing your enterprise's business and functional requirements. Policies have the same relationship to these other components that business and functional requirements have to the policies themselves. Every policy maps back to a business or functional requirement, and every procedure and standard should map back to a policy.

This process will be the first and most important project in your project portfolio. Keep this in mind later when you need to report the progress of your program to executive management; this will be the first win you're going to want to present to them. The building of your security documents will serve as a basis for identifying all of the other projects needed in your information security program. We'll go into greater detail on the security project portfolio a little later. For now, all you need to know is that the purpose of this process is to develop a prioritized listing of all the security projects that will be executed by the program. Let's begin by addressing the correlation between the functional requirements and the security policies.

Remember your functional requirements represent the embodiment of your enterprise's business requirements. Therefore, to ensure that the program is addressing the needs of the business, each policy must directly map back to at least one functional requirement. This is what will maintain the integrity of the pyramid. Let's quickly recap on the criteria before moving on to drafting the security policies.

- Policy development and ratification is the first project in the security project portfolio.
- Each policy must map back to at least one functional requirement; it is common to have several functional requirements met by a single policy.
- All of your subsequent documentation — processes, procedures, standards, and guidelines — should be derived from your policies.

Now that you understand the basic rules for building security policies, and their relationship to your business and functional requirements, we'll move on to drafting the first revision of your security policies.

Drafting Your Information Security Policies

Laws too gentle are seldom obeyed; too severe, seldom executed.

—Benjamin Franklin

The concept behind our book isn't to be an exhaustive resource containing all of the available knowledge for building an effective information security program. Instead, we're providing you with a logical framework and methodology for developing your own program. Accordingly, where applicable we'll try to steer you toward other resources that do a far better job on a given topic than we ever could. These resources are found in the appendix that covers recommended reading.

A dedicated reference on policy development can help you develop the necessary perspective and background for you to begin to draft your policies. We don't expect that you will become an expert overnight from merely reading a single book. However, the purpose of these reference sources is to provide context and perspective. If you have written a successful, comprehensive set of security policies in the past, then you have a head start.

The first step is to develop a committee of any stakeholders who are willing to participate in the process. Some may want to help you draft the policies while others may merely want to review them before they're ratified. Either way, you should identify these people and invite them early on. This will enable you to build consensus throughout the process, and address any issues that may arise. It will also allow you to agree on definitions for any general or vague terms you use within your policy statements.

You should have already identified your stakeholders and one or more of the following areas within your enterprise:

■ Legal counsel/law department
■ Executive management
■ Internal audit
■ Human resources
■ IT operations management

This process will help you to ratify your security policies once they have been completed. One benefit of this process is you will gain insight into what is most important to your enterprise directly from your stakeholders. You will also identify the level of change your enterprise will tolerate to its culture.

If your policies don't match the tone and culture of your enterprise, it isn't going to matter how brilliant they turn out to be. Failure to account for this factor can turn your program into big brother in a relatively short period of time. Successfully factoring the company culture into your policy development will lead to the perception of a responsible, proactive organization that has the best interest of the company in mind. The result is that most, if not all, members of your organization will work toward the mutual goals of the program and won't attempt to circumvent them.

Even if you fully understand the culture and the level of willingness to accept security practices, failure to convey that information in a written format that is acceptable to the organization will produce the same results as failing to understand the culture. Make sure the tone and tenor of any publication from the security office matches the culture of the organization. This is a difficult talent that is generally best suited to a human resource or policy specialist. Let's look at how a single functional requirement can spawn different policies that address the same issue (see Table 3.1).

As you can see, minor adjustments to a sentence can alter the tone and tenor of the message. This illustrates an important concept that is worth repeating: your policies must take into consideration the culture of the organization and be communicated in a manner that will be accepted

Table 3.1   Policy Phrasing Example

Functional Requirement	*Personnel with access to a processing facility that houses critical information may only enter these with appropriate authorization.*
Company Type	*Policy Statement*
Defense Contractor	Personnel will only enter designated areas corresponding to their level of clearance.
Travel Agency	Associates should only enter areas for which they have been given prior approval.

by the employees. The next step in our journey is to take your newly drafted security policies and get them ratified into law.

Ratifying the Security Policies

Your new policies will only be effective if they are ratified and endorsed by executive management. Most executive management will not be eager to sanction anything without approval from legal, audit, compliance, human resources, and other management. That is why we recommend you form a committee of these people to ensure their requirements are considered as you develop your information security policies. Most companies will have a process of formal approval for any policies that affect the entire organization. If you completed your assessment checklist, you should already have a feel for what this process is. Before we summarize this section, we'd like to take a moment and address the remaining information security program documents: standards, procedures, and guidelines.

Standards, Procedures, and Guidelines

We lumped these three categories of information security program documents together because they share similar characteristics that differ substantially from the policies.

- They are derived from your information security policies.
- They are very specific.
- They provide operational detail.
- They point to specific technical solutions.
- They are subject to periodic change due to their level of detail.

The intent of this discussion is to describe the mandatory elements of the information security program documents, not any specific manner for creating them. The reason is there are many excellent sources and methods for creating these documents. You will need to choose which one is correct for you and your organization.

Although we identified and described these earlier in this chapter, it's important to remember the key differences between these types of documents. Standards are detailed statements describing how the technologies you implement will meet the policy objective. Procedures are detailed statements describing how the processes you implement will meet the policy objective. Guidelines can be anything, but are typically refinements to either standards or procedures or things to consider during their implementation.

Build Security Documents Summary

We will end this section by reiterating the importance of taking the time to gather your requirements and generate thorough, comprehensive, and appropriate security policies, standards, procedures, and guidelines for your organization. They will provide the backbone for everything your information security program will accomplish. This is so important, that we want to take the time to summarize the steps necessary for arriving at this point.

- Incorporating your enterprise drivers (constraints and enablers)
- Transferring your drivers to business requirements
- Refining your business requirements into functional requirements
- Translating your business requirements into policy statements
- Performing a gap analysis against your functional requirements (policy requirements) and your existing policies and controls
- Mapping your existing policies against an existing framework (ISO 17799, CobIT)
- Drafting your information security policies
- Submitting them for review with legal, compliance, and audit
- Ratifying and implementing your information security policies
- Deriving and documenting the standards from the policies
- Deriving and documenting the procedures from the policies
- Ratifying standards and procedures
- Deriving and documenting the guidelines from the policies

Congratulations, you now understand all of the work that needs to go into the formulation of a strong set of security program documents. If you have followed the methodology, you are now in possession of the laws for your organization. The next section will address the designing of mechanisms for enforcing the new laws.

Building the Security Project Portfolio

From this point forward, we will assume you have developed and ratified a full set of policies, standards, procedures, and guidelines. These documents, and the results of the gap analysis you will perform, will form the basis of the security project portfolio. Attempting to build a project portfolio without these components could cause you to miss entire areas where you may need controls. Though you would probably identify some useful projects, the integration and value to the business would be inconsistent.

The security project portfolio is a list of all of the potential projects that need to be completed to fully implement your policies, standards, procedures, and guidelines. The portfolio is prioritized based on the risk each project is designed to eliminate or reduce to an acceptable level. Let's be honest, here. Unless you're lucky enough to have unlimited resources and funding, you will probably never complete all of the items you identify in your portfolio. We recommend you risk rate them according to the value they bring to the enterprise.

Performing the Policy Gap Analysis

Deriving projects from the policies, standards, and guidelines is accomplished through a gap analysis. In this process, you'll be comparing your enterprise's level of compliance with the policies you've adopted to any internal controls that already exist within the organization. This should be a comparison between the future-state (as illustrated by your security policies) and the current state of your environment. You should include both preventive and detective controls, as well as any standards that have been implemented throughout the enterprise. This process will involve understanding not only what your policy requirements are, but how your enterprise should best address the risks associated with each policy.

To perform a gap analysis, you will need to meet with the various groups responsible for implementing or maintaining these controls, and identify what they have done to meet the policy requirements. For example, if you have a policy requirement that eight-character passwords must be implemented on all systems then you may need to meet with the assorted engineers and administrators responsible for implementing passwords on all of the various platforms your enterprise relies on. In addition, these passwords may be implemented at varying layers within each platform. For example, password controls exist within the operating systems, networking equipment, applications, and databases used by each platform. Depending on how you do it, your gap analysis might show

Table 3.2 Policy Gap Analysis Worksheet

Functional Requirements	Policies	Existing Controls		Residual Risk	Exposure	Priority
		Preventative	*Detective*			
Req1						
Req2						

how effectively password controls are implemented for each platform, at each layer.

By doing this for each policy requirement, you would have a solid view of how effectively your enterprise meets your policy requirements, and what types of projects you may want to focus on to remediate any control deficiencies you find in your gap analysis.

After evaluating these controls, we would next determine the residual risk and the resulting exposure. These two criteria would establish the risk to the enterprise and the corresponding priority. See Table 3.2 for help completing this task.

The table above sums up the entire process. However, we should discuss one specific nuance before moving forward. Many policies are written with fairly general and vague terms and statements. This is useful for your policies to stand the test of time, but it does tend to make defining specific project requirements more difficult. If something can be interpreted more than one way, you can bet the farm that it will be. To prevent this, you should take any general or vague terms and statements from your policies and work to create an accepted definition for your environment. For example, the wordage "all systems," "as appropriate," or "approved personnel" are marvelous wordage for a policy, but can be too ambiguous to define concrete actions. The good news is that this is generally not a difficult or time consuming process and can be handled on a policy-by-policy basis. Further, as the world changes, these definitions can change along with it without requiring a complete rewrite of your policies.

Now do you see why having a strong set of security policies is necessary? We arrived at a critical juncture in the formation of your information security program. You are about to cross the boundary of theory into the world of practicality. All hands to the engine room...full steam ahead!

As stated earlier, the security project portfolio will represent all of the tasks that need to be accomplished by your program to achieve the mission. Due to the importance of this section, we are going to create a policy for a fictitious company and step through the project creation process. As always, we start with a sample scenario.

Example

You are employed at the OuiNukem Missile Corporation, the world's smallest nuclear arms designer and manufacturer. As the newly minted CISO for OuiNukem, you have diligently gathered your business drivers and derived the business and functional requirements. Using these two components, you draft and ratify a truly brilliant set of comprehensive security documents. Wow, is executive management impressed with you!

Within this set of documents is a policy statement that reads, "Personnel will only enter designated areas corresponding to their level of security clearance."

You know from speaking to your team that OuiNukem uses a sophisticated biometric retina-scanning product combined with a one-way locking mantrap for maintaining access control to sensitive areas. This was necessary due to the nature of the work the company performs and its customers, branches of the U.S. Armed Services. However, on further inspection of this control system you discover that no logs or surveillance camera tapes are maintained for the hundreds of entries and exits through the mantrap each day. In the past, this was never perceived as a problem because management believed the system was completely unbeatable. However, you realize that this lack of a monitoring control represents a high-risk issue that must be addressed.

Your mission, should you choose to accept it, is to distill a project for your new security project portfolio that addresses this policy and risk rate it for priority.

Analysis

To analyze this example, we provided an extensive analysis that is broken into the critical steps for developing your projects: define Ambiguities, evaluate current controls (gap analysis), determine residual risk, determine resulting exposure, and apply risk rating. We'll begin with defining the ambiguities.

Defining Ambiguities

We demand rigidly defined areas of doubt and uncertainty!

—Douglas Adams

To create a project that meets this policy we would begin by defining any ambiguities in the statement. From our example, the following items represent the ambiguities, along with the definitions, in the policy statement:

■ Personnel — any individual who works within the OuiNukem facility.

■ Designated areas — the Phoenix assembly plant and the Los Cabos Uranium enrichment facility.

■ Level of clearance — the level of clearance will be determined by the physical security office in conjunction with the United States Department of Defense.

To produce a successful project, the ambiguous nature of security policies must be eliminated prior to moving forward. By removing ambiguities, you will insure everyone views the important policy ideas and concepts in the same way. Just as your definition of the above phrases may have differed from ours at first glance, they may also differ from anyone else who has read this book as well. If one person believes that designated areas mean all locations and another person thinks they mean only the Phoenix plant, it will be impossible to scope your project appropriately. The only way to prevent this is to have everyone agree to the same common definitions.

Though defining these items may seem like a massive effort, you may find that many of the ambiguous terms in your policies will be re-used frequently. For instance, the term personnel may be used many times in your policies, but you will only need to define it once.

One last idea to keep in mind is there is no right or wrong answers to the definitions. The only element that matters is that all the people impacted by the definition agree to the way in which it was defined. Once we clarified any ambiguous statements, we'll evaluate the existing controls within OuiNukem.

Evaluating Controls (Gap Analysis)

As the example states the company employs a retina scan as the primary access control mechanism for sensitive facilities. Before identifying whether this control is sufficient, you must determine whether it possesses both preventive and detective capability (see Figure 3.8). Though the use of biometrics and mantraps definitely operate as a preventive control, there is nothing in place that provides any detective control capabilities. Currently, there isn't any electronic or visual record of access that has been granted or denied to sensitive areas. Does this sound like a problem? As the risk chart outlined, each statement must be evaluated for both preventive and detective controls. Currently the deficiency within OuiNukem's environment is a lack of detective controls for the policy. Before moving on there a few more concepts to keep in mind when evaluating controls:

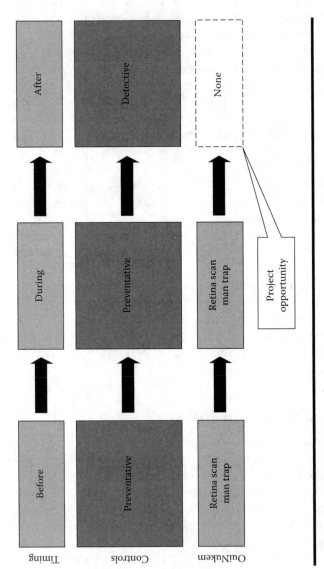

Figure 3.8 OuiNukem Controls

- The existence of a control does not mean that it is adequate; you must make this determination during the evaluation.
- If this policy had possessed both preventive and detective controls that are deemed satisfactory, this policy statement would not contribute to the creation of any projects.

To close out this analysis, we need to state the residual risk, the accompanying exposure, and the final risk rating.

Risk and Exposure Statements

These items are very easy and straightforward to create. In the case of the example, the residual risk and exposure statements could look something like this:

- Risk: The residual risk is the inability to determine if unauthorized individuals have entered sensitive areas of the company.
- Exposure: The resulting exposure is the potential for access, theft, or alteration of sensitive data or materials.

There is nothing terribly complicated or mysterious about these statements. To ease this process of creating residual risk and exposure statements, we have developed some guidelines. Each statement should:

- Provide only the amount of information needed to derive a risk rating; keep the statement clear and concise.
- Try to develop a consistent style for these statements that will aid in their uniform interpretation.

Once you have the risk and exposure statements, its time to apply a risk rating based on these inputs.

Risk Rating

Risk rating can be handled in a number of different ways. We have seen some organizations use a 1-10 scale, although others have attempted to build a complex model for evaluating risk. It's easy to miss the point when building complicated models. The objective is not the model itself, but to have a consistent process for rating specific risks, relative to all of the other risks analyzed during this process.

Because we like to keep things simple, we advocate the use of a high, medium, and low categorization system. This will allow you to view all the risks that comprise a specific category aiding in the development of projects that address multiple-like risk issues. Whichever mechanism you choose, pick one, and stick with it until you complete the design phase. Below is the risk rating we applied to OuiNukem's access policy deficiencies.

Risk Rating — High

Considering that the company deals in high-tech nuclear materials and secrets, the ability to determine a breach should be a high priority to the information security program. This is a personal determination that should be apparent. However, if you have any doubts, enlist the aid of others.

The final step, and the ultimate objective, is to produce actionable projects that will mitigate the risks identified while aligning to the business objective and priorities.

Deriving the Security Projects

This step is the derivation of projects from all of the policies evaluated in the policy gap analysis. Keep in mind we are using an example based on a single policy. In reality, you will be performing this exercise with all of your policies. It will be common for multiple policies to combine to form a single project. We will assume you completed the policy gap analysis worksheet for all of your policies and used a high, medium, and low categorization scale.

Quantitative Evaluation

After completing the worksheet, the first step is to group all of the risk categories together; highs with highs, mediums with mediums, and lows with lows. Don't despair with the total volume of risks as many companies will never get around to addressing the lows and a large number of the mediums. The point is to diligently work through the process, focus on the most critical items first, and after you implement enough of them, you'll eventually reduce your enterprise risk to an acceptable level.

After grouping the risks according to their rating, we will create a simple project name, type, and description to mitigate the risk. This process is a brainstorming exercise. Do not try to build detailed projects; use a simple name with simple definitions; we'll flush out the detail of each project later. The ultimate goal is to consolidate all of the risks into a smaller number of projects. You will repeat this step for every risk in the gap analysis worksheet (see Table 3.3).

Table 3.3 Policy Analysis Worksheet

Residual Risk	Exposure	Priority	Project Name	Project Type	Description

The worksheet allows independent assignment of projects per risk. The objective is to find risks that can be solved by a common project. As you address each risk, trends will begin to emerge that will allow the solution to be furnished in the form of a single project. It is in your best interest to create projects that are capable of addressing as many risks as possible. Don't arbitrarily lump risks together to achieve this goal. The risks must share a relationship. For instance, don't try and expand the scope of your firewall project to address risks associated with physical access. This is obviously a ridiculous example; we merely want to emphasize the need for establishing a balance between project consolidation and practicality.

The assignment of a project type (people, process, or technology) will aid in identifying the measures and controls that will be incorporated into a project; it quickly helps you determine the palette of available options. This easy task will aid you in providing the scope for the projects and give you an idea of the cost and resource requirements. We'll expand on this concept in the next action-packed section of this chapter; stay awake.

If everything has gone according to plan, you are now in possession of a completed gap analysis worksheet. The next move is to consolidate the projects into a single list, eliminating duplicate entries; this will be your security project portfolio.

Eliminating the duplicate entries provides the individual projects, but the number of occurrences of each risk aids in the prioritization of each project; the more occurrences of the project in the gap analysis worksheet, the higher the execution priority of that project. The other primary consideration for prioritizing projects within the portfolio is the rating of the contributing risk. Below we have an example of the quantitative security project portfolio and the steps taken to complete it.

Taking all of the listed information, let's distill the guidelines for the quantitative prioritization of the project queue. Below are the steps:

- Determine the number of occurrences in each of the risk-rated columns for every project.
- Calculate the total number of occurrences for each project.

■ Using the risk rating, move from high to low, to determine the relative priority.
    – Rank the projects based on the ones that address the largest quantity of high risks. The items marked high the most win.
    – If two projects address the same quantity of high risks, use the total quantity of medium risks to determine the ranking. The most mediums win.
    – If there is still a tie, choose the project with the greatest quantity of low risks. The most lows win.
    – Under rare conditions, if they are still tied then so be it. Wait until later in the chapter when we perform the qualitative evaluation to break the tie.

Because this can be confusing, below is an abbreviated sample portfolio with the occurrence section complete (see Table 3.4).

Applying the guidelines, the first row has 20 occurrences of risk that were scored with a risk rating of high in the project analysis worksheet; making it the number one priority for the project queue. The number two priority is the personal workspace security training and awareness project due to the total number of high-risk occurrences using the medium risk occurrences as a tiebreaker. The tiebreaker was needed because both the personal workspace security training and awareness project and the centralization of access control project had the same number of occurrences of high-risk items. The personal workspace security training and awareness project wins the tiebreaker due to having 12 medium occurrences versus 11 for the other project.

After successfully completing the quantitative analysis and ranking of the security project portfolio, we will move on to building your final project portfolio with the inclusion of qualitative considerations.

Qualitative Evaluation

A qualitative evaluation of the security project portfolio will take various esoteric factors into consideration that can lead to the re-prioritization of projects. This evaluation is more an art form than a science and will require considering the following factors:

■ Quick wins — a quick win is a project that can be achieved quickly with a limited expenditure of energy and resources. Their true value is the capacity to exploit the marketability of the accomplishment to aid in building momentum for the program.
■ Timing — this factor addresses the issue of resource allocation. Certain projects will be bigger than a breadbox, resulting in the consumption of large portions of resources. This consideration can

Table 3.4 Quantitative Security Project Portfolio

Priority	Project Name	Project Type	Description	Number of Occurrence			
				High	*Med*	*Low*	*Total*
1	Perimeter Security	Technology	Installation of standard firewalls and derivation of necessary rules	20	5	2	27
3	Centralization of Access Control	Technology	Centralize and standardize the multitude of access control mechanism for the organization	15	11	5	31
4	Log Review Practices	Process	Design, develop, and implement standard procedures for the reviewing and archiving of system logs	7	6	2	15
2	Personal Workspace Security Training and Awareness	People	Provide training to the organization regarding personal practices in the handling of data and systems, focus on raising the awareness of the need for strong passwords, log out procedures, clean desk policy, and illegal software	15	12	12	39

be accommodated by altering the timing of execution for a project. Another major consideration is the projects that are time-constrained due to regulation. The priority of these projects may need to be altered to support a date that is mandated by law.

■ Politics — a project may address a large number of risk elements, but the remediation will be too costly in terms of political capital. These projects are also extremely wasteful in their consumption of energy. These types of projects may be more successful after the program has built some momentum. The scheduling of these types of projects needs to be addressed in a strategic manner.

■ Funding — money makes the world go round. A project may not have the financial backing necessary to be successful. Once again, a high number of risk occurrences does not equate to the finances to mitigate them. It provides excellent ammunition for acquiring the necessary funding, but that's a completely different conversation.

■ Resources and skills — for every project you must perform a cursory evaluation of required resources and skills necessary to execute the project successfully. Skills are always the difficult aspect of this evaluation. If your organization lacks the skill, the amount of resources becomes moot. When in doubt…buy them.

■ Dependencies — some projects within the portfolio may be dependent on other projects that have yet to be started. Obviously, this type of situation would affect the project priority.

■ Culture — the final aspect to consider for the qualitative analysis of the portfolio is the organization's culture. As you implement projects, the awareness and acceptance of security practices will change within the organization. This makes cultural acceptance of various controls a timing issue. You must evaluate the control and anticipated implementation date to determine if the organization will accept it. This timing can also be altered by a people project aimed at increasing the education of the organization toward an upcoming project.

See Figure 3.9 for more information.

Many additional factors can influence the priority of a project. Each organization will be different and will possess additional unique considerations that may not be listed. This isn't necessarily a major issue; these items tend to present themselves with only a minimum amount of detective work. Evaluation is a proactive step that you should take in the budgeting and approval process.

Your ability to include these factors in the development of your portfolio will prepare you to address the objections that may be raised by others while acquiring funds or approval. Don't forget you're not the

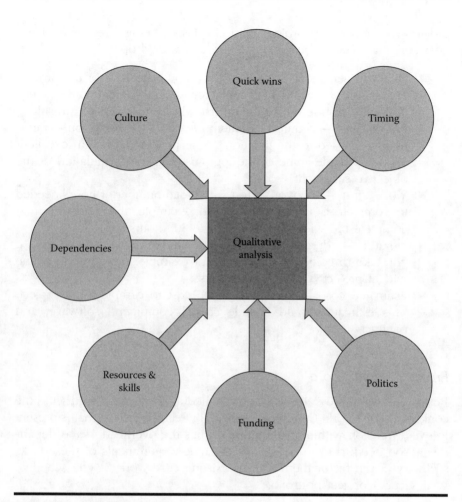

Figure 3.9   Qualitative Analysis

only one looking for funding within the organization. Any funds directed toward your program will not be applied anywhere else in the enterprise. Therefore, not everyone will be as supportive as you would hope (refer to Chapter 1, Assess: decision makers, champions, and obstructionists).

Cursory Project Scoping

Right now, you have a list of project titles with a brief description. That by itself is a major accomplishment. However, it's insufficient for proper planning and approval. That leads us to the concept of cursory project scoping. Cursory project scoping is a high-level definition with metrics for the projects. You need to complete a cursory scoping for each of the projects in the security project portfolio. Listed below are some of the questions that need to be included in the cursory scope.

- Objective statement — what is the overall objective of the project? This should be a SMART statement regarding the intent of the project. It should include the problem that will be resolved as a result.
- Background — a quick statement regarding the background information that led to the creation of the project. This is an excellent area to provide some of the logic used in the formulation of the objective statement.
- Work effort — the work effort is the total number of hours needed to complete a specific project. For example, the work effort to complete the widget project will be 800 hours.
- Duration — duration is the calendar measurement of the time it will take to complete a project. For example, the duration of the widget project will be eight weeks.
- Estimated cost — the approximate cost to complete the project. This estimate should include capital equipment, software, and contract support.

Projects Versus Core

Before we can address the next topic, scheduling, we need to discuss the concept of core work. Core work is the daily recurring work that is present in every function within an organization; it's the overhead of the department. You need to have an idea of the time requirements of these tasks so that you can factor them against existing core work as you schedule your security project portfolio.

Scheduling (First Three Years)

Scheduling for anything can be broken down into short-term and long-term. Security is no exception. Your goal in this scheduling exercise is to create a short-term schedule (one year or less) and a longer-term schedule (two to three years). As with everything else in our methodology, begin with the end.

Start with your security project portfolio and try to imagine which projects will be completed in the next three years. Write a number that represents the corresponding year next to the items to be completed in that period. It's that easy. This is the commonsense filter. You will find there is no need for additional information; merely adjust the projects so they execute in a manner that appears to make sense. You should now have a number next to every project in the portfolio. Next, we apply the practicality filter (see Figure 3.10). There are three major practical constraints that will need to be accounted for in the scheduling of the portfolio: project dependencies, resources, and funding.

- Project dependencies — the easiest factor to account for is the dependency one project may have on another. For example, a television broadcaster cannot determine the playoff match-ups for a particular professional sport until the regular season games have been completed. The playoffs are dependent on the regular season games.
- Resources — a rough estimate of the required resources to execute a project may reveal its timing needs to be altered. Your resource pool is likely fixed necessitating that a schedule for executing projects is arranged in a manner that doesn't create a deficit. For example, if you have a pool of twenty people and you attempt to execute three projects, requiring seventy people simultaneously, it probably won't be successful.
- Funding — the most brilliant idea in the world is useless without the cash to execute it. This is the final practicality filter. Is the cost of the project justified by the results? The logic behind the project has to include the financial rationale for its inclusion in the portfolio.

Each of these constraints will be refined as you generate detailed scope for the associated projects. Remember this is a cursory assessment to provide strategic scheduling for your program.

Capital Budgeting

Your accounting and finance departments will already have a capital expenditures request process. If you haven't already done so, you should learn what that process is, and what forms or financial analysis spreadsheets they require. Your project requests should follow whatever your enterprise's existing processes are.

OK, now that you have a completed security project portfolio that has been both quantitatively and qualitatively risk rated, its time to share it with the rest of the organization.

Approval of the Security Project Portfolio

Your security project portfolio will only be useful if those who will affect the funding and approval process accept it. Those who will affect the funding and approval will be the decision makers you identified earlier. As we stated earlier, your role is similar to an insurance salesman and

Figure 3.10 Scheduling Constraints

your security project portfolio, along with all of the rationale used to develop it, is the end product that you are selling. However, don't forget your portfolio contains those projects that will bring you as close as possible to the end-state you identified in your gap analysis. The goal during the sales of the portfolio is to get the final portfolio to match as closely to the original as possible; get as close to the perfect world as you can. So, how do we accomplish this task?

As always, we have several guidelines for accomplishing this task. Many of these have been passed down from sales professionals to sales professionals ever since cavemen started selling volcano insurance.

- Believe in your product.
- Know your product.
- Know what others are buying.
- Identify the buyers and the roadblocks.
- Sell through momentum.
- Sell through others.
- Ensure that your logic for prioritization is understood.
- Ensure that it's sold before you attempt to sell it.
- Always present in person.

Believe in Your Product

Before attempting to sell anything, review your portfolio and ensure the work performed in developing it has a high degree of quality. Quality lends credibility to the entire program in addition to the portfolio. Focus on the elements that are driving the logic in prioritizing the projects. This law is of greater importance if you have not established any credibility within the organization. Quality speaks louder than words.

Ensure That Your Logic for Prioritization Is Understood

Every potential customer will challenge you, either directly or indirectly, on the logic that you have applied to the portfolio. Take the time to teach the customer how you derived the prioritization though drivers, business and functional requirements, policies, standards, guidelines, and risk.

Know Your Product

The first law has to be: know your product. What is it you are selling to the customer? The answer should be: something they really, really need or something that they really, really want. Never attempt to sell based solely on fear, uncertainty, or doubt (FUD). Though these can be mildly persuasive in the short-term, they seldom (if ever) provide the satisfaction your customer will be expecting at the conclusion of a project.

Know What Others Are Buying

Selling anything becomes much easier when you understand the motives of the buyer prior to presenting the pitch. What will excite the buyer? What pains will your product alleviate for the buyer? What is the direct benefit to the buyer? The buyer is not the organization but the individual charged with making the decision. Don't ever forget that people will generally operate in their own self interest. Identify what would make that person's job easier and use that information in preparing your sales pitch.

Identify the Buyers and the Roadblocks

Every organization will have several different kinds of potential customers. They break down into the following categories:

- Those who will buy your offerings
- Those who will not buy any of your offerings
- Those who can apply pressure to individuals who won't buy your offerings

Those Who Will Buy Your Offerings

These are the easy ones. These people will generally have a vested interest in all, or a component of, the program. Another category of easy sells are those who overtly broadcast their pains and needs, which can be satisfied by your portfolio.

Those Who Will Not Buy Any of Your Offerings

In every organization, there will be individuals who will not buy any of your projects. These are the roadblocks. Once you have identified individuals who fall into this category we suggest you go around them. Though you could engage with these people, it will be easier to circumvent them in the long run. If this is not possible, evaluate your support and power versus the political power of the roadblock and remove it if possible.

Those Who Can Apply Pressure to Individuals Who Won't Buy Your Offerings

Everyone in the organization has someone to whom they report. Everyone has peers within the organization. Once you have established that individual as a roadblock, identify his superiors and peers to determine the next best road for selling the program. Be careful when taking this approach for it can have severe consequences. No one will appreciate the perception of a sneaky individual.

Sell through Momentum

Selling through momentum takes advantage of the herd mentality. This is the need for people to belong to the majority on a particular item or concept. Take advantage of this by selling to the easy sells first to establish the momentum to add people to the cause.

Sell through Others

This is the idea of getting others excited about the possibilities of your portfolio. If you can generate enthusiasm and excitement for your projects, it will be possible to enlist that person's aid in selling it to others. Don't be shy. Tell him how he can help and be as specific as possible.

Ensure That It's Sold before You Attempt to Sell It

This is our way of rephrasing Sun Tzu (the art of war): don't engage in battle until the battle has already been won. For our purposes, this means to spend the time performing a pre-sales function to make sure you're prepared to win the sale. Talk to people and educate them through casual conversation. This will make them part of the club so when the formal pitch is given they are already sold.

Always Present in Person

That says it all. Do not rely on documentation or proxies alone to sell the product. Customizing the sales to the customer must be done in person. Make sure they get the true and complete message. The only way to guarantee this is to be there in person and walk them through the logic.

Summary

All of the work you performed to this point has been in preparation for this step in the methodology: approval of the portfolio. We have discussed many important ideas and concepts and this is no exception. Each project in the portfolio reflects a portion of the entire information security program; for every project you fail to sell, you lose a portion of your program. Failure to gain approval for the majority of projects within the security project portfolio will result in a program that is nothing more than a paper tiger lacking any true value to the organization. Therefore, take your time, be strategic, and focus on selling as much of the portfolio as possible.

Annual Portfolio Review

Your brand new, shiny portfolio will age the second you write it down. That's because many of the issues and factors that are the relevant drivers today may not be as important tomorrow. Every year you will need to perform the entire portfolio creation process. Keep in mind that each subsequent year will be easier because you will be able to leverage your current long-term plan and most likely your existing policies.

The state of your security policies will determine where to begin in the methodology. If your policies are current and do not require updating because the prior year, the review can begin at the gap analysis between controls and policies. Otherwise, you should go back to the beginning and perform the gap analysis of the existing policies to what is needed for the new environment. This is an excellent case for writing policies that can stand the test of time.

Build the Communication Plan

Congratulations. If you made it this far you most likely will be the proud owner of a ratified, fully funded, and executive-sponsored security project portfolio. The final step for completing the design of your information security program is to build the communication plan.

The communication plan is the design and development of the communication mechanisms used throughout the life of the security program. We need to address this concept during the design of the program to furnish the vehicle for maintaining project momentum, removing obstacles, and, finally, for reporting. In this section, we create the channels; Chapter 5, Report, will discuss their optimal use.

The plan for the information security program serves a multitude of purposes other than merely informing the organization of accomplishments and events. If properly planned and coupled with the portfolio, the communication plan can be a powerful tool within your arsenal. It can serve the purposes of marketing, education, and occasionally politics.

The marketing function is the primary use for the communication plan. The principal use for the plan is to promote the information security program. Few people understand the need or the power of self-marketing within an organization. It is the key to funding, acceptance, and ultimately the success of the program. The well-designed, thoughtful, security project portfolio you created is a marketing opportunity. Few areas within the enterprise will possess such a well-organized and logical approach to addressing their mission. After all the pain you have endured to this point, why would you miss this opportunity? The other marketing use for the plan is in the promotion of individual projects.

Eventually, questions will arise regarding the status or intent of projects as you begin to execute them. The communication plan should encompass a mechanism for addressing these questions. We've seen organizations that actually create glossy brochures that explain and instill support for their projects. So when there are questions, they have sanctioned material readily available to distribute regarding the project. Though this is an extreme example, it illustrates the opportunity to leverage the communication plan to gain support and acceptance of an individual project. Another aspect of the plan that is valuable is security awareness.

Once you have established the various channels for distribution, any information from the program can use them. Awareness material can be easily disseminated through this mechanism. Think of it as a shotgun approach for sending out various bulletins that, over time, will alter the way people go about their daily jobs. Finally, the last use for this tool is politics.

Most people like to play politics in the shadows of an organization; they certainly don't want anyone to discover the activity because it is generally frowned on. Your newly created communication plan presents a means to reveal individuals who are hindering your program through politics. The various channels of communication will provide you with a wide selection of tools to deal with these hindrances.

Potential Channels for the Communication Plan

Every organization will be different in the available routes of communication. You need to determine, based on the size and complexity of the enterprise, what is appropriate for your program. Listed below are some ideas that will aid you in developing your communication plan (see Figure 3.11).

- Executive updates — a regular forum for providing security updates to the highest-level executives within the organization.
- Stakeholder updates — a regular weekly or bi-weekly update of the information security program to the program stakeholders. You can accomplish this through a written status report, but we recommend a meeting.

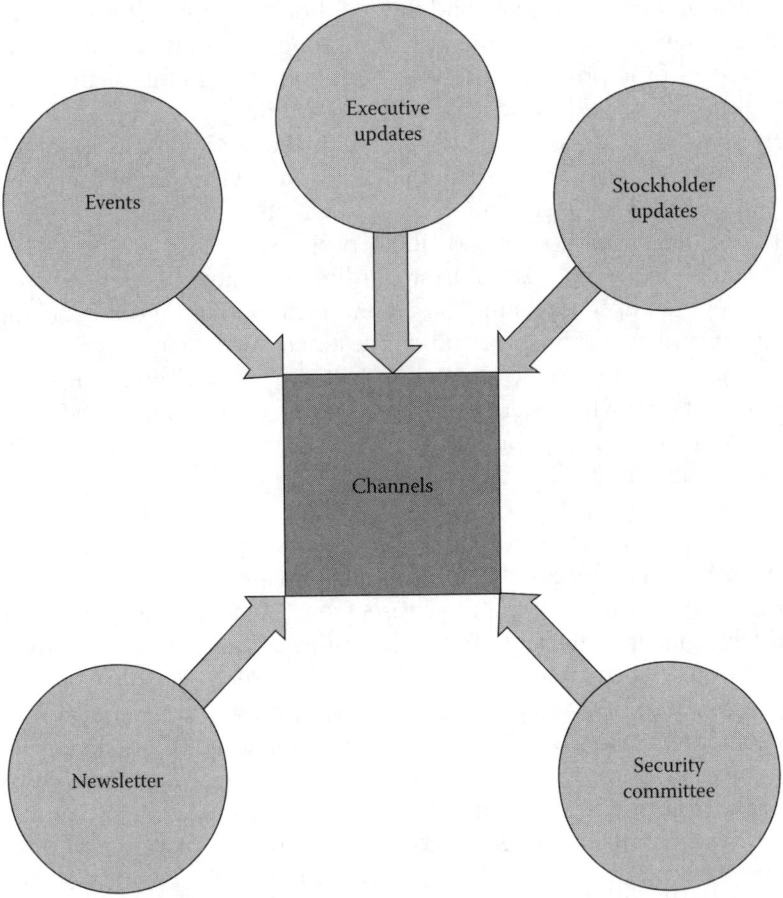

Figure 3.11 Communication Channels

- A security committee — a group comprised of individuals from different areas of the organization who are charged with various aspects of security.
- Newsletter — a publication highlighting upcoming projects, training, and accomplishments. This can take the form of a flyer or company intranet.
- Events — these are gimmicks that involve raffles, sweepstakes, and contests.

The communication plan is a very personalized area of the program that will be unique to your organization. We suggest you enlist the aid of the marketing department within your organization to assist in its design if you feel deficient in this area.

Chapter Summary

In this chapter, we have covered a large number of concepts, procedures, and tools to design your information security program. Though there are many ways to achieve this goal, we presented you with the process we have found to be the most effective and successful.

Our approach is linear, providing an easily explained checkpoint at each juncture of the methodology. Further, this approach ensures that the program aligns to the needs and functions of the organization. Though there are many steps in the process, it ultimately boils down to three primary objectives:

1. Creation of your security documents
2. Creation of the security project portfolio
3. Creation of the communication plan

Up to this point, each chapter has been cumulative building on information from the prior chapter in a serial fashion. Chapter 4, Execute, and Chapter 5, Report, operate parallel to each other. Though we can't present them simultaneously, please keep in mind that they will happen together.

In closing, we want to say that the fun part is about to begin. We will leave behind the world of preparation (assess, plan, and design) and move on to the realm of getting things done (execute)!

Strap on your seat belts, Skippy. The fun's just beginning.

Design Checklist

The design checklist is a bridge between this chapter and Chapter 4, Execute. The information that will be furnished in this checklist will be needed to make decisions in Chapter 4. Not completing this questionnaire will reduce the value of future chapters, because they will rely on the information gathered. The answers do not have to be lengthy, just enough to remind you of the thought process that went into the formulation of the answer. To aid you in this process, we have limited the responses to one or two sentences. Take the time and complete this exercise (see Table 3.5).

Table 3.5   Design Worksheet

FOUNDATION CONCEPTS			
Personal Assessment	*Sufficient Skill (Y/N)*	*Book Review*	*Affected Methodology Phase*
Critical Skills			
Analytical			Design
Organizational			Design, Execute
Sales			Design, Execute
Financial Planning and Budgeting			Design, Execute, Report
Critical Knowledge			
Opportunity Cost			Design, Execute, Report
Security Documents			Design, Execute, Report
Risks, Threats, and Vulnerabilities			Design, Execute, Report
Types of Security Controls			Design, Execute, Report
Gap Analysis			Design, Execute
SMART Statements			Design, Execute
Types of Projects			Design, Execute

Table 3.5   Design Worksheet

DESIGN METHODOLOGY	
Enterprise Drivers	*Constraint or Enabler*
Describe in a single sentence each of the primary drivers for the enterprise.	
Business Requirement Statements	

The additional forms that were discussed in this chapter can be found in the design worksheet appendix. These documents are an extension of the design checklist and will be needed to successfully negotiate the next chapter.

Chapter 4

Execute

Overview

You spent a great deal of time and energy building the customized factory that is your information security program. Now it's time to start delivering the product. The execution phase of the methodology is the process of delivering the projects from the security project portfolio; this is the tangible representation of your program. To accomplish this task we will focus on four major concepts:

1. Project execution
2. Incorporating security into projects
3. Vendor evaluation/selection
4. Preparing the marketing material to publicize the program accomplishments

In Chapter 3, Design, we concentrated heavily on creating a security project portfolio based on the requirements of the business. We then prioritized them by performing a risk assessment.

Using another sporting analogy, it's like filling a stadium, fielding a team, hiring a coaching staff, and finding yourself up at bat. Proper execution is all that stands between a strikeout and a home run. In this chapter, we will focus on hitting the home run. It is important to note that at this point in the methodology there isn't any wiggle room left. In execution, you either get it done or you don't; there is no in between. The mechanism we will use to ensure you are successful is project management.

There are a multitude of project management philosophies, models, and concepts. If you were to distill the commonalities of all of these methodologies, you would wind up with a consistent set of truths for running initiatives, a set of characteristics for executing successful projects. In this chapter, we will identify these project management truths to aid you in executing your security project portfolio. It may be surprising to find a chapter on project execution in a security book. However, we feel it provides synergies that will be important for your program; we have found a strong correlation between a project that has all the foundation elements necessary for execution and the ability to incorporate security successfully into an enterprise. Once you understand these fundamentals, we will show you how to leverage that new knowledge to incorporate security into every endeavor in which you are involved. From there, because the areas of project execution and information security require such specialized skill sets, the next section of the chapter will discuss how to evaluate and select the right product and people vendors. Finally, after disseminating the execution, security incorporation, and vendor evaluation/selection concepts, we will delve into preparing the marketing of your newfound success.

One last idea we would like to cover is how you, as an individual, can best participate in the process of executing your projects. Gaining an understanding of the attributes associated with a successful project will enable you to ensure the completion of the portfolio regardless of your level or degree of participation. Depending on the size and organization of your program, your participation within projects will vary. The execution of your projects may be handled directly by you, your staff, or a different group within the company. In any case, you'll have the ability to determine if any single project is in jeopardy. As usual, we'll start off with the foundation concepts for execution.

Foundation Concepts

Preview

The information we will cover in the foundation concepts for the execution phase include both critical skills and critical knowledge. Below are the critical skills we will discuss:

- Executor
- Commander
- Communication
- Tactician

- Research
- Analysis

Many of these critical skills should look familiar to you because we introduced them in Chapter 2, Plan. We will elaborate on them again here to show how they are applicable to the concepts of execution discussed in this chapter. If you need a refresher on these attributes, refer to Chapter 2, Plan.

This chapter will also discuss different applications of the skills depending on your role and involvement in the project execution process. We will discuss two different roles. The primary role will be responsible for the overall execution of the security project portfolio; this is generally the chief information security officer (CISO) for an information security program. The other role will be a person directly involved in the execution of projects. This role can vary, but is often a project manager or staff member of the information security program. In any case, this person is personally accountable and responsible for the successful completion of an individual project.

We will also define the knowledge required to successfully complete the execution phase. While a comprehensive discussion of these materials is beyond the scope of this book, we will give you a general overview of the areas we believe are critical success factors in the implementation of an information security program, and will point you toward a few recommended resources for more information. These critical knowledge areas include:

- Overview of project management methodologies
- Benefits of a project mentality for your information security program
- The project management triangle
- Technical control layers

Critical Skills

Executor

The ability to get things done will be critical to the success of your program. The executor skill is the ability to manage obstacles, resources, and priorities to meet the original objective for any project. Also referred to as a GSD (Get Stuff Done) degree, this skill can only help you in your career. Without it, your program will never establish the necessary momentum to grow and succeed, and future support from executive management will be more difficult to acquire as time goes by. As a newly minted CISO or a member of an existing information security office, we believe that time spent learning this skill is time very well spent.

Commander

The commander pertains directly to leadership and the ability to inspire and motivate others. Whoever is charged with executing the projects in your information security program must possess the commander attribute and the demonstrated skill to use it effectively. A CISO must possess this skill to inspire, motivate, allocate, reallocate, and align the troops as needed to meet the objectives of your program.

Communication

> Communication is everyone's panacea for everything.
>
> **—Tom Peters**

Communication skills are the combination of the two attributes described previously: writer and presenter. During the life of a given project, there will be a need to relay the status, accomplishments, and the value that the project brings to the organization. Further, communication skills will be paramount to publicize the success of your projects. You can have the most successful projects in the entire organization, but if no one is aware of their existence, it is detrimental to future endeavors. Returning to the sports analogy: though it's satisfying to hit a home run, it's better for future contract negotiations if the stands are full and the cameras are rolling when you do it.

Tactician

The skills of a tactician will vary depending on your role in the execution process. You will either be monitoring the entire project portfolio or be directly immersed in the execution of one or more projects. As a CISO your role will probably consist of making tactical changes that will affect the portfolio such as resources, funding, schedules, and scope. When directly involved in the execution of projects, the tactical skill is used to facilitate alterations to the design, technology, tools, and assignments associated with a project.

Research

The ability to research will be applicable to the execution phase primarily in the area of risk analysis and risk reduction. Threats are constantly developing and evolving. The ability to research effectively will allow you to stay abreast of current trends, issues, and developments that can impact your organization. Additionally, the ability to analyze the risk surrounding a specific project is also research intensive. The smallest detail of a project can expose a high level of risk.

Analysis

Once the research material is collected, it must be analyzed and applied to determine the risk associated with the initiative. This skill will be indispensable during the risk analysis portion of a project.

Critical Skills Summary

Though we can share the attributes and traits that will aid in successful execution of your projects, the ability to deliver a product that conforms to security and operational requirements, is an art unto itself. We attempted to provide some of the basic ingredients necessary to successfully execute and secure any endeavor. The key is to find the right balance for your environment. As always, our intent is to keep things simple, relevant, and useful.

Critical Knowledge

Overview of Project Management Methodologies

> If you can't describe what you are doing as a process, you don't know what you're doing.
>
> **—W. Edwards Deming**

Our definition of a project management methodology is any organized, repeatable process used to complete work in an efficient and controlled manner. This definition is broad and will probably not conform to the exact tolerances of our friends at the Project Management Institute (PMI). However, our intent is not to regurgitate the Project Management Book of Common Knowledge (PMBOK), though it is an excellent reference. Instead, we will focus on a few key characteristics of well-managed initiatives. This knowledge will aid you in assimilating the characteristics as we describe and use them in our methodology. You're probably asking yourself, why are these guys spending so much time selling me on the concept of running everything as a project?

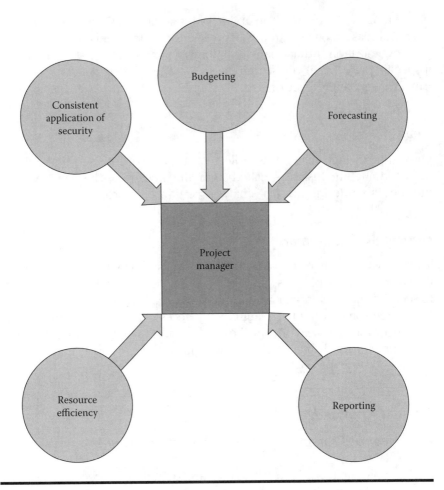

Figure 4.1 Benefits of a PM Mentality

Benefits of a Project Mentality for Your Information Security Program

There are many benefits associated with operating under a project mentality. They include big concepts like accountability, responsibility, visibility, and repeatability. But those don't necessarily resonate with real humans who have real work to accomplish. So let's boil it down to something that is a little more relatable — a project mentality provides the following as shown in Figure 4.1.

Budgeting

The essence of every successful project can be found in the planning and development of detailed requirements. This detail provides all of the components necessary for accurate estimation of costs. For example, if you were to plan a trip to the grocery store using a predetermined shopping list, it will be much easier to estimate the amount of the final bill.

Forecasting

Forecasting is also derived from the planning and development of requirements. The detail you capture in your requirements provides the necessary information to estimate the total work and duration of an initiative. With these components, you'll be able to determine the beginning and end dates for your projects, allowing for the strategic planning of the entire portfolio.

Reporting

Because you spent the time planning and identifying the deliverables of each project, you built the criteria for success or failure into each project. These metrics lend themselves directly into the communication plan. We'll discuss additional items that can be added to reporting during the methodology section on execution.

Resource Efficiency

Resource efficiency is based on the detailed quantification of work that is inherent in a formal project planning. Since you spent the time building the requirements, schedule, and budget, you have the ability to shift and re-prioritize resources in the most efficient manner. An additional benefit that can be tied to resource efficiency is the ability to evaluate the work effort of each individual resource.

If the tasks for a project are detailed and the scope is determined, you now have a built-in benchmark for all of the project participants. This will allow you to evaluate, measure, and re-deploy resources to maximize the execution of tasks.

Increase the Consistent Application of Security

The ability to consistently apply security to projects is derived from two different elements of a project. First is the high degree of definition and scoping that are the trademark of any project methodology. Before you can incorporate security controls into a project, you must know what it is you are attempting to secure. Different projects will require different controls. For example, if you were building a bank vault, the type of lock needed would differ substantially from the lock you used for the front door of your home. The second aspect of projects that lend them to the consistent incorporation of security is they represent a repeatable and predictable mechanism of execution.

Our definition of a project methodology includes the phrase organized, repeatable process. Because every project should be executed following the same rules each time, it will provide an opportunity to build in the necessary controls, checkpoints, and deliverables. These items will ensure that the security requirements have been met and the controls adequately address your security policies.

Summary

Though we focused on five elements of a project mentality, there are many more benefits associated with this mode of working. Throughout this chapter, we will try to point out some of the more nebulous benefits. Before moving on, we'll recap the five primary benefits.

1. Budgeting
2. Forecasting
3. Reporting
4. Resource efficiency
5. Consistent security application

The Project Management Triangle

The project management triangle is a required core concept for anyone who can be impacted by a project. This concept will provide common ground for everyone involved or impacted by the project. This concept is not just for project managers. Even if you never manage a project, a clear understanding of the inter-relationships of these components will aid you for the rest of your career. Let's explore the triangle shown in Figure 4.2.

Each side of the project management triangle represents a different constraint affecting a project. As one side of this triangle changes, at least one other side must change to compensate. As we address each of the sides of the project management triangle, we will build an example one piece at a time to illustrate the concept culminating in a final example.

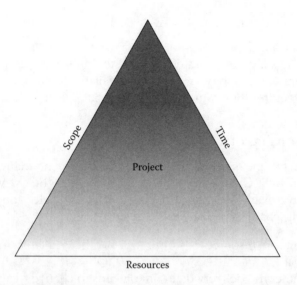

Figure 4.2   PM Triangle

The sides of the project management triangle are scope, resources, and time.

Scope

The ultimate objective of the project is defined within its scope. For example, we would like to build a white picket fence made from pine. It should encompass the entire property and have a gate at the entrance. These simple requirements serve to define your project scope.

Resources

Resources can be money, people, or equipment. These are the tools utilized to accomplish specific tasks within the project. For example, Bobby and Suzy are available to help with your fence, which will require approximately $500 for materials and tools.

Time

Time is the time available to complete a project. It is usually given as a deadline by someone or some thing that has a vested interest in the project's completion. For example, the sponsor has requested the fence be completed by Wednesday.

Cumulative Example

To recap: our small project is to build a white picket fence made from pine by Wednesday. It should encompass the entire property and have a gate at the entrance. Bobby and Suzy are available to work on the project, which will require approximately $500 for materials and tools.

Inter-Relationship of Components

Any change to one side of the project management triangle must be compensated by a change to at least one other side. Below we will take the cumulative example, change one side of the triangle, and explain the compensating changes available as a result.

- Change in resources — Suzy will not be available for the fence project.
    - Either the delivery date (time) needs to change to accommodate the reduction in resources, or
    - The scope of the project needs to be reduced to accommodate the reduction in resources and maintain the original schedule.
- Change in time — the project must be completed by Tuesday.
    - Either the resources need to be increased to accommodate the reduction in schedule, or
    - The scope of the project needs to be reduced to accommodate the reduction in schedule while maintaining the original resources.
- Change in scope — the fence must be constructed of high tensile steel cable.
    - Either the resources need to be increased to accommodate the additional complexities of the scope while maintaining the original schedule (time), or
    - The schedule (time) of the project needs to be increased to accommodate the increase in scope while maintaining the original resources.

The Project Management Triangle Summary

As we demonstrated, changes to one side of the project management triangle must be compensated for by a change in at least one other side. Regardless of the role you play in a project, this perspective on execution will continue to aid you throughout your career. The numbers of permutations are finite and easily manipulated to address the issues and changes that are an inevitable part of business life. With this view on projects, you now have the basics for evaluating and modeling the affect that change can have on projects.

This is an important concept to understand because changes to a project may have a negative impact on the final product. These types of changes can manifest in various ways. The most common is to reduce the scope or requirements, resulting in a reduction in the functionality of the product. This reduction usually impacts the security elements first. This is due to the desire to maintain as many of the original benefits as possible, while meeting the new constraints that have been inflicted on the project. For example, we don't need access control for this version; we'll put it in the next version. It still works without password protection.

The final concept we need to cover in foundation concepts is a holistic approach to building security controls into your projects. It is a layered method of breaking down the various levels of technology to ensure they are addressed when gathering the security requirements for a project. We refer to this model as the technical control layers.

Technical Control Layers

Many information security professionals choose to view the implementation of internal controls of an enterprise in a layered model. This defense in depth approach typically involves the implementation of similar controls at various technical layers within an information technology (IT) environment. We present this concept in the form of a five-layer model. Regardless of the type of project, the security considerations and controls will be found in at least one of the five layers of this model. Following this approach, the technical control layers can be defined as follows:

- Databases
- Applications
- Networking and middleware
- Operating systems
- Physical security and environmental controls

Each layer contains a number of internal controls that can be implemented in conjunction with similar controls at other layers. For example, authentication controls exist within:

- Physical security and environmental controls (e.g., data center card keys)
- Operating systems (e.g., user accounts and passwords)
- Network connections (e.g., user accounts and passwords)
- Applications (e.g., user accounts and passwords)
- Databases (e.g., user accounts and passwords)

Figure 4.3 illustrates some of the internal controls that can be implemented within each technical control layer.

DATABASE:
- User, Service, & Default accounts
- Profiles, Roles & Group assignments
- Special privileges (DBA, DBO, etc)
- Access rights of objects & Resources
- Access rights to objects & Resources
- Global security configuration
    - Environmental variables
    - Audit log configuration
    - Table configuration
    - Encryption
    - Password controls/intruder detection & Lockout

APPLICATION:
- User, Service, & Default accounts
- Profiles, Roles & Group assignments
- Special privileges (Administrator, Supervisor, Manager, Operator, etc.)
- Access rights to screens and transactions
- Interfaces to/from other systems
- Access to command prompts & System utilities
- Input controls (Buffers, Input validation, Batch totals, Importing data)
- Output controls (Distribution, Extracting data)
- Global security configuration:
    - Environmental variables
    - Audit log configuration
    - Table configuration
    - Encryption
    - Password controls/intruder detection & Lockout

NETWORKING (NOS, SERVICES, & DAEMONS)
- Open ports
- Vulnerabilities of services running on open ports
- Patches & Upgrade maintenance (O/S, Firmware & Middleware)
- User, Service, & Default accounts
- Profiles, Roles & Group assignments
- Special privileges (Administrator, Manager, etc.)
- SNMP configuration
- Firewall objects & Rules
- Encryption/VPN configuration
- Configuration of network interfaces (NIC's)
- Domain naming services (DNS)/Windows internet naming services (WINS)
- Configuration of remote access systems (i.e.,VPN, Citrix, Wireless, Modem)
- Global security configuration
    - Environmental variables
    - Audit log configuration
    - Encryption
    - Password controls/intruder detection & Lockout

Figure 4.3   Full Five Layer Control Model

OPERATING SYSTEM:
- O/S Version and Patches
- Configuration of trust relationships
- User, Service, & Default accounts
- Profiles, Roles & Group assignments
- Special privileges (Administrator, Root, NON-CNCL, etc.)
- Access rights of users & Groups
- Access rights to O/S & System files
- Access rights to application source and program executables
- Access rights to application data files
  - Global security configuration (Domain and local)
  - Environmental variables
  - Audit log configuration
  - Encryption
  - Password controls/Intruder detection & Lockout

PHYSICAL SECURITY & ENVIRONMENTAL CONTROLS:
- Physical security (Card key access)
- Monitoring & Alarm mechanisms
- Power management
- Air conditioning & Cooling (H/V/AC)
- Fire & Water damage prevention
- Physical security (Doors/Windows/Walls)

Figure 4.3   (continued)

A layered view of internal controls, such as the example shown above, allows the identification of the right blend of internal controls necessary to avoid or mitigate a given risk or threat. This concept can play a powerful part in allowing you to identify the appropriate blend of functional and technical requirements in any of the projects within any project. We'll show you how to accomplish this task later in the methodology.

Summary

All of the critical skills and knowledge outlined in this chapter are designed to help you with two key concepts. The first is to give you the base skill and knowledge requirements to successfully execute your projects. The second is to provide the ability to incorporate security into all projects within the organization. With this in mind, we will now enter the methodology section.

Methodology

Preview

This is it, the moment that we have all been waiting for: executing projects. This is the physical manifestation of your entire information security program. This is what the rest of the organization will see, touch, and feel. In the methodology section, we will cover the detail of how to successfully execute any initiative. Once you understand the execution portion, we will leverage your new understanding to present the different tools and techniques for incorporating security into all projects. Then, we will shift the conversation to a discussion on vendor evaluation and selection. This is an area of increasing importance as more work is outsourced as companies attempt to control costs using contractors and vendors. Lastly, we will help you start the necessary preparation of marketing materials from the successes that the execution chapter will furnish. The areas we will cover include:

- ■ Project execution
- ■ Incorporating security into projects
- ■ Vendor evaluation/selection
- ■ Preparing marketing materials

We have one final idea we would like to share prior to moving into the methodology. The techniques and ideas we are presenting are not limited to the execution of an information security program. Though our focus is on the execution of your security project portfolio, the methodology we will espouse is applicable to the successful completion of any new idea; it doesn't have to be a formal project. Learning these ideas now will aid you in everything you will do for the rest of your career.

Project Execution

Now that you know all of the projects that are included within the information security program, we will shift our focus to individual projects. In order to accomplish this task, we will discuss the critical success factors for a project, review the different project types, and elaborate on their intricacies. To facilitate this conversation, we must first provide a frame of reference to properly support it. The tool we'll use is a development methodology structure.

Development Methodology Structure

A development methodology is a structured and systemic method for the definition, development, test, and deployment of new or changed elements within the organization. Though there are many different methodologies, each possessing their strengths and weaknesses, they generally boil down to the same critical components. This is where we are going to focus the discussion. We will not argue the merits of a spiral versus cascading methodology; these models merely represent the manner in which the development iteration is accomplished.

Regardless of the method and timing employed, they all rely on stages that will look similar to the ones we will describe (see Figure 4.4). This perspective is invaluable to an information security officer because it provides the ability to view any initiative and determine the point of development and the tools at your disposal for securing it.

Listed below is a brief overview of the various stages of a development methodology along with the opportunities to incorporate security into the process. Later in the chapter, we will expand on the security opportunities in, "Incorporating Security into a Project."

Define

The define phase (commonly referred to as proposal, envisioning, or initiation) is the beginning of every project. This phase begins with the definition of the project encapsulated in the project objective statement. This is a broad declaration that states the intended purpose and describes the final product. It will culminate in a series of documents that describe the intent of the project and the requirements that drive it.

Security Opportunities

- Verify the security requirements are driven by the security documents: policies, standards, procedures, and guidelines.
- Ensure security requirements are included before the project leaves this phase.

Design

The design phase (commonly referred to as analysis or planning) is the point where the requirements and objectives for the project are translated from general statements into specific elements of work to be performed. This is a blueprint for the project including architectural diagrams, a formal project plan, and budget estimates. Don't forget all four of the architectural precepts should be addressed at this point: people, process, technology, and facilities.

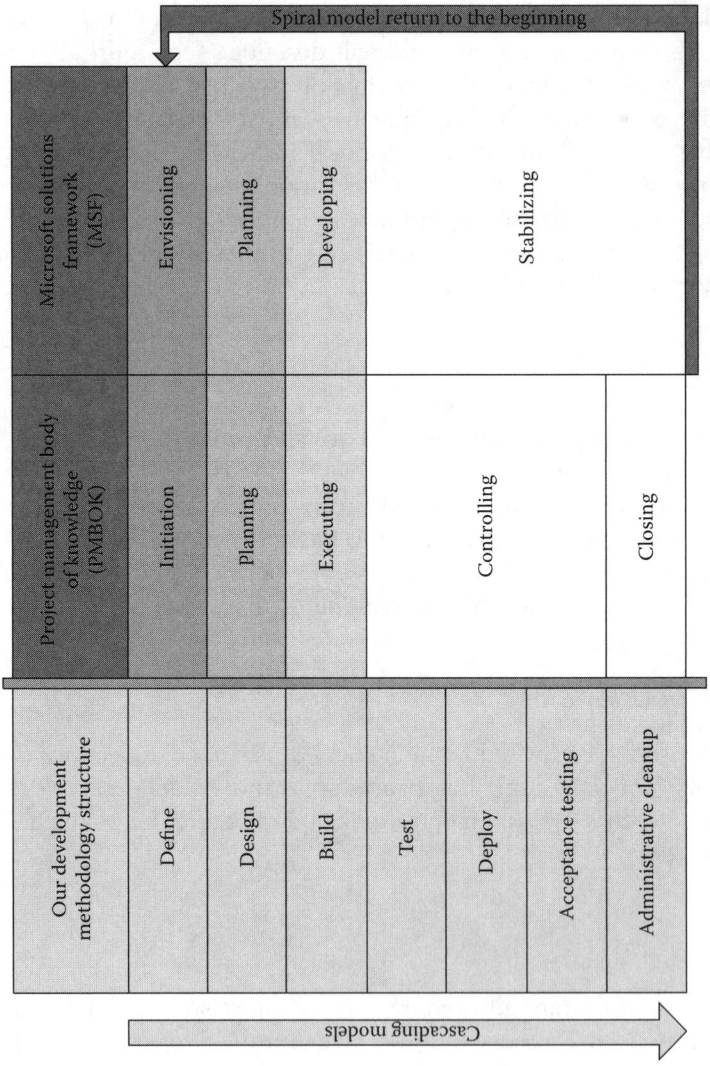

Figure 4.4   Model Comparisons

Security Opportunities

- Perform a risk analysis of the design.
- Make recommendations that will ensure the design adequately addresses the security requirements.
- This is also an excellent time to build future checkpoints into the project plan.

Build

The build phase (also known as execution or development) is the point in the project where the team begins to execute the physical tasks associated with the project plan. If the effort is a software development project, this is where the programmers start to write code. If the effort is a network infrastructure project, this is where the team starts to assemble equipment. There isn't much more elaboration for this point in the project; this is where things start to get done.

Security Opportunities

- Measure the completed product against the security requirements. Make sure the project team did not take any short cuts to meet the project schedule.
- Reconcile the risk analysis to the product. Verify that the risk analysis from the design phase is still valid for the current product. If not, modify the risk analysis to reflect the product in its current state.
- Make recommendations to mitigate unacceptable risks.

Test

> Test fast, fail fast, adjust fast.
>
> **—Tom Peters**

The test phase (also known as controlling or debugging) is the point in the project where the design is verified against the functional and technical requirements. It is a measurement of expected performance to actual performance. The information derived from this phase is then used to alter the product to ensure the correct functionality. The means by which this is accomplished will vary based on the development methodology your organization employs.

Security Opportunities

- Success in the earlier phases of this process will make security efforts in this phase much easier. Pay me now or pay me later…one-way or another you are going to pay.
- Ensure all test results are documented.
- Reconcile the risk analysis to the product. Verify that the risk analysis from the build phase is still valid for the current product. If not, modify the risk analysis to reflect the product in its current state.
- Make recommendations to mitigate unacceptable risks.

Deploy

The big day has arrived and it is time to unleash your new project into the production environment. This part of the methodology is commonly referred to as go-live, deploying, or stabilizing. If you exerted enough energy at the beginning of the project, gathering requirements and driving the design from them, this phase should be a non-event. For those of you who didn't, the project is probably culminating into a lot of sleepless nights. The moral of story: measure twice and cut once. The energy expended early in the project will pay massive dividends in the form of a successful project.

Security Opportunities

- This is the last opportunity to measure the final product to determine its compliance to the security requirements.
- Reconcile the risk analysis to the product. Verify that the risk analysis from the test phase is still valid for the final product. If not, modify the risk analysis to reflect the product in its current state.
- Make recommendations to mitigate unacceptable risks.

Acceptance Testing

This phase of the project is often overlooked in many IT organizations. It is generally considered a software development concept, but it is often employed in most project management methodologies. This phase is comprised of re-administering the test plan (developed in the test phase) and reconciling the results to the originals. They should be identical. If not, roll back the deployment and determine the cause for the deviation.

Security Opportunities

■ Any changes made at this point will require another reconciliation of the risk analysis.
■ Make recommendations to mitigate unacceptable risks.

Administrative Cleanup

The last step in any project is completion of the residual administrative tasks. The types of items that fall into this phase include:

■ Finalization of all documentation
■ Ensuring an orderly transfer of knowledge to the responsible operations area
■ Lessons learned
■ Final review of accomplishments with the executive sponsor

Development Methodology Summary

There are different flavors of concepts and methodologies for project execution. When you distill them into their core functions, they all have the same basic components. They will all have a phase for defining, designing, building, testing, and deploying a project though these phases may use different names (see Figure 4.5). A distinct benefit for a security professional attempting to build a program is it allows you to integrate into any existing organization that has formal or informal processes for the completion of work. Just remember, as long as these major stages are addressed your chances for success will increase dramatically. For any methodology to be effective, it must cover the areas described in the phases above, and it must include certain critical success factors.

We will now move on and furnish detail on the critical success factors allowing you to consider the impact of these elements in the development methodology structure. The other benefit of this approach is it will enable you to compare and contrast these components relative to your own company. Now that we have presented the concept of a development methodology, let's move on to the discussion of the critical success factors.

Critical Success Factors for a Project

The critical success factors for a project are the ingredients that increase the probability of success for an initiative. You may complete a project

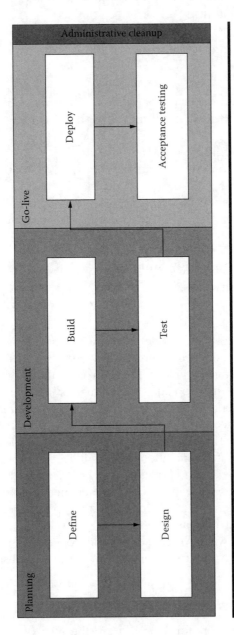

Figure 4.5   Development Flow

without them, but your chances of success will be greatly diminished. Depending on the complexity and size of the project, the amount of each ingredient will vary. Listed below are the most valuable critical success factors for a project:

- Project requirements
- Governance model
- Management support–sponsorship
- Establish team
- Shared vision
- Formalized project plan (Gantt chart)
- Identifying and working through the lull of doom

Some of the items above may look familiar if you have read other books on IT auditing, information security, or application development. These critical success factors (in one form or another) are also common to a System Development Life Cycle (SDLC). An SDLC is really just another type of project methodology in this regard. Therefore, if you practice project management you are in essence going through many of the same steps included in an SDLC. Since we are going to discuss the critical components of project management, you will automatically get exposure to a basic SDLC for your program. This is where we feel our approach is different from other security books. Instead of merely discussing why the incorporation of security into an SDLC is important, we will actually show you how to build an SDLC and then incorporate security into it. We will begin with the single, most important aspect to any endeavor: project requirements.

Project Requirements

Project requirements provide the necessary detail and criterion to determine exactly what needs to be built, providing an exact end-state for the deliverable. Executing a project without formal requirements is the equivalent to trying to construct a multi-story building without blueprints.

What is odd is many enterprises run projects without ever formally identifying the requirements. We feel this is caused by six basic reasons:

1. The process can be time consuming and most projects are reactive; people want to see immediate results.
2. It's harder to do. It requires a large degree of discipline and energy.
3. It eliminates the wiggle room on projects. They force the delivery of the exact item promised.

4. It defines accountability. The use of formal requirements is analogous to making a promise. Some people are terrified by this prospect.
5. Some people simply don't know where to begin. For whatever reason, they don't know how to identify or gather the very requirements for the projects they are responsible for implementing.
6. Finally, some people don't understand the benefits associated with formal project requirements. If they did, we believe they would want to do them every time.

Benefits of Formal Requirements

The list above gives some common reasons why some enterprises execute projects without expending the necessary effort to develop or document formal project requirements. Further, we alluded to the amount of effort associated with this task. Now we'll show you why we believe the time and effort are worth the investment.

▪ They provide a blueprint to guide your construction effort — as we stated above, you wouldn't construct a building without a blueprint. Formal requirements establish the end-state of the deliverable, providing a defined goal to strive toward. It is always easier to plot a course when you know the destination.
▪ They represent a contract between the program and the organization — once the requirements are approved, they represent the agreement between everyone involved with the project. This enables the project to lock-in on the objective and proceed with minimal deviation.
▪ They provide metrics for determining project success — since the requirements define the end-state for the project, they automatically provide a benchmark to determine if the final deliverable conforms to the original goal of the project. When the project is completed, merely compare the delivered product to the requirement statements, line by line, and measure the degree of compliance.
▪ They serve as a communication tool — formally documented project requirements provide the perfect distillation of a project and its stated objectives. As a result, you may decide to share them with management or other stakeholders of your program as appropriate.
▪ They serve as a consensus-building tool — the requirements of a project provide a tangible culmination of all the ideas and concepts associated with a project. The acceptance of this document is tacit acceptance of the project itself. If you worked with the various stakeholders for the project to gather them, then they will have a

much higher degree of support for its completion than if you develop them in a vacuum.

■ They provide a mechanism to ensure the inclusion of security into the final product — like any other area associated with a project, security will have requirements that need to be incorporated into the design of the final deliverable. Formal requirements provide the mechanism to ensure the security elements are considered during the design instead of retrofitting them on completion of the project.

The list above provides a synopsis of the benefits associated with project requirements. Additionally, there are a number of smaller benefits that can be associated and extrapolated from each of the major benefits that will vary based on your organization.

Now we discussed the role, importance, and benefits of requirements; here are the building blocks for identifying and gathering project requirements.

Building Requirements

Let's start this section with a question: what makes a good set of requirements? Each methodology has a different definition and manner in which it is assembled. Ultimately, they are all attempting to accomplish the same goal — the quantification of work to be performed and the constraints and criteria that need to be met by the initiative.

In our opinion, anything that can meet this definition is an effective set of requirements. Experience has taught us regardless of the presentation method, a good set of requirements share the following characteristics:

■ Representative — all of the requirements should be accepted by the participants and sponsors of a project.
■ Sufficiently detailed — requirements should possess only the detail needed to relay the concept no more, no less.
■ Related — a requirement should be related to one or more subordinate requirements (we'll elaborate on this subject a little later).
■ Documented — all requirements should be clearly documented.

The following items represent what we believe to be the building blocks of project requirements:

■ Objective statement
■ Business requirements
■ Functional requirements

- Technical requirements
- Security inclusion
- Project electives
- Gathering methods
- Packaging and publishing

Objective Statement

An objective statement is collected for every project within the security project portfolio during the design phase of our methodology. However, when the time comes to initiate a project, you should always verify that the objective statement you identified earlier is still valid for the project. This statement is the definition of what is completed within the project. It is the basis for all the requirements that you will gather.

Business, Functional, and Technical Requirements

In Chapter 3, Design, we introduced two of the three types of requirements you will need to understand to successfully create a comprehensive requirements document for each project. The two types included are the business and functional requirements as shown in Figure 4.6.

The difference between these types of requirements and those presented in the design chapter is in their application; these requirements

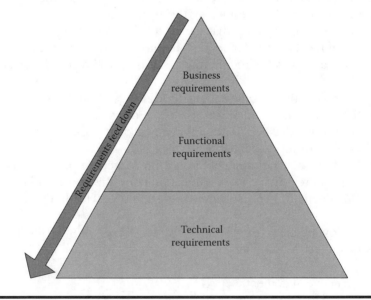

Figure 4.6   Requirements Flow

are specific to projects, not the entire information security program project portfolio. Therefore, prior to moving on to the technical requirements, we will first present a quick refresher on the definitions of these two types.

Business Requirements

The business requirements define the elements of the project that can be derived from the project objective statement. This will provide the business justification for committing to the initiative. It represents the top of the pyramid in the hierarchy. These statements will feed the functional requirements.

Functional Requirements

The functional requirements are the characteristics of a solution that support the business requirements. They will describe the manner in which the solution achieves the objectives of the project. The functional requirements are related to the business requirements in a one-to-many relationship; one business requirement will probably drive multiple functional requirements. This ensures the integrity of the project scope and the relevancy of the overall project requirements.

Technical Requirements

Technical requirements are the attributes and characteristics that must be included into any aspect of technology to fulfill the project objective. This can include statements such as: the solution must operate on a Windows 2003 server operating system or the solution must support Triple DES encryption. These statements operate as clear guidelines and constraints for evaluating various technical solutions. The technical requirements maintain the integrity of the project scope because they are derived from the functional requirements; one functional requirement will drive multiple technical requirements.

Security Inclusion (Security Requirements)

With all of this talk about project methodologies, you may have thought we forgot about security. Quite the contrary! Most books discuss building security into an organization through an SDLC, but fail to explain how to accomplish this task. To build security into the organization through an SDLC or project framework, you must understand the total process and the various points where security can be integrated.

The single, best way to ensure that security is incorporated into each initiative within the enterprise is through the requirements process. Whether your enterprise follows a formally documented project methodology or a more informal process, requirements represent the single best tool your information security program has at its disposal.

The security requirements are any statements that support a security policy, standard, procedure, or guideline. They should fall into one of the three types of requirements shown above (business, functional, or technical) to best work within your project methodology. This is how you will institutionalize the practice of building security into every project. The results of these practices will yield the following benefits:

- Comprehensive analysis — requirements provide a comprehensive view of the end-state for the project, allowing the best available diagnosis for security requirements.
- Benchmark for security — the security requirements provide a measurement device to determine the level of compliance for the project. This part can provide significant value to the organization and is described in Chapter 5, Report.
- Accountability — the security requirements provide a means for establishing accountability of the project team to ensure adequate security controls have been built into the project scope.
- Education tool — the process of building security requirements into a project increases the awareness toward security by everyone participating in the projects. This includes management, project managers, business analysts, application developers, and system engineers. Over time, this process helps to educate people about internal controls, risk identification, risk avoidance, and risk mitigation.

Though this sounds great as a concept, you may be asking how to accomplish this task. If you recall from the foundation knowledge section, we introduced the idea of a five-layer model in the section on the technical control layers. The benefit of using this model is it will provide a comprehensive guide for ensuring you do not exclude any potential area of security.

The manner in which you employ this model is to map each of the security-driven requirements to each of the different levels outlined in the model. Using an example, we will correlate the requirement statements to the model in the form of a diagram.

Scenario

Let's assume They-Go-To-Eleven (TGTE) Inc. is a manufacturer of high-end guitar amplifiers used by the loudest (and richest) rock bands on earth. TGTE employs a layered approach to implementing security require-ments (internal controls) into their projects and view technical control layers using the five-layer model described earlier. With this in mind, we'll move on to the project and the various security requirements.

One of their security-driven business requirements is to ensure all employees are held to the highest levels of accountability. This, in turn, translates into two specific security-driven functional requirements that can be implemented across several different technical control layers, as follows:

1. Security-driven business requirement.
   ■ All employees are to be held to the highest levels of accountability.
2. Security-driven functional requirements.
   ■ All employees must be uniquely identified and authenticated to any company-owned computer systems.
   ■ All access attempts will be logged. All transactions performed by users will be logged.

Figure 4.7 illustrates how the above requirements might map to a layered model of internal controls.

The two security-driven functional requirements shown in the above example translate into several project security requirements (internal con-trols) that exist within each technical control layer.

■ Unique user accounts and security group assignments within all layers.
■ Passwords within all layers.
■ Intruder detection/lockout controls can be deployed at the oper-ating system and networking, and middleware.
■ Audit logging controls can be implemented in all five of the technical control layers shown in this example.

The next level of considerations to include in building your project requirements are the project electives.

Project Electives

Project electives are the exception to the rule when gathering require-ments. Though they are reflected as requirement statements for the project, they do not directly support the overall project objective. These items will benefit your security program, but not necessarily the project itself. Be very careful when including electives because too many of them will lead to scope creep and confuse the vision for the project.

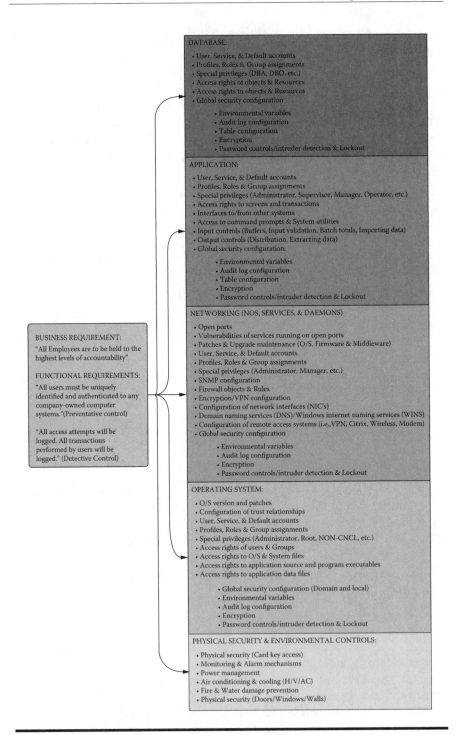

DATABASE:

- User, Service, & Default accounts
- Profiles, Roles & Group assignments
- Special privileges (DBA, DBO, etc.)
- Access rights of objects & Resources
- Access rights to objects & Resources
- Global security configuration
    - Environmental variables
    - Audit log configuration
    - Table configuration
    - Encryption
    - Password controls/intruder detection & Lockout

APPLICATION:

- User, Service, & Default accounts
- Profiles, Roles & Group assignments
- Special privileges (Administrator, Supervisor, Manager, Operator, etc.)
- Access rights to screens and transactions
- Interfaces to/from other systems
- Access to command prompts & System utilities
- Input controls (Buffers, Input validation, Batch totals, Importing data)
- Output controls (Distribution, Extracting data)
- Global security configuration:
    - Environmental variables
    - Audit log configuration
    - Table configuration
    - Encryption
    - Password controls/intruder detection & Lockout

NETWORKING (NOS, SERVICES, & DAEMONS)

- Open ports
- Vulnerabilities of services running on open ports
- Patches & Upgrade maintenance (O/S, Firmware & Middleware)
- User, Service, & Default accounts
- Profiles, Roles & Group assignments
- Special privileges (Administrator, Manager, etc.)
- SNMP configuration
- Firewall objects & Rules
- Encryption/VPN configuration
- Configuration of network interfaces (NIC's)
- Domain naming services (DNS)/Windows internet naming services (WINS)
- Configuration of remote access systems (i.e.,VPN, Citrix, Wireless, Modem)
- Global security configuration
    - Environmental variables
    - Audit log configuration
    - Encryption
    - Password controls/intruder detection & Lockout

OPERATING SYSTEM:

- O/S version and patches
- Configuration of trust relationships
- User, Service, & Default accounts
- Profiles, Roles & Group assignments
- Special privileges (Administrator, Root, NON-CNCL, etc.)
- Access rights of users & Groups
- Access rights to O/S & System files
- Access rights to application source and program executables
- Access rights to application data files
    - Global security configuration (Domain and local)
    - Environmental variables
    - Audit log configuration
    - Encryption
    - Password controls/intruder detection & Lockout

PHYSICAL SECURITY & ENVIRONMENTAL CONTROLS:

- Physical security (Card key access)
- Monitoring & Alarm mechanisms
- Power management
- Air conditioning & cooling (H/V/AC)
- Fire & Water damage prevention
- Physical security (Doors/Windows/Walls)

BUSINESS REQUIREMENT:

"All Employees are to be held to the highest levels of accountability"

FUNCTIONAL REQUIREMENTS:

"All users must be uniquely identified and authenticated to any company-owned computer systems."(Preventative control)

"All access attempts will be logged. All transactions performed by users will be logged." (Detective Control)

Figure 4.7   Full Five Layer Control Model with Example

The type of elective that is easily justified, and very important to a information security program, is the establishment of metrics for the purpose of marketing the program.

Marketing Metrics

Marketing metrics are the quantifiable information used to prove the value and worth of your program. Though this is important to any type of program in an organization, it is highly applicable to information security. As we discussed in earlier chapters, the value of an information security program is often difficult to quantify and explain to others. Using marketing metrics will aid in defining and proving the value of your organization. Wherever possible, you'll want to identify project deliverables that can provide statistical proof of risk avoidance or risk mitigation — the primary goals of an information security program. The best means of achieving this objective is by incorporating this concept into your requirements. Below are some example requirement statements that would provide a wealth of marketing metrics. We will discuss how to utilize the results that statements like this would collect later on in this chapter and in Chapter 5, Report.

- The solution must reduce the number of individuals who need to enter the data center by at least 30 percent.
- The solution must conform to all HIPAA requirements and guidelines.
- The solution must be capable of providing enterprisewide reporting of all access attempts, whether successes or failures.

Methods for Gathering Requirements

Gathering requirements is a straightforward process we will present in a straightforward way. During the process, there will be many participants contributing to the requirements document. However, only one person can be responsible for construction and assembly of these requirements. This ensures that the final documentation is consistent and uniformly interpreted. Let's move on to the process of gathering requirements (see Figure 4.8).

The first step in determining the requirements for the project is to build a sample document (i.e., a straw man) that others can review and build on. It's far easier for others to add to an existing document than to come up with things from scratch. So, using the project description derived during the cursory project scoping, document all of the business and functional requirements relevant to this project that you can think of. The

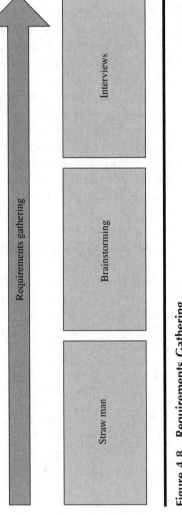

Figure 4.8 Requirements Gathering

amount of requirements you will be able to derive will be based on your level of knowledge in the areas specific to the project. Do not worry if you don't get all of them because it would be virtually impossible for one person to completely scope an entire project. Your intent here is to build a straw man to fuel further conversations. Once you have accomplished this task, the next step is to schedule some brainstorming sessions with knowledgeable professionals.

These brainstorming sessions serve several purposes besides gathering requirements. First, they allow you to gain additional insights into elements that can potentially affect your project. Second, they provide the opportunity to float an idea to the public to measure the acceptability of a new initiative. Third, they provide an opportunity to begin gaining consensus and advocates for the new project. The last step is the interview process.

The interview process is the means by which you refine the existing requirements to accommodate the parties affected by the project. This mechanism will aid in the resolution of disputes between parties, increase communication and awareness, and gain consensus among the major stakeholders. This step becomes more important when the project has a political element associated with it.

Now that you have gathered the various type of requirements, it is time to consolidate them into a consumable, uniform document.

Packaging and Publishing

The requirements document is your contract for the project and should reflect the hard work and time that has gone into its preparation. For maximum effectiveness, this document should be presented in a consumable format that is consistent from project to project (see the Requirements Sample Appendix for an example). Like any good contract, the intent of this document is to remove any room for ambiguity; you are defining the scope of work for the initiative.

Another function of a clean requirements document is a sales brochure for the project. It can be distributed to any interested party and executive management to reinforce the image of your security office as an effective instrument of change within the enterprise.

Since it incorporates the ideas and concepts from all of the relevant parties, it will provide a mechanism for establishing expectations and deliverables for the project. Note that once the requirements have been approved, all parties are committed to delivering their associated requirement responsibilities. People are watching; you better get it done! To get it done, you'll need to know how to interact with your team. That leads us to the next critical success factor: project governance.

Project Governance Model

The project governance model of a project methodology defines the roles and responsibilities under which all projects are executed. There are many different ways to define the model, but they all should share the following characteristics:

- Clearly identifies and defines roles and responsibilities
- Addresses all levels of the project from the line engineers to the executive management level
- Establishes defined channels of communication
- Provides a reporting framework
- Provides an escalation path for resolving project issues

All of these factors will aid in the overall success of projects, as well as provide the information security program with more valuable tools. These tools include a role on the project teams for participation from the security office or the ability to set precedence if that role is lacking. Another tool is the ability to gather project-specific information faster. Since there will be defined roles, responsibilities, and communication channels, it will be easier to acquire the information needed to make effective security requirement recommendations. Project governance models will ensure security concerns are identified and escalated early in the project execution process. This provides more time to proactively resolve security-related matters, reducing the likelihood of impacting the project schedule.

Once you have identified all of the roles and responsibilities for executing your project, the next step is to understand and solidify the level of management support.

Management Support — Sponsorship

> Management must speak with one voice. When it doesn't, management itself becomes a peripheral opponent to the team's mission.
>
> **—Pat Riley**

This is a critical factor. Any project initiated without the full support of management is doomed to failure. For this discussion, management is defined as those individuals who have the responsibility, authority, and funding to either get the project completed or to stop it dead in its tracks. The requirement for management support is magnified when dealing with projects outside security. It provides an escalation path and a single point of accountability to ensure the security requirements are met for every project. Once you have management support, you are ready to build the execution team.

Establish a Team

Few great things are ever achieved by one individual; it takes a team. Project work is an example of where this rule applies. The establishment of a good project team can make even a scary initiative successful. Let's take a look at the attributes needed for a successful team and analyze these factors to determine their pros and cons.

The same considerations applied to determine the size and structure of your security team can be used in determining project teams. The first component to consider is the size of the team. Small teams are usually agile, allowing them to adjust to fluid situations when the scope of the project is moving. The amount of time and energy needed to manage a project will increase as the size of the team grows, eventually to a point of diminishing returns. The objective is to find the balance between effectively executing a project and the effort to coordinate its resources. We prefer to start with a smaller team and add to it as needed.

The composition of the team is going to have the largest impact on its size. Additions to the core project team are made to compensate for a perceived technical deficiency. Select only the minimum number of individuals required to meet the needs of the team. They don't all have to be superstars, just good at their particular discipline (it's not always the most talented team that wins the championship, but the right mix that works best together). If you are already doing this, you are ahead of the game. Many organizations do not take the time to analyze the composition of their teams. Take the time to build good teams and it will pay great dividends as your projects move along the project pipeline.

Now that you have built the execution team, it's time to share the vision with everyone.

Shared Vision

> On this team, we're all united in a common goal: to keep my job.
>
> **—Lou Holtz**

In sports, every team has a shared vision of success. It is reflected in a common drive to win a championship title or a trophy for the level of competition. Whether it's the Super Bowl, World Series, or the World Cup, every player on a winning team shares the vision that constitutes success. Though a security project is probably not as exciting as these professional championships, it shares the same dynamics for success. The first rule of every project is to share the vision.

Take the time to explain what everyone should be working toward and how each individual will play a role in the successful achievement of that vision. Since we are discussing security projects, this is an excellent time to make sure the project team is well versed in the security aspects of the vision for every project within the enterprise. Over time, this will become a natural part of the organization's culture to consider security in the shared vision of everything that is built.

Formalized Project Plan (Gantt Chart)

Before beginning this section, we would like to issue a small disclaimer: project plans are a tool; they are not the project. A formalized project plan is a valuable tool to provide forecasting and resource leveling for a project. It will aid you in the following manner:

■ Share the vision and the plan of attack.
■ De-conflict resources.
■ Plan the work effort.
■ Measure the planned-work to the actual-work completed.
■ Provide progress reporting.

For the purpose of security, the Gantt chart is a treasure chest of information. It will provide a sanity check of the security requirements to the actual work planned. The plan, like everything else in the project, must be driven by requirements. If you are uncomfortable with the requirements, the plan won't make the project any better. Failure at the requirements formulation stage will translate into failure at the project planning stage. All of the benefits we list below are base-lined using the project requirements. If the requirements are strong, then the chart can provide insights into:

■ The feasibility of the execution plan. If the plan isn't feasible, chances are security will not meet the project requirements.
■ The competency of the execution team. The logic, organization, and order of the plan speaks volumes about the team members.

- The validation that the security requirements are included in the execution of the project and the manner of inclusion.
- The ability for the security office to build checkpoints into projects. Project plans are usually stratified by phase, providing an opportunity to build in a security gate for evaluation.

The next topic we would like to discuss is an anomaly we like to refer to as the lull of doom. While the lull itself is not a critical success factor, the avoidance of it is.

Identifying and Working through the Lull of Doom

Every project will encounter the lull of doom. Sounds dramatic huh? The lull of doom is our term for when projects lose their momentum right after the completion of a large portion, generally just before the last mile of the initiative (see Figure 4.9). This is the point where most of the major issues have been solved, and their associated tasks completed. This is where your team starts to slack off because a great deal of the energy and excitement has diminished. This is the same as running the best 22-mile marathon in history...the only problem is marathons are 26 miles long. Your job is to identify the lull and drive your team through it to a point where they can sense the finish line and regain their excitement and enthusiasm. The place to look for the lull is after the deployment or acceptance testing phase of the development methodology.

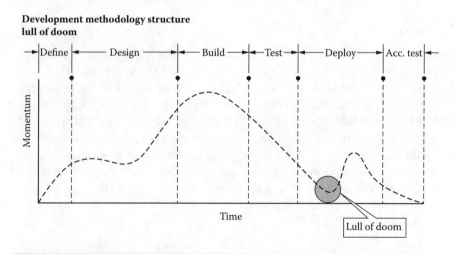

Figure 4.9   Lull of Doom Graph

Critical Success Factors Summary

The critical success factors for a project are numerous and diverse. Your use of these tools and techniques will vary based on the size, complexity, and the unique characteristics of each project. The objective is to find the balance between need and practicality. Like any process, excessive bureaucracy or procedures will hamper the execution and efficiency of the project, too few and the project may not ever get off the ground. Use the critical success factors as a checklist for what should be addressed in each project. Then determine the level of applicability for your endeavors. To extrapolate on the concept of critical success factors, we will move on to some examples of every day types of projects where the critical success factors are either missing or improperly balanced.

Warning Signs for Projects

> I always tried to turn every disaster into an opportunity.
>
> **—John D. Rockefeller**

This is a compendium of different types of cataclysmic project outcomes we've seen and how to recognize them before the inevitable disaster. In order to make them more relatable and ease your identification with them, we have coined certain terms to describe these types of initiatives. In their entirety, we affectionately refer to all of them as train wrecks.

Train Wrecks

This is our term for describing projects that are clearly doomed to fail. These projects are missing at least one, and often many, of the critical success factors needed for them to succeed. Not only will these projects fail, they are also incredibly difficult to ensure security is properly embedded in the solution. If one of your projects fits this category, stop it now and fix it. If you can't stop it, warn the stakeholders and prepare for damage control. If the project belongs to someone else and you are responsible for securing it do not despair. The entire next section will discuss the techniques for securing these kinds of projects.

As we identify specific examples of these train wrecks, let's start small and move to the larger ones.

Desperado

The desperado is an initiative that does not have any visibility, thus negating any opportunity for support or input; for that matter, few people know of its existence. It is driven by one person and encompasses only that individual's objectives and requirements without any regard to the rest of the organization. Another major flaw attributed to this mode of operation is resources.

The desperado uses resources in an ad-hoc fashion because a formal utilization would draw too much attention to their endeavor. The critical success factors often missing from the desperado include:

- Shared vision
- Formal requirements
- Governance model
- Project team
- Management support
- Formal project schedule
- Packaging and publishing

Hoover

The hoover is a known project understood by one person. The title comes from the fact that all of the work on the project is conducted in a vacuum. The missing critical success factors for a hoover include:

- Shared vision
- Packaging and publishing

Wiley Coyote

This is one of our all-time favorites. We call this type of project failure a Wiley Coyote because of an unreasonable amount of complexity built into the project scope. Just as Wiley Coyote would design the most elaborate solutions that were incapable of capturing the Road Runner, many projects will build the most incredible solutions that don't come close to meeting the objective. The Wiley Coyote is also our favorite because it underscores the importance of identifying and documenting a solid set of project requirements. These projects often do not document formal requirements because either the idea is incomplete or the project does not make sense. Missing element:

- Requirements!

Death March

The death march is a project that never seems to end. You've seen these types of projects before; you know the ones that have been going on for the past five years. They cycle through resources, managers, designers, subject matter experts (SME), but no one seems to be able to complete the project. The reasons for this type of project include:

■ Weak or no objective statement
■ Meandering requirements
■ Shared vision
■ Formal project plan

Quick Sand

The quick sand project is the initiative so mired in bureaucracy, procedure, and micro-management that it is encumbered by its own methodology. This is when the critical success factors are either missing or out of balance. They may all be present, but the degree of use is counter-productive. The probable cause for quick sand is:

■ One or more misused critical success factors

Hail Mary

The Hail Mary is a desperation attempt to solve a critical problem without adequate time to plan and execute. These types of projects are generally the result of reactive corporate executive management practices; don't be one of those people. Like all projects, the Hail Mary is dependent on the project management triangle. What makes these projects different is it is virtually impossible to balance or to compensate for the extreme needs of the project. This can include any or all of the factors:

■ Time
■ Resources
■ Scope

You can call these types of projects anything you want. The point we're trying to make is these projects are missing one or more critical success factors resulting in an imbalance or complete disregard for the project management triangle. You want to identify these projects early and take the appropriate corrective action. Table 4.1 illustrates the projects we discussed with the associated missing or improperly balanced critical success factors.

The last topic we will cover for execution is the intricacies associated with the different types of projects as discussed in Chapter 3, Design. These include projects that affect people, processes, and technology (see Figure 4.10).

Table 4.1 Missing or Improperly Balanced Critical Success Factors

	Desperado	*Hoover*	*Wiley Coyote*	*Death March*	*Quick Sand*
Formal Requirements	☑		☑	☑	☑
Governance Model	☑				☑
Sponsorship	☑				☑
Defined Team	☑				☑
Shared Vision	☑	☑		☑	☑
Formal Project Plan	☑			☑	☑
Packaging and Publishing	☑	☑			☑

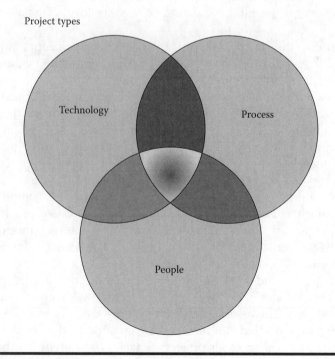

Project types

Technology

Process

People

Figure 4.10   Project Types

Project Types and Their Intricacies

Your security project portfolio is comprised of the three basic types of projects discussed in the chapter on design: people, process, and technology. It is common for a project to have characteristics and elements that are a mixture from multiple project types. However, there is always a primary driver used to determine the project type.

Once you identify the project type, you will need to make minor adjustments to your development methodology to accommodate the unique traits of each type. Each of these project types have intricacies and quirks that need to be considered when in the definition and design phases of a project. Additionally, certain tools will lend themselves better to one type of project versus another. This section is intended as a cheat sheet to aid in the formation of the security projects.

Common Guidelines for All Projects

No matter what type of project you are attempting to execute, the guidelines and concepts outlined in this section will aid you in successfully accomplishing your project. These give the extra little kick that will make your projects run smoothly. These elements have either a direct, or an indirect, effect on the implementation of security for the initiative.

■ Review the factors of the project management triangle for balance — this is a quick sanity check to verify the task is achievable. It doesn't have to be an elaborate analysis, just a gut check.

■ Review the initiative to determine the level of use for all of the critical success factors — review the organization of the project and team to determine missing or improperly used critical success factors. If one or more are missing, and needed, force the project to incorporate it. Compensating for the lack of critical success factors is not recommended. We've made it very clear that these components are necessary to avoid problems and complications.

■ Ensure the availability of a qualified SME — every project needs an SME. Not a self-proclaimed expert, but one recognized by the organization and peers to be an expert. The ultimate design of the project will only be as good as the SME.

■ Project risk and impact analysis — each time an organization begins a new project there will be risks associated with its successful execution. This is different from security risk. These types of risks refer to items that can hinder the execution of the project such as dependencies on other projects or lack of resources. Further, there will be an impact on the organization as a result of the new thing the project is creating. Both of the items need to be analyzed and reported to the stakeholders of the project to shift the accountability for these variables to the appropriate levels of the organization.

- Identify obstructionists — every organization has people within it who lack the necessary skill, sense, and maturity to contribute in a positive manner. We're not saying who they are...just that they exist. Your project needs to be free of these types of people either as part of the team or an element along the critical path of a project.

These guidelines are consistent amongst all projects and using them will aid you in identifying and circumventing project risk. Next, we will focus on the guidelines that are generally applicable to people projects.

Common Guidelines for People Projects

People projects are unique because the primary focus is to alter the behavior and practices of individuals rather than inanimate objects or processes. Since individual human reaction can be unpredictable, it adds complexity and variations to every project of this type. The guidelines we are going to address are directed toward managing and normalizing the human element of these projects. We will begin with the cultural considerations of the organization.

- Cultural considerations — each people project needs to consider the culture of the organization they will affect. A strong understanding of the culture will allow you to predict the response certain changes will evoke from the population, allowing you to alter or tailor the message to increase the level of acceptance. For example, a company with a relaxed family culture would have an adverse reaction to regular, random drug testing if the message was not delivered correctly. By understanding the potential reaction early, it will allow the message and delivery to be tailored to accommodate the culture increasing the likelihood of acceptance.
- Management support — most managers will be very interested in projects that affect the employees and the manner in which they produce the work; always reaffirm management support for these endeavors. Though this needs to be done for all projects, people projects are especially sensitive. Once they are bought into the project, they can be instrumental in selling the benefits of the changes. Many employees look to management for guidance, direction, and support. Management can provide the assurance many employees will require to accept the change.

■ Manner of communication — people projects will typically impact a large, diverse audience. As a result, you will be limited to the mechanisms at your disposal. Most mass communication systems will not provide a mechanism for you to control the spin that will result from a large amount of people attempting to interpret the message. The only solution for this problem is to select a tool that provides the clearest, most concise, delivery of the project message. This tool should allow for some type of personal feedback and issue management. For example, the company has decided to implement a clean desk program. In order to distribute the message, the CISO has determined that a tiered communication approach to management is the best manner in which to communicate. The idea is to present the written material to the various levels of management to address their concerns and issues, and to have them perform the same function with their employees. This will deliver the same communication documents, control the employee spin, and allow each manager to give the appropriate assurances to their team. The result will be the clean desk program is enabled and everyone understands the what, why, and how of the project.

Common Guidelines for Process Projects

Process projects are unique because they often overlap and intertwine with other processes that currently exist within an organization. The more one process interacts and depends on another, the greater the complexity and number of considerations must be addressed by the project to avoid damage. To alleviate some of these complexities, we developed the following guidelines.

■ Highly scoped — though scoping is always necessary, process projects require an additional level of granularity to avoid the potential of scope creep. Process projects can be like a loose thread on a sweater; you pull out the first one, which leads to the second, third, fourth. Applying a fine degree of scoping to the project will help to establish the boundaries reducing the potential scope creep.
■ Keep it lean — during the development of new processes, it is easy to over-build and over-complicate them. Compartmentalize the project to accommodate the project requirements with the leanest available solution. It will be easier to maintain, communicate, and deliver the final product minimizing the impact to the organization.

■ Responsibility and authority of the process — don't forget to build the roles and responsibilities into the new process. Every process needs defined roles and the associated responsibilities to maintain and execute the new process. For example, if the project were to create a new process for ordering a stapler, there would be several new roles and responsibilities that would be required to execute the new process: requestor, fulfillment, finance, and approvals. This deliverable is often overlooked leading to confusion and inconsistency once the project is completed and the process becomes operational.

■ Tools — a picture is worth a thousand words never applied more than when discussing process projects. Your tool for accomplishing this task is the flow chart. We recommend flow charts and pictures whenever possible; they are irreplaceable when discussing processes. Use them well and often.

■ Great is the enemy of good — before embarking on a process project come to terms with the idea that the perfect process does not exist. It is nearly impossible to account for every variable and complexity of a new process. However, it is important to design a good process; do not over analyze, and delay the project in an attempt to create a great process. It will be far more efficient to deploy a good process and handle minor variables as they present themselves after the process has been released to operations.

Common Guidelines for Technology Projects

The majority of available security controls will often be based on technology. This will result in a majority of projects launched by your program to fall into the technology category. Like other types of projects, technology projects have their own idiosyncrasies.

■ Company technology profile — the company profile is its propensity toward various technologies. Does the company prefer to be on the bleeding-edge or stay in the realm of tried and true? The company's technology profile will determine the available options considered for the final solution. This information is available from the assessment checklist you completed in Chapter 1, Assess.

■ Technical SME — due to the variety of available technologies and their associated complexities, technology projects tend to require a higher degree of specialization. A common pitfall is to use the first available body in this role rather than identifying and acquiring a resource that is highly skilled in the needed discipline. Remember that technical projects generally produce a tangible deliverable that would be very difficult and expensive to change once deployed. As a result, choose these people wisely.

■ Information quality — most technologies will be delivered as a product from a vendor. The goal of most vendors is to sell a product, not to solve your problem; though the good ones will do both. The information provided by vendors needs to be carefully evaluated because it has a tendency to possess a great deal of marketing hype. This will become more complicated as the number of vendors competing in a product space increases. The easiest solution to this problem is to review material from unbiased sources. An additional method is to gather all of the information on a product from multiple sources and reconcile it all to find the common message.

■ Gap diagrams (differential diagrams) — as we said in the design chapter, you will use this concept over and over, and over. In this particular case, we are speaking of the gap between the current state and the proposed state of a technical solution. Though this process should be used in all projects, it is especially important in technology projects due to the cost, energy, and complexity associated with them. Two diagrams that display the different states will allow a quick analysis to determine if the requirements of the infrastructure can be met and determine the overall suitability of the design for the environment.

Project Type Summary

Every project can be categorized into one of the areas listed above. Keep in mind these guidelines can be mixed and matched to accommodate the unique characteristics of your project. For example, you may determine a project is a process project, but has a heavy reliance on technology. In this case, use the appropriate guidelines from both categories.

Incorporating Security into Projects

Hopefully, you are beginning to see the correlation between executing a project and the ability to incorporate security into that project. As we move forward, we'll start to focus solely on the security aspects leaving the pure execution elements behind. We will approach this conversation from two different perspectives. The first will be directed toward the tools that can be employed to build security in a properly structured project, while the second will be focused on the techniques that will compensate for a project that is missing critical success factors. The other slight difference in this section is we will address projects as a generic definition; they may be projects from the security project portfolio or any other initiative emanating from within the organization. Before delving into these topics, we would like to take a moment and discuss the idea of expectations and consequences.

Expectations and Consequences

> High expectations are the key to everything.
>
> **—Sam Walton**

Building an information security program and reducing the risk to an organization is not easy; that's probably why you purchased this book. It becomes even more difficult when working with other entities within the organization that may not understand or appreciate the role of security. The first step in the process is to establish the expectations of the information security program within projects. No one is going to know what you need or expect until it is communicated to them.

This message must be clear, consistent, and concise. It should outline the role of security within a project and the expected deliverables necessary for adequate risk reduction; set the expectation. Address any questions and clarify any misconceptions. Once the project members know what is expected, what happens if they fail to comply?

This question is answered by your mandate and the organizational alignment of the information security program; both questions should have been answered in the assessment checklist. If your program has adequate clout to establish a consequence that is commensurate with non-compliance, do it. Communicate the ramifications for non-compliance and make sure everyone involved understands the serious nature of the role of security. Operating under these conditions will be covered in the following section on Adding Security to a Properly Structured Project. If your program does not posses the political muscle to establish meaningful consequences for the lack of compliance, then the following section on securing a project with missing components will provide techniques for compensating.

Tools for Adding Security into a Properly Structured Project

Let us congratulate you if this area applies to you and your organization. Since your organization has the necessary framework supporting its development initiatives, we will direct this conversation toward the tools that can be employed to incorporate security into your projects. We illustrated the major points on this subject during the discussion on the development methodology structure, but we felt it was important to reiterate the key points. Listed below are some opportunities for building security into the various phases of a project, along with a description of the tools that will facilitate this activity, when all of the prerequisites are present.

Define Phase

Security Opportunities

- Verify the security requirements are driven by the security documents: policies, standards, procedures, and guidelines.
- Ensure security requirements are included before the project leaves this phase.

Enabling Tools

- A formal requirements document — a well-articulated definition of the business, functional, and technical requirements for the project will illustrate how the policies and standards will be addressed. This document will provide an opportunity to ensure security requirements are included and reconcile them to the security documents. If they are missing, this is your opportunity to make sure the project requirements are complete by including them.
- Publishing your security policies — a series of security policies that are readily available to the population of the company. This will increase the likelihood that others will consider the policies when formulating the project requirements.
- Training — training programs designed to relay the contents of the security policies that are easily consumable by laymen. This increased level of awareness will improve the likelihood of security inclusion within a project.
- Governance model — a clear set of roles and responsibilities for the information security program will set and maintain the manner in which security will participate for every endeavor. The role of security within the organization can be highly confusing; this simple document will alleviate this condition.
- Authorization — add a security sign-off for each phase to ensure the information security program is involved in any add, change, or deletion to the information systems for the organization; projects

are merely a convenient choke point. If you view the implementation of internal controls as a layered model, you can create a security checklist that asks pointed questions regarding the implementation of specific internal controls at each of your technical control layers. This checklist can be used at the various stages of your project lifecycle to ensure the appropriate internal controls are implemented to meet the functional requirements you identified earlier. As a reference you can use in the creation of a customized security checklist for your organization, we have included a sample for your consideration in the SDLC Checklist Appendix.

Design Phase

Security Opportunities

- Perform a risk analysis of the design.
- Make recommendations to ensure the design adequately addresses the security requirements.
- This is also an excellent time to build future checkpoints into the project plan.

Enabling Tools

- Gap diagrams (differential diagrams) — this is the process of diagramming the current state in one diagram and presenting the proposed changes in a second diagram. These two diagrams allow a quick gap analysis of the solution to determine if it is sound and conforms to the security documents.
- Security checklist — this is a document that is designed by the security office with the intent of guiding laymen through the pertinent questions and issues surrounding security for the project. This is an excellent tool for bubbling up security concerns early in the process for rectifying. An example of this document was referenced in the SDLC Checklist Appendix.
- Perform a formal risk analysis — the concepts and techniques associated with a formal risk analysis are beyond the scope of this book. With this in mind, we recommend two ways of addressing this need. First, use a security checklist and perform a risk analysis on the findings. Second, perform a full risk analysis on the entire project. The first option is far less time and cost intensive making it a viable solution for an organization with a small security team or one that is time constrained.

- Project plan (Gantt chart) — the Gantt chart for the project should outline all of the major tasks and the associated schedule for their completion. It is a powerful tool that will enable the security office to track the progress of a project, as well as ensure the incorporation of security requirements into the final product.

Build Phase

Security Opportunities

- Measure the completed product against the security requirements. Make sure the project team did not take any short cuts to meet the project schedule.
- Reconcile the risk analysis to the product. Verify the risk analysis from the design phase is still valid for the final product. If not, modify the risk analysis to reflect the product in its current state.
- Make recommendations to mitigate unacceptable risks.

Enabling Tools

- Requirements document — this is the foundation for the project. You should be able to tie the final product back to the requirements point-by-point.
- Gap diagrams (differential diagrams) — the final product should match the future state diagram completed in the design phase.
- Project plan (Gantt chart) — verify every step in the project plan was completed. Any steps skipped, usually in the name of budget or schedule, represent a potential nonconformance to the original design.
- Arsenal of compensating controls — know what tools and solutions are currently available within your environment that can be utilized as compensating controls. This can include logging and log review, training, virtual local area networks (VLANS), firewalling, or any other commonly used mechanism employed within your organization to reduce risk. The key to this suggestion is to have the facilities built before you need them.

Test Phase

Security Opportunities

- Success in the earlier phases of this process will make security efforts in this phase much easier. Pay me now or pay me later...one way or another you are going to pay.

- Ensure all test results are documented.
- This is probably the most important checkpoint.
- Reconcile the risk analysis to the product. Verify the risk analysis from the build phase is still valid for the final product. If not, modify the risk analysis to reflect the product in its current state.
- Make recommendations to mitigate unacceptable risks.

Enabling Tools

- Application and network scanners — don't reinvent the wheel. Take advantage of the plethora of available scanning products. The inclusion of these tools presents an unbiased third party evaluation that can be helpful when addressing issues that may be politically sensitive.
- Formal test plans — most projects are tested in an ad-hoc fashion, usually by individuals without formal training on testing procedures. The best way to alleviate this concern is through formal test plans. These test plans should be derived from the formal requirements and should produce repeatable results.

Deploy

Security Opportunities

- This is the last opportunity to measure the final product to determine its compliance to the security requirements.
- Reconcile the risk analysis to the product. Verify the risk analysis from the test phase is still valid for the final product. If not, modify the risk analysis to reflect the product in its current state.
- Make recommendations to mitigate unacceptable risks.

Enabling Tools

- Physical inspection — a physical inspection of the total system and the affiliated components will give you the final level of confidence in the product.
- Documentation — the inspection should be driven by the requirements document, the project plan, and the final state diagram. Make sure all of the necessary elements have been put into place and function as they were designed.

We found these are the tools and techniques to be the most useful and applicable for incorporating security into projects. You will note all of the tools build on each other as the project moves from phase to phase. Therefore, inclusion at the earliest stages of a project will make your life much easier. If you find yourself engaged later in a project, determine the current phase and play catch-up with your tools. The fact that you will be able to identify the current stage of the project, and what steps should have been taken, will provide a point of reference with which to work. This idea is useful when working in an environment that employs a structured development methodology. What happens if they don't? Let's move to the next section and find out.

Tools for Adding Security into a Project with Missing Components

The previous section dealt with securing projects that operated under an ideal project framework. The sad fact in our experience is more projects are run haphazardly than in a structured, systemic fashion. These projects are generally missing one or many of the critical success factors. In this section, we will discuss techniques to compensate for a lack of missing components, collaterals, and tools.

Missing Requirements

Our initial response to this particular problem is: thanks for playing, but there is some hope. This is the only element within a project methodology for which there is no alternate means of compensation — you just need to tackle this one head on. If you don't have requirements, you do not know what is being built. If you don't know what is to be built, you certainly can't secure it. So what do you do in these situations? You must get the objective and the supporting requirements formally committed in writing. Missing or poorly written requirements represent a significant risk to the project and ultimately, your program. As we stated earlier, project risk needs to be escalated to the sponsors so the accountability is shifted to the appropriate level of the organization. Most sponsors will not be willing to accept risk born from omission; the lack of a critical success factor will generally be motivation to get the situation corrected.

Missing Governance

Any project that has not established a formal governance model is essentially the same as a baseball team taking the field without anyone knowing what position to play. So how do you reduce the risk of this situation?

- Establish a primary contract — since there isn't any established leadership for the project, create a virtual leader for yourself. This will cut through the noise and confusion of the project and transfer it back to the individuals who created it. Place all of your requests and requirements with this individual and hold them accountable for the delivery. Brutal, but effective.
- Rely on project documentation — use the project documentation as your SME for the initiative. Any discrepancies in the project need to be directed back to the documentation for explanation. This will force the project team to maintain the documentation and provide you with a view into the project without any of the confusion surrounding it.

Missing Sponsor

The sponsor provides a single point of accountability for a project. It is common for projects that have a low probability of success to lack sponsorship as no one wants to be associated with a loser.

- Escalation — if you go far enough up the organization structure, ultimately one person can make the decision. Keep escalating the issue until a sponsor is named for the project who is directly accountable for its execution. If that means you keep going until you reach the board of directors, so be it. They will probably be very interested to find out that money is allocated to an initiative no one is willing to own.

This is yet another example of missing critical success factors, but what if they aren't missing individual components, rather an entire development methodology?

Missing Systems Development Life-Cycle Methodology (SDLC)

This is a common occurrence. Not as common as missing requirements, but common. Hopefully, we've sold you on the necessity of a development methodology to the information security program. The problem is many IT professionals haven't necessarily come to the same conclusion. The result is there will be many initiatives and projects run without them. The approach for handling this situation is a sequential escalation of force. The first step is to ask the participants to document and define their development methodology.

The development methodology the team has employed for the project may be perfectly legitimate. In this case, you need to determine the points of interaction for building security into the project. If it is not definable or defendable, this needs to be brought to the attention of the sponsor. This is an inherent risk to the project and represents a risk to the enterprise, something you cannot possibly certify. If the sponsor does not intercede, then it's time to escalate this issue to executive management.

If the approach fails to make sense with executive management, a correction will be made allowing you to perform your function. However, if executive management supports the project in its current incarnation or doesn't want to be bothered with the issue, there is another way to achieve risk reduction for the project.

The solution to this problem is to apply the same necessary deliverables to these efforts as you would to your own projects. The project team doesn't need to know you are marshalling a development methodology. They will simply view your requests as documents necessary for security sign-off of their project; the good news is that is all they really are.

- Detailed documentation — require the project team to furnish the same types of documentation at the same level of quality you would expect from a properly run project.
- Interviews — if the project team fails to build the documentation required for a proper risk analysis, conduct a series of interviews to extract the information and build your own documents. This is a tricky area because eventually you will often know more about the project than anyone else, making you the de-facto project manager. Remember your focus here should be risk reduction, not execution.
- A project schedule — this is a high-level schedule that marks the milestones for the initiative. The higher the degree of detail, the better.
- Utilize a third party technical guru — this is a spiffy little political maneuver you should use infrequently and with great care. Sometimes difficult messages are better received when the messenger is an independent third party. Further, these individuals are viewed as having a higher degree of expertise. This may not be the case, but it is usually the perception. Sometimes hiring a consulting firm to perform an independent analysis will have more credibility with executive management and create momentum for you.

Security Incorporation Summary

We'll be the first to admit some of the techniques we discussed in this section are a bit Machiavellian and may lead to your removal from a Christmas card list or two. But let's be frank — the primary objective of an information security program is not to be popular; it's to reduce the risk to the organization. The consequences of failing to meet the primary objective can have disastrous results for the organization. That does not mean you cannot perform your function in a congenial manner. If you are creative and thoughtful in the use and deployment of these tools and techniques, you and your program can perform your primary task and be viewed positively by the rest of the organization.

This concludes the discussion on execution and securing projects. Before addressing the topic of "Preparing the Marketing Material" we need to review one final related concept: the use of vendors in both execution and risk reduction.

Vendor Evaluation/Selection

> True genius resides in the capacity for evaluation of uncertain, hazardous, and conflicting information.
>
> **—Winston Churchill**

We have incorporated the vendor evaluation/selection process into this section because vendor selection is a natural part of most organizations, particularly when dealing with both execution and security. The ability to both execute projects and perform security functions tends to require a high degree of specialization; as a result, outsourcing will be a common occurrence. We break vendors down into two distinct categories: products and people.

Product Vendors

Our definition for product vendors is any external entity whose primary business is the sale of a tangible product or service. To properly select a vendor, we came up with a procedure to ensure the product selected meets the needs it is intended to satisfy.

- Never purchase anything without requirements. Requirements for a product are just as important as requirements for a project. They establish the business need and the definition of the solution capable of fulfilling it. Do not allow any potential vendors to participate creating the requirements; chances are they will be skewed to that vendor's advantage. Always create your requirements internally before including an outside organization to participate.
- Review industry material to determine applicable vendors. Use every mechanism at your disposal to understand the product space,

its occupants, the maturity of the products, and the relative leaders. Identify the short list of potential vendors; three to five participants should be a workable number.

■ Reconcile your requirements with vendor material. Take your requirements and perform a cursory reconciliation against readily available vendor information. The goal here is to match apples with apples, and oranges with oranges. This practice allows you to include elements that may have escaped your attention during the requirements building process. It is also the last opportunity to purge a vendor from the short list prior to contacting them.

■ Contact the potential candidates and conduct phone interviews. Selecting a product is like hiring new employees. They will be joining the company and performing critical services designed to enable the business. Do not treat this process like a trip to the grocery store. Your intent is to determine the fit of the product or service for your organization, as well as the vendor who will support it. A great question to ask during this exercise is who the vendor considers to be his primary competitor? It will usually be the same; they will all be chasing the space leader. In the event you get a new name, maybe they should be researched for inclusion in the short list. Further, the manner in which they address their competitor will provide indications to their level of professionalism.

■ Send requirements to vendors as a questionnaire. After establishing a communication channel with the vendors, send a copy of your requirements to them as a questionnaire. Have the vendors explain how their solutions meets each of the requirements. Force them to answer the questions concisely usually with one or two sentences. This practice will negate their ability to cut and paste exciting marketing dribble into the response. If the vendors don't wish to participate or comply with your request, you have learned a valuable lesson about them and may not want to engage in a business relationship. If they respond in a timely manner, this shows the degree of interest they have in pursuing a relationship. The final benefit of this practice is it provides another opportunity to reduce the short list to an even shorter list.

Bake-Off

Competition is not only the basis of protection to the consumer, but is the incentive to progress.

—Herbert Hoover

A bake-off is a practical comparison of products or services conducted within your organization. The first step in the process is to build a detailed, applicable test plan derived from your requirements...of course. You can use the vendors to aid in the test, but do not allow them input or modifications to the test plan. Keep in mind, this exercise is expensive in terms of time and energy. Therefore, minimize the number of participating vendors to two or three, include only those who have a realistic chance of winning.

- Always add training — sometimes it's free. There is a little known secret when negotiating on products. Many vendors will give free training in an attempt to close the deal. A new product is of little use if your people do not know how to extract the maximum benefit from its use. Always ask for reduced pricing or free training; the worst answer that you'll receive is no. Training is a low-cost, high-margin product for the vendor; there is usually some room for negotiation.

- Always add lab equipment — it's generally heavily discounted. When negotiating for capital equipment make sure you inquire about the acquisition of identical products for a lab. Many vendors have a heavily discounted price list for equipment purchased for use in non-production environments. Though they won't sell at these discounts for your production needs, they will consider selling it for a lab or staging environment.

- Negotiations — prior to beginning negotiations, perform an honest assessment of the size and marketing clout associated with your organization. If you are a large company with tremendous brand power, vendors are more likely to be flexible in their negotiations than if you are a small ten-person company. The other component when measuring your negotiation tactics is to evaluate the stature of the vendor. If the vendor is a small player new in the space, he is likely to work harder and make more concessions to gain your business. These are generalities, but they may save you money. Do not feel badly about working a hard deal with a vendor if your company carries a great deal of clout. The vendor will realize additional sales power by adding you to the client list which vendors love to publish. Your company name will be used in every sales pitch for the next five years.

- Close the deal — closing the deal has to do with selecting a vendor and ending negotiations with the remaining competitors. The easy part is informing the victors of their newly acquired customer. That leaves the remaining bake-off partners who were not selected. Don't leave them guessing. Most vendors expend a great deal of time, energy, and money attempting to win your business. Be professional and let them know as soon as possible. Further, be honest why they were not selected. They may not agree with your assessment, but at least they can leave the situation with some valuable information that can be used for future sales.

We spent the past few pages presenting a formula for evaluating product vendors. Though the selection of any type of vendor shares similar traits, people vendors have some unique aspects that will need further exploration.

People Vendors

People vendors are companies that specialize in the sale of knowledge. They will provide your organization with an expert on a particular subject for either a fixed bid or an hourly rate. These are consulting companies ranging in size from the big four accounting firms to small boutique companies. The services are beneficial because they allow your organization to gain immediate access to expertise in a specific area where it may be deficient. Several tendencies need to be acknowledged and avoided. The first of these tendencies revolves around the view that people have toward the delivery of a product.

Human nature is to equate the delivery of a product with success without measuring the true value of the deliverable. Consultants rely on this. These organizations will always deliver a product; it may not be what you asked for, but they will deliver; this delivery capability is often mistaken for success. This statement can be substantiated by reviewing any number of companies and the preponderance of dust-laden binders full of useless gibberish created by past consultants. The dust isn't simply from age, rather from irrelevancy. The other tendency associated with engaging consultants is the failure to understand the need the consultant is supposed to fulfill.

This misunderstanding is generally attributable to the customer failing to define his own needs prior to engaging a consultant. This issue is exasperated by a final tendency, which is to defer the decision on requirements and needs to the consultant.

A consultant is a knowledge expert; that is why you have engaged his services. As a result, consultants are capable of providing insights toward the organization's needs. It is important to listen to their council, but reserve the right to determine the needs, requirements, and deliverables for your own organization. Do not defer this power or leadership to a consultant. The most important issue is to enforce the delivery and ensure the product delivered meets your needs. In order to facilitate this philosophy, we have developed a similar procedure for selecting people vendors.

- Define deliverables prior to the engagement. If you do not fully understand your own needs, you cannot expect a consultant to deliver it. Take the time to develop a strong vision of the end-product and drive your consultants toward it. If you need help with this process, then the engagement should be an assessment to help refine the idea. In that case, the final product is a document that accurately reflects the end state of your next project.
- Requirements for the engagement. In case you haven't been paying attention, nothing in our universe starts without explicit requirements. Build your requirements for the engagement and share them with the consultancies. This will protect you from receiving a product you don't need.
- You are buying expertise, not another pair of hands. One of the primary motivators for adding consultants to the staff is an increase in the demands on your organization. When this situation occurs, it increases the pressure to bring someone into the organization quickly. This can lead to a knee jerk response of adding someone indiscriminately or worse underutilizing a highly skilled and expensive consultant. Regardless of the pressures of the situation, always measure the skills of the new consultant against the initial requirements.
- Bake-off: never use a single source for acquiring anything for your program. People vendors, like products and services, need to be short-listed and pitted against each other to allow the fabulous process of capitalism to work its magic. Make sure each participating vendor knows who the competition is.
- Review resumes and interview candidates. As we stated in the section on product vendors, adding a consultant is no different from adding a new member to your team. You need to conduct the same level of due diligence when selecting consultants as you would when hiring a full-time employee. As with any employment candidate, you need to review the resumes and conduct interviews to determine the validity of stated skills, as well as the fit with the existing team. Just don't treat the process differently because of the manner in which you pay the bill.
- Negotiations: once you select the candidate(s) who are best capable of meeting your requirements, the next step is to negotiate their services. Always start with identifying the people you want prior to discussing money or rates with the vendor. This is even more important if you are dealing with a large consultancy that has a

very large pool of available resources. Do not let the negotiations be driven by the billable rate; the talent must be the driving factor.

■ Price versus quality: the reason you negotiate quality before pricing is to set the standard of measurement for the desired talent. Once you have a resource that meets your requirements, you can start discussing rates. Keep in mind this strategy has a breaking point. The harder you negotiate on rate, the lower quality individual you will get.

At a certain point, it is not profitable for a vendor to provide a certain caliber of consultant for the negotiated rate. Be realistic about the rate you are willing to pay, and what the vendor is willing to accept for the level of skill required for the job. In the event you cannot reach an accord regarding the individual and the rate of pay, it is not the end of the world; look elsewhere.

Do not be afraid to walk away from the negotiation; vendors will often find a way to make the sale. That is why you performed the bake-off; you need to establish alternate channels for product in case a vendor is unable to meet all of your needs.

Prepare the Consultant

You spent a great deal of time and effort to get the right person for the job; don't quit now. The consultant is like any new employee to your organization. They are unaware of the organizational structure, culture, personalities, politics, or even where the bathroom is located. For this engagement to end well, you must do your homework and prepare the consultant for the job.

Because you have a detailed requirement document along with a stated objective, it shouldn't be difficult to gather all of the background information and tools necessary for the consultant to be successful. Once you have all this information, spend some time with your new employee establishing the framework for the engagement. This should include your expectations, the history that led to the work, the relevant participants, the expected deliverable, and the schedule for completing the work. In our experience, this is the single greatest point of failure for the engagement of contractors.

Vendor Summary

We would like to emphasize that every business transaction needs to be a win-win for both parties. The ideas and guidelines we presented are merely the tools for ensuring this outcome. We attempted to level the playing field for the consumer because sales people negotiate and sell every day. One final concept affiliated with the execute phase is the preparation of marketing material for the next chapter.

Preparing the Marketing Material

If a tree falls over in the woods and there isn't anyone to hear it, does it truly make a sound? The same can be said for the information security program. In this chapter, you learned two important skills: how to get things done and how to secure the work of others. Both of these accomplishments, when done correctly, represent victories for your program; they need to be shamelessly publicized to anyone who will listen. Let's start with the major talking points.

Getting Things Done

We are of the opinion that anyone who can complete work in an orderly, strategic fashion is rare in many organizations. You established the expectations for the program when the security project portfolio was created. As you complete projects in this portfolio, you need to ensure that at least executive management and your stakeholders are aware of the success. Remind them that you met your stated goals and objectives as planned. The mechanisms for accomplishing this objective were established in the design chapter where we discussed channels of communication. The message communicated should include the fact that you completed an objective and if the metrics gathered during the execution of the project are available, use them. These metrics will continue to provide marketing material as the benefits of the initiative are accumulated over time. Don't forget, victory will bring supporters; everyone loves a winner. One victory will make future victories easier by building momentum for the program. The other aspect of this chapter that merits marketing is the risk reduction efforts for projects.

Risk Reduction

This is the primary mission of the information security program. Even if you are given direction to the contrary, risk reduction is the heart and soul of security. Anytime the program measurably improves the risk profile for the organization, it must be communicated. This is the ultimate value of the program to the organization. Never miss an opportunity to demonstrate that value.

All you need to know right now is to gather the information that will be distributed through your communication channels. We will develop the strategies and presentation models in the next chapter.

Chapter Summary

We covered a great deal of territory with this chapter. However, these items can be distilled into four major categories. Let's quickly review these major topics.

1. Project execution
2. Incorporating security into projects
3. Vendor evaluation/selection
4. Preparing the marketing material

Proper utilization of these concepts, tools, and techniques will lead to the timely completion of projects within your security project portfolio, the reduction of risk for the enterprise, and the staging of materials for your upcoming marketing campaign. We guarantee incorporation of these concepts into your professional life will reap huge dividends toward your success; it did for ours.

Chapter 5

Report

Overview

We covered a great deal of material so far, starting with the assess phase and culminating with the last chapter on execution. During this process, we have shown how to assess your environment, develop your program, and design and execute initiatives aligned with the needs and functions of your enterprise. At this point, it is time to share your results with the various stakeholders of your organization.

We feel even the most brilliant, effective, and cost-effective information security program will be of little value to your enterprise if you are unable to communicate your ideas, your program's status, the status of your various initiatives, your enterprise's risk posture, and your enterprise's audit and compliance status to the audiences who need to know this information.

We define reporting as any form of communication from your program to any individual or group outside your program. Reporting can take many forms and can be distributed through many channels. Regardless, the objective is the same: distribute a desired message to a desired audience to evoke a desired reaction. To accomplish this goal, we will provide a mechanical process for effective reporting.

This process is formula based allowing a broad application and repeatable results. This process will include the following steps:

- Identify your need.
- Determine your intent.
- Establish your desired reaction.

- Determine your target audience.
- Determine your appropriate delivery mechanism (both packaging and presentation).
- Follow-up on your message to measure the actual reaction to the desired reaction.
- Close the deal.

We will start by identifying your motivations for communicating information about the various elements of your program. Based on your identified need, we will move to the intent of your report. The next step in the process is to determine the desired reaction driven by your intent. With an identified desired reaction for your report, you will be able to move to targeting the audience best suited for the desired reaction. With the desired audience identified, you can determine the appropriate delivery mechanism to reach the objective of the report. To close it all, you will follow up on the message to measure whether the actual reaction met your desired reaction, which will allow the necessary adjustments to the message to close the deal. Closing the deal is the last step in the process where you bring your efforts across the finish line. This is a procedural approach to delivering your information with predictable results. To prepare you for these topics, we will begin with the foundation concepts.

Foundation Concepts

Every section of this book is preceded with foundation concepts. This section should provide you with why you need to know it, as well as a brief description of each idea.

The information we will cover in the foundation concepts for the report phase includes an elaboration of the attributes outlined in Chapter 2, Plan, that are applicable to reporting:

- Writer
- Presenter

We will also define the knowledge required to complete the report phase. A comprehensive discussion of these materials is beyond the scope of this book and will require additional sources. These topics include:

- Primary rule of reporting
- Basic report components
- Delivery mechanisms
- Marketing concepts

Now that you know what is in store for you, let us begin with the critical skills for a report.

Critical Skills

To facilitate this conversation, we will begin with a review of the definitions for the attributes of each critical skill and their importance to the objective of this chapter.

> All speech, written or spoken, is a dead language, until it finds a willing and prepared hearer.
>
> **—Robert Louis Stevenson**

Writer

The writer must be capable of communicating thoughts and concepts in an orderly, structured, written form such as policies, procedures, and guidelines. Because the majority of your material will be relayed in written form, the ability to write effectively becomes a very important skill. The team will need someone who can craft a message in a concise and timely manner, which communicates the desired concept as intended.

Presenter

The presenter must be capable of communicating thoughts and concepts in an orderly, structured verbal form such as initiatives, training, meetings, and sales presentations. This attribute will be valuable when the method of delivery is verbal. Written communiqué is not always the proper mechanism for delivering a message. In situations where the response of the audience is unpredictable, verbal delivery is the preferable method.

Critical Knowledge

Primary Principle of Reporting

Regardless of the type of report or the delivery mechanism, this principle is applicable and useful. It provides a direction and a philosophy that should be utilized for every communiqué. It is an old concept that is generally associated with presentations:

- Tell them what you are going to tell them.
- Tell them.
- Tell them what you told them.

The precept is basic, but it provides a useful roadmap for the dissemination of information. This manner of reiteration will ensure the major points and ideas within your reports are delivered. Now that you have an outline to follow for any report, let us move to common reporting components.

Basic Reporting Components

You will give many different types of communications throughout the life of your program. These can include administrative information, such as executive presentations, sales meetings, budget proposals, and audit and compliance reports, as well as operational information such as unauthorized access attempts and Internet firewall activity. Each one will be unique based on the message, intent, audience, and desired response. Below we distilled the various components of a report that can be mixed and matched based on the medium, message, and audience. Not all of these components need to be present in each report you issue.

- Executive summary — the executive summary should be a synopsis of the entire document. This portion should be concise and to the point. It should present the overall concept, with enough information to illicit the desired reaction.
- Problem statement — the problem statement is the portion of a document that clearly outlines the reason for your communication. It does not need to be a problem as much as a motivation. For example, this document will present an overview of the various types of firewalls with the intent of providing a common frame of reference for future discussions.
- Statement of facts — the statement of facts should outline all of the relevant facts that need to be considered to address the topic. Present them in a neutral manner allowing the reader to accept the information as merely a statement of fact.
- Analysis — the analysis should present the logic used to determine any potential solutions. It is best to present this as a step-by-step linear discussion that allows for the easy assimilation of concepts. Additionally, you should try to minimize the amount of technical nomenclature and other distracting elements. Keep it simple and to the point.
- Potential solutions — do not state a problem without presenting a recommendation for a potential solution. The analysis section should lead your audience to the same conclusions you came to. Outline any potential solutions in a manner that only highlights their

differences. Do not attempt to provide a comprehensive dissertation on each solution. This section should also include your recommendation for the preferred solution. Of course, if your analysis section is crafted properly, the audience will reach the same conclusion before they are presented with your recommendation.

■ Call to action — this is often the missing element for most reports. Don't ever forget the report was created to illicit a response from the audience. The call to action tells them what is needed to solve the problem. It directs their actions and participation creating a roadmap for the necessary actions. If you do not provide this guidance, the resulting actions may not be the desired ones.

These components can be used individually or as a group based on the type of report you are creating. Try to use as many as possible but only use what is needed to deliver the message.

Delivery Mechanisms

The delivery mechanisms are the different methods used for the delivery of information to a target audience. It can take the form of a written report, a private one-on-one meeting, a dedicated internal Web site, output from a security testing tool, a presentation, a class, a game, or even an informal hallway conversation. Anything goes so long as it meets the objective of communicating the message. The communication plan created in the design chapter will be the vehicle for distributing reports in this chapter. Without a delivery mechanism, the quality and content of your reports are lost. If you have not built your communication plan yet, or you feel it is insufficient, now is the time to stop and rectify the situation.

Marketing

You need to understand marketing to ensure your information security program always looks good; it's that simple. Reporting is the tool you can use to make your program shine when you are successful. When the program hits rough spots, it is also the tool to smooth out situations. Think of how a politician uses the press to aid in achieving an agenda. Now think of the same politician using the press to provide damage control when he has done something wrong or unpopular. We are not suggesting you use it for propaganda, but you need to understand this is a powerful tool for how the information security program will be perceived. Therefore, be careful what is published and to whom. One of the concepts from marketing we advocate heavily is the concept of branding.

Branding

Branding refers to any unique or readily identifiable characteristics of your work. Every report you release, every presentation given, should be readily identifiable with your program. It should instill confidence in the quality and effectiveness of your program and the content of the material presented. There are three steps to branding that we will elaborate on below:

1. Establish the brand — determine the visual characteristics you wish to be identified with your information security program. Once you have selected a certain look and feel for the information that leaves your program, all of your communications should then conform to this standard. Next, work to establish a benchmark of quality for the material presented. Make sure everyone on your team understands the standards and enforce them with brutal determination. Once you brand your program, any deviation may cause people to misunderstand your message, which may cause them to see your communications as inconsistent, useless, or worse — untrustworthy. Consistency is often seen as a cornerstone of trust so developing a consistent look and feel to your messages can assist you in developing credibility with your program's stakeholders. Again, once you have a pre-defined brand, you should ensure that all of the reports from your office are using it.
2. Quality control — a brand is of little value if it is applied inconsistently to your communications. As a result, you should build controls around the creation and distribution of all materials emanating from the information security program. Below are some mechanisms to ensure a consistent brand:
   - A review process for any communications about your program
   - Controls over who owns the communications with your various audiences
   - Templates and standardized formatting
   - Source control for all of your templates and past reports

It only takes a couple of poorly written and distributed reports to have a negative effect on the perception of your brand. Make sure you put the proper controls in place to ensure the integrity and consistency of your reports. The last step in the brand process is to get feedback on what others think of your brand.

3. Brand perception — though you may have a great brand, and a process to ensure its consistency, people can be fickle in their interpretation of any material. For example, go to a movie theater

and ask ten people who saw the same movie what they considered to be the message of the film — chances are you will get ten different answers. Because of this, you must constantly solicit feedback from the audience of your reports to determine the perception of your branding efforts.

The next item to discuss in your marketing efforts is using the metrics gathered throughout the projects you have already identified and completed.

Metrics

The metrics we use for marketing are the statistics we gathered from the completed initiatives or the market data we are using to prove a point. Be careful in your selection and use of this data because not all data is of equal value.

Where feasible, we recommend you use quantitative data (facts) that can be supported by technical analysis or other data sources. Qualitative data, on the other hand, should be used sparingly as this information is often based on intuition or gut feel, and can be difficult to support or justify.

Damage Control

The final use for marketing techniques such as branding and metric reporting is political coverage. This may help you and your program to avoid potentially unpleasant situations where you may have presented information requiring action to management, but their non-committal response results in a breach or other security-related incident. The best way to describe this concept is through an example.

Scenario

The information security office of StimCo, a manufacturer of all-natural herbal stimulants for aspiring authors under deadline, has performed an audit of the current operating system patch levels for the organization's Unix-based server farm. The findings from this audit showed that 90 percent of these systems are un-patched, thus making the organization susceptible to a myriad of attacks. This analysis was communicated to upper management along with recommendations to correct the situation. However, this information went unheeded and StimCo was hit by a worm, and is now forced to execute a portion of their disaster recovery plan to get business functionality back.

Analysis

Despite your very best efforts, executive management did not take action on the information you presented. However, one thing to keep in mind is due diligence was exercised by your information security program through your communication of your audit findings and recommendations. As a result, the accountability for this disaster is shifted from your information security office to executive management.

The moral of this story is to communicate the right message, to the right audience, at the right time. This will help protect your program even under the worst conditions.

In this section, we discussed a number of tools and techniques, but marketing is more a frame of mind than an action to be taken. Reporting is the tool that enables the marketing of your program. The tool will only be as effective as the preparation and care given to the materials and strategies that go into their formulation.

Summary

In the critical skills and concepts, we covered the basic techniques and concepts of reporting. Next, we will utilize these ideas in the methodology section.

Methodology

Thus far we have provided simplified formulas or processes for achieving a desired goal and the reporting process will be no different. We will walk you through a process for the planning and delivery of information from the information security program.

The report creation process will lead you through a series of steps designed to maximize the impact of the material you wish to present from your program. Further, we hope to change your perspective on reporting from simple data compilation and regurgitation into a strategic exercise to promote the value of the information security program. We will help you identify the differences between administrative and operational reporting, what types of communications typically fall into these categories, and how to develop a reporting strategy for this type of information.

During the report construction process, we will point out different considerations for the different types of reports. Additionally, we will focus on what we believe to be a commonly overlooked driver in business communications: identifying your target audience. Different audiences require different methods, techniques, and tools for accurately delivering

Report construction process

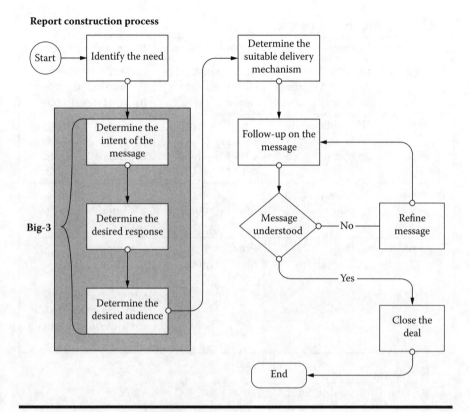

Figure 5.1   Report Construction Process

the target message. We will review the major categories of audiences and some strategies for successfully delivering your message.

Now that you have the itinerary, let's get started with the report construction process.

Report Construction Process

We will present a consistent repeatable process for achieving a specific objective. In this case, our focus will be reporting (see Figure 5.1). If you expected to see a section on sentence construction and grammar, you are sadly mistaken. The construction process is a series of concepts and questions that will aid in the determination of the big three of reporting: desired intent, desired audience, and desired response. This is the underlying precept from which we derived this process. We will elaborate on this idea later. For now, all you need to know is these three items are the driving force behind the steps listed below. All of these address one or more of the big three.

Table 5.1 Big Three Examples

	Desired Intent	Desired Audience	Desired Response
Example 1	Evaluate expected support on a new project	Staff members of the audit department	Gain the support of the audit department for your new initiative
Example 2	Get additional funding for the program	Chief executive officer Chief financial officer	8 percent increase in the annual budget for the security program
Example 3	Acquire project resources	Operations management	Get engineers assigned to your project
Example 4	Shift accountability	Executive management	For executive management to understand the situation and that they are responsible for the consequences of inaction

- Identify your need.
- Determine your intent.
- Establish your desired reaction.
- Determine your target audience.
- Determine your appropriate delivery mechanism (both packaging and presentation).
- Follow up on your message to measure the actual reaction to the desired reaction.
- Close the deal.

Table 5.1 provides some big three examples.

Our definition of reporting is any form of communication from your program to any person or group outside your program. With that in mind, let us get started with the first step in the process: identifying the need that is driving the delivery of data.

Identifying the Need

I look for what needs to be done. After all, that's how the universe designs itself.

—R. Buckminster Fuller

The first step in the report creation process is to determine the need or motivation that is driving this endeavor. We are not talking about the my-boss-told-me-to-do-it stuff. We are talking about the more strategic or tactical need that is providing the impetus for this action. Regardless of the source of the assignment, you should attempt to match the deliverable to a specific need of the information security program. The need is the primary motivator for undertaking any reporting task. It can fall into many different categories and take many different forms, such as:

■ The program may have a need to inform executive management of a particular threat to the organization so they may take action or make a business decision.

■ You may have a need to shift the accountability for a specific item to a higher level within the organization.

■ You may have a need to increase the level of education on a particular topic to fuel a future conversation.

If this concept appears to be vaguely familiar, it is because it is. The process used for identifying the need is the same one used in many other portions of this book, specifically, during the design chapter when you identified the business drivers for your security policies, and during the creation of objective statements for your projects. It follows a predictable formula. The repetition of this process should make your prediction on the next topic easy. The next step is to gather the requirements for the communication, and this is achieved through the determination of your intent for it.

Determine Intent

> A truth that's told with bad intent beats all the lies you can invent.
>
> **—William Blake**

Intent for any communication is the response that is desired from the delivery of information to a specific target audience. In other words, what would you hope to accomplish from publishing this data? The best way to illustrate this is through an example.

Scenario

■ Need
  - Gain support for a new objective for an enterprise anti-virus solution.

- Intent
  - Illustrate the prevalence of virus incidents in similar organizations.
  - Emphasize the inadequacy of anti-virus protection within your organization.
  - Outline the potential financial impact to your organization from a virus incident.
  - Shift the accountability for a potential incident to operations management.

Analysis

We developed a single overarching need (objective) that provides focus and guidance for the intent (functional requirements) of the report. This model is hierarchical in that one objective will spawn multiple intent statements.

Each intent statement directly supports the need that is driving the report; the statements range in value from general education to political maneuvering. Keep in mind the deliverable at the end of the process is a single report targeted to a specific audience. Therefore, keep the intent statements focused and relevant to the identified need for that report. Now that we know what is needed, and the intent of our message to meet this need, we will move to identifying how we want people to react to the information presented.

Desired Reaction

When distributing information, it is important for you to fully understand the type of reaction the information may produce. This is a simple concept, but one that is often overlooked. Many people issue or distribute reports without any idea of the response the report will generate. This can lead to haphazard, unpredictable responses that will put your information security program in a reactive position. So, you must ask yourself, I am not a mind reader, how do I predict the reaction to my reports before I distribute them?

The key is to be proactive with your reporting and to utilize the same premise we used throughout the entire information security program; begin at the end. Before you set off to build a report, identify what the ideal reaction could be, then drive work backwards to derive the correct path for achieving that reaction. Working in this manner enables the following:

- It provides a roadmap for the manner in which the report will be created.
- It enables you to identify the target audience for the report.

- It provides insights into how many different reports will be needed to deliver the desired reaction.
- It allows for the preparation of follow-up questions or action items the report will produce.

Now that you know the importance of identifying the desired reaction, let us explain how to use the intent of your report to create them. The way in which we will accomplish this is through desired reaction statements. Desired reaction statements are one-sentence descriptions that correlate an owner to a specific reaction, as well as a quick overview of the reaction itself. There are three primary considerations when generating desired reaction statements:

- You will have at least one, and possibly multiple, desired reaction statements for every intent statement.
- Every desired reaction statement should include only one type of owner for the reaction.
- Every desired reaction statement must include only one reaction.

These considerations are illustrated with an example. We will build on the anti-virus example we used above in the need section.

Scenario

- Need.
- Gain support for a new objective for an enterprise anti-virus solution.
- Intent.
  - Illustrate the prevalence of virus incidents in similar organizations.
  - Emphasize the inadequacy of anti-virus protection within the organization.
  - Outline the potential financial impact to the organization from a virus incident.
  - Shift the accountability for a potential incident to operations management.
- Desired reaction statements.
  - Management should gain a new level of concern for the potential of a virus incident within the organization.
  - Management should become uncertain the organization is capable of withstanding a major virus incident.
  - Management should become supportive of an enterprisewide anti-virus solution.
  - The report must present enough information so executive management accepts the responsibility if they choose not to act on this information.

Analysis

You will note all of the statements tie back to the intent statements. In this case, we used a basic one-to-one correlation, but there can be many desired reactions of every intent statement. The next concept that is illustrated is the association of an owner to a desired reaction.

The owner is generally not an individual, but a distinct group or level of responsibility within an organization. The owner to a desired reaction is also a one-to-one correlation. If you find you need multiple parties to react in a similar manner, then you have identified the need for multiple reports. Don't forget: reports should deliver a desired message to a desired audience to illicit a desired response. Don't mix your audiences or your messages.

You now should understand the role the desired response plays in the planning of your reports. Further, we identified the relationship to the other components of the process: objective and intent. Continuing with the logic of beginning at the end, we're ready to determine the desired audience.

Determine Target Audience

The target audience is the reason for all of the planning you have done to this point. The target audience is a body of individuals who will provide the desired reaction, which is, after all, the purpose for the report in the first place. This part should be very easy because they were identified through the prior components of the process. However, we would like to address the importance of selecting a target audience and elaborate on some subtleties associated with the various audiences within your organization. These are clearly generalizations; you should take the time to research the various audiences in your enterprise and learn their traits.

Internal Audiences

The first category of audience is the internal variety; these are your co-workers. This is any group of employees within your organization. We will start at the highest level of management and work our way down the organizational chart to staff personnel. To be consistent in our comparisons, we will address the following considerations for each group:

■ Motivations — this element addresses the issue of the driving force behind this group. What is their mission or agenda? What hot button issues will generate the desired response? For example, the accounting department will be driven by the reduction of expenses for the organization.

- Traits — various groups within the company tend to share similar characteristics, actions, and views. An understanding of these traits will aid you in customizing the delivery of your message.
- Focus — the focus of any group directly correlates to their perspective of the organization. For example, an individual working in the mailroom may be interested in the company's financial statements, but his focus is not the company's finances; that exciting topic belongs to the CFO and finance.
- Tips for effective communications — this section will present a series of tips and concepts based on the focus and motivations of each group we address.

Now that we have the agenda, let us begin with a discussion of the highest level of management.

Executive Management/Board of Directors

We have grouped executive management and the board of directors together because they share similar motivations, traits, and focus. This is the highest level of management within an organization. Let us review their motivations.

Mission

The mission of executive management is the ongoing viability and profitability of the organization. For the information security program, their motivation will stem from the mitigation of risk while minimizing the impact to the organization's bottom-line. This group is especially sensitive to regulatory compliance issues or any issue surrounding due care and due diligence.

Traits

These people are seasoned professionals with a clear understanding of the industry and the business they manage. They want direct answers without any window dressing; they don't have the time. This group is usually extremely bright and quick to determine the focal point of any issue. Additionally, this group can be somewhat overwhelming in their ability to correlate large numbers of variables in very short periods of time. More often than not, they can draw logical conclusions from data points that previously eluded your analysis and ask questions that leave you scratching your head.

Focus

These individuals will be fixated on the profitability, stockholder equity, and continued prosperity of the enterprise. Not only is this group concerned with the financial viability of the organization, they are also responsible for setting the strategic direction. They will always have one eye on the current situation and the other eye looking down the road.

Tips

Listed below are some tips for presenting materials to executive management. We found these guidelines extremely useful regardless of the distribution mechanism for the information.

- Be factual — this is clearly rule number one. Never present information to this group that you can't support. Though communications to this audience will most likely not require supporting detail, make sure you have it available in the event it is requested.
- Be direct — keep all of the material concise, direct, and to the point. A good rule of thumb is one page — period. You will not impress this group of people with long, flowery reports. They only require the information necessary to form an educated opinion, nothing more. The time you take from this group is very expensive to the organization in terms of opportunity cost and dollars; be mindful of this fact and don't waste their time.
- Trended information — information that presents trends over time is far more valuable to this group than individual data points because they focus in the strategic development of the organization. Trended information tells a story and provides insight into the direction the enterprise is going.
- Keep it high level — this audience makes decisions that alter the course for the entire organization. As a result, they are interested in a macro view of the issues, not a bunch of minor details.
- Use charts and graphs — the saying, "a picture is worth a thousand words," must have originally been uttered before the very first board meeting. Keep things brief, concise, and to the point. A well-crafted diagram or graph can achieve all three of these objectives.

Summary

Be extremely careful when addressing this group with any type of report. Mistakes at this level of the organization can undo months, and sometimes years, of success.

Senior Management

Senior management is the next level down on the organization chart. This typically includes vice presidents, junior vice presidents, and directors. Though they share some similar objectives with upper management, their mission and focus are somewhat different.

Mission

The mission of senior management is to enact the strategies outlined by executive management. These plans are manifested through the annual plans and budgets. This group is the bridge between the strategic planners and the tactical execution for the organization.

Traits

These people have risen to a comfortable level in the organization either by political maneuvering or by accomplishment. In either case, they are motivated, result-driven people. This group is highly adept at protecting themselves and their organization. Information is a vital component in this practice. Therefore, they will pay attention to items they feel will aid them in promoting their agenda.

Focus

Senior management will be focused on the accomplishment of their annual plan and the compliance with the established budget. More specifically, they will be interested in the information security project portfolio, obstacles to accomplishing the projects, and the budgets of the individual projects. This group will be more concerned with the elements of the project management triangle (time, resources, and scope) than any other potential audience because they are the largest components that tie directly back to their budgets and annual plans.

Tips

The tips for dealing with this group are varied because of the way they may have ascended to the position. Merit is not the sole manner by which people are promoted. Below are some tips to help guide you.

- Research the audience thoroughly — because it is difficult to categorize this group, you must research the individuals who comprise it to determine the most effective manner to present your information.
- Focus on triangle elements — because this group focuses on macro issues of the organization, they will be most interested in schedules, resources, and scope.

■ Keep it at a high level — it may be tempting to add detailed background information to your reports to this group, but it may not be what they want or need. Only supply the necessary amount of information needed to deliver the message. Remember, this is still an upper management group.

■ Avoid technical material — this is an associated concept to the prior tip. Technical material is used as background information to the message you are attempting to deliver. This group is not interested in the technical aspects of the latest security widget. If you have this type of information in your report, you have either the wrong audience or the wrong level of information.

■ Be proactive with bad news — this group is both highly political and focused on long-term planning. As a result, the sooner you can present bad news, the more time senior management has to work out contingencies for dependent plans. The last thought on this topic is it is difficult to find fault when bad news is identified and disclosed rather than attempting to conceal it. Don't let senior management find out about the bad news second hand. Being proactive and communicative with potential difficulties will help them react quickly, and may even add to your credibility.

■ Don't give superfluous information — this goes back to the idea of only presenting the information needed to deliver the message and to answer any anticipated questions. Keep it as simple and direct as possible. They will not be impressed with pages and pages of minutia. The more information you offer to this group, the greater the opportunity to put your foot in your mouth; this can be a painful experience with this level of management.

Summary

The level of risk associated with distributing information at this level is still high; not as high as with the executive management and the board of directors, but high enough to severely damage the creatability of the program and your personal career path. Therefore, be careful when dealing with this group. They are accustomed to individuals telling them what they want to hear. As a result, they tend to be very skeptical of all information presented, in an attempt to separate fact from fiction. Don't take it personally; merely present your information in as direct and succinct a manner as possible.

Middle Management

Middle management is comprised of individuals who manage the various program areas within an organization. They typically have titles such as manager, supervisor, or section chief. This is a very important group because they comprise the largest segment of management within an organization. This group will require frequent communication from various channels to keep your program moving smoothly.

Mission

These are the day-to-day people who ensure the strategic plans from senior management are executed in the tactical plans of the department. They are concerned with the efficient, cost-effective execution of the department's objectives.

Traits

These people will fall into two distinct categories: war heroes and Dilbert managers. The war heroes are usually individuals who have excelled in a number of different positions within the department they now manage. This means they understand the nuts and bolts of their organization and the potential impact of various changes. They will know how to get things done and who to use to best accomplish any task.

The Dilbert managers are the opposite of the war heroes. These are the people who moved up the food chain through years of service and attrition, not through merit. This doesn't mean they aren't good managers, just that the chances of this occurrence are highly reduced. They are probably the same obstructionists they were when they were one of the troops, just scarier because now they have some power.

Focus

Middle management is concerned with the continuance of their particular operation or mission. This will be as varied as your organization. For instance, the manager of network operations will be focused on the 24/7 availability of the network resources while the manager of the accounting department will be focused on the accuracy of data and the deviation from budgets. Before you provide any data to this group be sure to understand the focus of the specific manager.

Tips

The tips for dealing with this group are varied because of the wide array of work focus that is represented by this group. Though they are different, they share some similarities that we shall address in the tips below.

■ Pragmatic perspective — you have just crossed the boundary from the high-level, strategic thinkers to the people who have to make the strategies work. This group, through necessity, must have a real-world perspective on their departments; theory rarely results in meeting a deadline. They are all about execution; they have to be because their jobs depend on it. Keep the information presented to this group realistic and applicable.

■ Sensitive to negative press — these managers are responsible for delivering a product that is consumed by another part of the organization. As a result, they are like small businesses unto themselves. For instance, the manager of network operations is producing a service (network availability) consumed by the rest of the organization. They will be very concerned about the perception others, specifically senior management, have about their group. Always consider this factor when creating your reports.

■ Apprehensive of change — because this group is focused on the execution of their mission, anything that could potentially hinder that mission (change) will be viewed skeptically. Because these people are generally experts in delivering their product today, they will be reluctant to alter any aspect of what they perceive as successful.

■ Tactical mindset —this group is concerned with maintaining the capabilities of their current operation. As such, their planning window tends to range between a three- to twelve-months time-frame. Most of these new initiatives will be the tactical execution of the strategic plans developed by higher levels of management. With this perspective, remember this audience will require far more detail and substance when compared to the upper levels of management. Theoretical debates may be good fun, but this group will be far more concerned with how to use the information you give them.

■ Detail to substantiate position — the daily work of this group will put them in close proximity to the minutia of details present in every department. Any information presented to middle management will require back-up data to support the position delivered. Be aware any information that is distributed will be shared with their subordinates and analyzed for accuracy.

■ Accuracy of detail — because this group will have the resources to review every aspect of the report, the level of scrutiny that each fact receives will be substantially higher than information presented to upper levels of management. The only defense against this review is to verify the accuracy of your information and the presentation of the data.

■ Defensive posture — the last aspect of middle management we would like to discuss is their propensity to be highly defensive regarding their group. Just as they are sensitive to any bad press, this group often will not tolerate negative criticism of their team or its individual members. Though this is a form of bad press, their response will be closer to an angry parent than a defensive manager. The reason for this is it provides a moral high ground from which to mount their attack.

Because security reporting often identifies deficiencies within the organization, it can place people on the defense very quickly. Make sure your reports state the facts objectively and avoid direct reference to individuals or teams. For instance, it is preferable to illuminate deficiencies with the change control process, but avoid singling out any specific team that manages the process. This approach will neutralize the moral indignation some middle managers use. Lastly, be sensitive to the communication channel you select when delivering potentially sensitive or aggravating information. If you need to deliver bad news, do it in private, not in a large open forum where they may feel the need to fight back.

Summary

There is risk associated with reporting to this group. This group may own the resources you will be interacting with to complete your projects; their continued support and good will is vital. This issue will be intensified if you designed your information security program to not have operational duties. The last group we will address is the staff level of the organization.

Technical Engineering Staff

The technical engineering staff is comprised of all the people who make the technology within an organization work. We singled out this group because they have their own specific intricacies and eccentricities.

Mission

The mission of this group is to make all of the various technical components and applications work. These people have very little time or interest in theories or strategies unless it aids them in completing the tasks.

Traits

As you recall from our discussion in Chapter 1, Assess, this group is usually comprised of on-off people; these are the bit heads. Because technology is an exact discipline, this group will see the world as a series of black and white decisions. They will not be interested in such things as politics or in the business itself, only what they need to accomplish their jobs. This type of individual will appreciate meaningful details that help establish a definitive position for a topic. This is why this group will seem to have an insatiable appetite for information.

Focus

They focus on completing their jobs while incorporating technology, innovation, and anything else they may view as interesting. This is good for your information security program. Generally, security has characteristics that fall into these categories. It has interesting, innovative technology that will get this group's attention.

Tips

- Be specific — the interest a specific group has will be limited to their area of knowledge and responsibility. They are not going to care about global issues unless it impacts them directly. Keep your topics specific and relevant to the group you are addressing.
- Be supportive — this level of employee has to deal with the realities of all the plans that are devised by management. The issues you are raising with this group were probably created by someone outside the engineering team and left for them to solve. It is advisable to empathize with the group, but when reporting, focus on the solution not the problem.
- Be technology agnostic — technology zealots can be as irrational as any other fanatic can (just ask any Mac user). You never know who is a reasonable pundi and who is a militant. The best rule of thumb is not to take any definitive position on technology — just stick to the issue and try to avoid references to specific technologies. Like politics and religion, you will inevitably alienate someone.
- Avoid philosophical debates — this group will have expertise in their chosen discipline. As a result, they will have developed deep seeded convictions on how to apply their trade. Further, they are experts with high levels of detail and information resources at their disposal. This combination makes for a less than optimal debate situation for you.
- Be accurate — this group, more than any other, is going to research your details. They also will be able to judge the veracity of your information because of their specific expertise. This issue speaks directly to your ongoing credibility.

Summary

The summary for this group is elementary. Be accurate and direct with these people; they'll appreciate it.

Employees

The non-technical staff are any employees who do not fit in one of the aforementioned groups. These people perform the various functions the company needs to stay in business.

Mission

Perform the day-to-day tasks each department requires. They are not involved in the strategic or tactical planning for the organization, just the execution of their own work.

Traits

Generally, these people will not have a strong technical background nor will they have a strong understanding of security concepts or practices. Their primary expertise will be their portion of the business and the manner in which they perform their duties.

Focus

Their focus will be extremely narrow and specific to their own tasks or anything that can affect them.

Tips

- Non-technical — this group will not relate to highly technical material, therefore don't present them with technical information.
- Avoid complex concepts — do not bombard this audience with multiple security concepts. Deliver each concept by itself in terms that are as simple as possible. Don't forget this group has other issues contending for its attention other than security.
- Relatable — present your material in a context that is familiar and relatable to the audience. This practice is useful for all of the target audiences, but it is imperative for this one. Because they will be the least familiar with security concepts and technology, you need to distill the information into a consumable format for this audience. Analogies are a great tool for presenting to this audience.

Summary

The employee group is going to be your largest and most diverse internal audience. This factor will create significant variances in the personality, skills, and temperament of this group that will be distinct to your organization. Use the information outlined above as a guide, but take the time to understand your unique audience prior to presenting any information to them.

Internal Audit/Regulatory Compliance Office

Mission

Many enterprises have a dedicated internal audit function that serves to assess and monitor the enterprise's efforts toward governance, legal and regulatory compliance, and other business processes as directed by either the audit committee or executive management. Additionally, an internal audit function generally serves to assess and monitor both the design and the effectiveness of the enterprise's internal control structure. Many, if not all, of the policies you developed as part of your information security program fall under this internal control structure.

Traits

Generally, these people have strong business backgrounds and a modest level of expertise in one or more technical areas. They tend to be excellent communicators, big-picture thinkers, and take their work responsibilities very seriously. Internal auditors usually own one or more professional licenses, such as Certified Public Accountant (CPA), Chartered Accountant (CA), and Certified Information Systems Auditor (CISA), and usually belong to one or more professional associations that require them to uphold a strict code of professional conduct and ethical behavior.

Focus

Their focus tends to be on their audits and any special projects they are currently working on, although they are required by the aforementioned codes of conduct to look out for and report unethical activities to management. Most are eager to learn about new technologies and techniques, and enjoy working with technical personnel.

Tips

- Unique backgrounds — many auditors begin their careers in other areas in business and transition to internal audit to learn more about enterprise-level issues and business processes. Some get into auditing straight out of school. The very best of them have some business experience, and can see issues in the context of the enterprise. These auditors will typically work with you to identify any risks and internal controls that may need to be implemented or improved as part of their audits. However, others may not have this background, and may get distracted by more trivial issues. As a result, you should always get a sense of each auditor's background before presenting material to them as part of their audits. Your job here is to help them understand what they're looking at and give some sort of perspective to any issues they may find.

- Generalist — this group may not understand highly technical material at first, but can usually figure it out with a little guidance. They can usually understand multiple security concepts simultaneously, but be prepared to explain any new, complex, or esoteric technologies or processes.
- Inquiring minds — as a group, internal auditors are naturally inquisitive and tend to ask many questions. However, be very careful about how you answer them as they may sometimes ask for things they don't really need. This is because they may not know exactly what to ask for, but they usually have a very clear idea of what control they are trying to test. Working together, you should be able to identify and get them what they need.
- Supportive — this group, probably more than any other, will be supportive of your efforts to implement an information security program. Internal audit is typically a great place to look for champions for your program.
- Be factual — as with the executive audience, never present information to this group that you can't support. Auditors will usually ask for detailed supporting documents, and getting this information can take a lot of time if you're not prepared. An easy way to ensure you are able to give them what they need is to ask them to provide you with a document request list prior to the start of their audit fieldwork, and establish a mutually agreed upon date to give them everything.

Summary

The auditor group can be strong advocates for your information security program, and we recommend teaming with them from the very beginning to ensure their audit plans directly correspond to your program implementation goals.

External Audiences

External audiences are the stakeholders and third parties that have relationships with your enterprise requiring occasional communication from your information security program. These can include:

- Government agencies/independent auditors/regulators
- Stockholders/owners
- Customers and clients

We've grouped these various entities together based on their similarities in the mission, focus, and traits. We'll begin with government-related entities.

Government Agencies/Independent Auditors/Regulators

This group consists of auditors who typically require formal communications.

Mission

Generally, this group is focused on your enterprise's compliance with some sort of criteria, whether they are existing laws, government or industry regulations, or Generally Accepted Accounting Principles (GAAP).

Traits

These people tend to be very formal and business-like in their conduct and mannerisms. They will have a clear mission and will be focused on its completion.

Focus

Much like internal auditors, their focus tends to be on their audits and any special projects they are currently working on, and are usually required to uphold a strict code of professional conduct and ethical behavior. Accordingly, they are bound by these codes to report any unethical activities they become aware of to management.

Tips

- Unique backgrounds — like internal auditors, these people sometimes begin their careers in other areas in business and move into an external compliance or audit role to learn more about industry-wide issues and business processes; others choose this career straight out of school. The very best of them have some business experience, can see issues in the context of the enterprise, and will typically work with you to identify any risks and internal controls that may need to be implemented or improved as based on their testing. However, others may not have this background, and may get distracted by more trivial issues. As a result, you should always get a sense of each person's background before presenting material to them as part of their testing. Your job here is to help them understand what they're looking at and give some sort of perspective to any issues they may find.

■ Generalist — this group may not understand highly technical material at first, but can usually figure it out with a little guidance. They can usually understand multiple security concepts simultaneously, but be prepared to explain any new, complex, or esoteric technologies or processes.

■ Inquiring minds — external auditors are typically very inquisitive and tend to ask a lot of questions. However, be very careful in how you answer them as they may sometimes ask for things they don't really need. They may not always know exactly what to ask for, but they usually have a very clear idea of what controls they are attempting to test. Working together, you should be able to identify what is needed.

■ Supportive — this group may be supportive of your efforts to implement an information security program, but may or may not have the ability to support it. This group is typically a great place to look for influencers.

■ Be factual — as with the executive audience and internal audit never present information to this group that you can't support. External auditors will usually ask for detailed supporting documents, and getting this information can take a lot of time if you're not prepared. An easy way to ensure you are able to give them what they need is to ask them to provide you with a document request list prior to the start of their audit fieldwork, and establish a mutually agreed upon date to give them everything.

Summary

The external auditor group can be reasonably strong advocates for your information security program. However, unlike internal auditors, you don't have the luxury of being able to work with them to co-develop audit scopes and timing. Treat them well, communicate with them formally, and you will be fine.

Stockholders and Owners

Realistically, you will probably never communicate with this group directly. That responsibility is reserved for executive management. However, you may occasionally receive an inquiry from executive management to answer a specific question the stockholders or owners may have about your program. Your executive management will know how to communicate with this group and will almost certainly guide you in packaging the information for them.

Customers and Clients

These good people are of the utmost importance to your organization, but do not fit in one of the aforementioned groups. These are the people who purchase or use the goods and services your organization provides.

Mission

Each customer or client of your organization has their own unique needs, wants, and mission. However, we suspect that if your sales and marketing departments could have their way, their mission would be to spend as much money as possible on your goods and services.

Traits

Generally, these people will not have a strong technical background nor will they have a strong understanding of security concepts or practices.

Focus

Their focus is on the perceived value of your organization's products and services, customer support, and how you treat sensitive information you collect from them. For financial institutions, online businesses, insurance companies, companies doing business with California residents, hospitals, medical product or medical research companies, non-profit agencies, and basically any other type of enterprise, this means exercising the appropriate level of due care with any Personally Identifiable Information (PII), Protected Health Information (PHI), or other sensitive information your organization may be required by law to protect.

Tips

- Essential to your enterprise — obviously, your enterprise only exists because of this group. As a result, you should always double check with your marketing, legal, or public relations departments before attempting to communicate directly with this group. Odds are your enterprise already has an existing process or policy for this.
- Sensitive — individuals within this group may have no real reason to trust you or your organization, and therefore can be highly sensitive to issues that negatively affect them. In the rare event you have the opportunity to communicate with them directly, be as positive as possible in all communications with them, focusing on successes and achievements where applicable.
- Keep all communications simple and direct — customers and clients have the widest backgrounds in terms of their understanding of security issues, therefore you should keep all communications as simple and direct as the topic will allow.

Summary

The customer and client group is your largest and most diverse external audience. This factor will create significant variances in the personality, skills, and temperament of this group that will be distinct to your organization. Use the information outlined above as a guide, but take the time to understand your unique audience prior to presenting any information to them.

Target Audience Summary

Selecting the correct audience for the intent of your message is critical. However, every audience has an inherently different degree of risk associated with it (see Figure 5.2). For example, furnishing bad information to executive management could result in a loss of your position, whereas, bad information submitted to middle management may only result in a loss of creditability. Always match the intent of the message with the correct level of your audience.

Now that you have identified the target audience capable of meeting the desired intent and giving the desired reaction, we can now select the most appropriate medium for delivery.

Delivery Mechanisms

The delivery mechanism is the way in which we relay information. This includes the manner of packaging and presentation. The packaging of

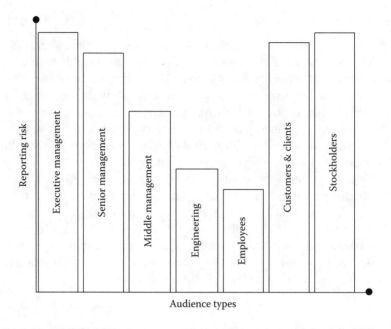

Figure 5.2   Report Risk

information relates to the template or report type used to relay the message to the target audience. The delivery mechanism is the physical presentation of the information. For instance, you may choose to deliver a project summary report using e-mail. The project summary is the package and the e-mail is the presentation method. We will start by covering some of the various report types (packages) common to information security.

Administrative Reporting

Administrative reports are communications that help to build support, communicate status, or request assistance with one or more aspects of your program. There are many types of administrative reports used to deliver information relative to your information security program. The type of report you use will be based on the intent of the message and the target audience. The idea that best captures the spirit of this section is form follows function. Based on the type of message and the audience it will be aimed at (function), you should always choose the most effective reporting format possible (form). Below are some of the more commonly used administrative report types we will discuss:

- ■ Executive reports
- ■ Proposals

- Status reports
- Internal marketing reports
- White papers

Executive Reports

Executive reports are generally high-level program status reports that demonstrate trends over time for specific elements of the information security program. Some of the common intents for this report style include:

- To gain or maintain the support of executive management
- To bolster confidence for you and your program
- To prepare executive management for a request for funding
- To prepare executive management for a substantial change in your information security program

The common audience for this type of report is:

- Executive management
- Senior management

The best way to demonstrate this concept is using a scenario with the accompanying report.

Scenario

You are the newly appointed CISO for Debt-Mart, a financial company whose primary product is issuing credit cards to high-risk college students. The majority of your business is run online, and as the new CISO you are interested in testing the effectiveness of the existing controls surrounding your Internet presence. To accomplish this task, you wish to engage a third party to perform a comprehensive security assessment of your external networks. A test of this nature was never conducted at Debt-Mart in the past, and you are concerned about the ramifications, perception, and acceptance of this practice. To prepare the organization for this concept, you plan to communicate your desire for a project of this nature with upper management.

The first communication you want to make falls under the category of executive report and has the following objectives: gain support of upper management, prepare them for the pending funding request, familiarize them on the effect this will have on the company culture, and any potential risks associated with this type of assessment.

Analysis

You are presenting something completely new and rather complex to executive management. As a result, you determine a personal one-on-one meeting with several of your executives is the best method to educate them and build support for your initiative. You understand that internal audit has expressed concern with Debt-Mart's Internet security because of several audit findings from last year's audit, and you've received internal audit's support of this proposed assessment. You have already received a rough pricing estimate from several security firms specializing in this sort of project, and have put together a quick cost analysis. Your one-page executive report contains a high-level overview of the scope of the proposed assessment, an estimate of the cost, a rough timeline for performing the work, and the benefits this assessment would bring (where you mention you have internal audit's full support). In addition to this one-page assessment, you also understand that the executives you are meeting with are very busy and extremely non-technical, so you prepare two high-level diagrams in advance. Figure 5.3 is a visual showing Debt-Mart's three physical locations in relationship to the Internet. Figure 5.4 shows some basic control areas that will be tested during the assessment you are proposing.

As you walk your executives through the scope of your proposed project and discuss your one-page executive report, you refer to these

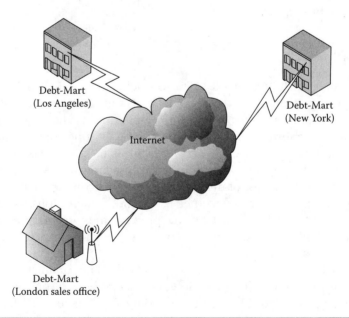

Figure 5.3   Executive Presentation One

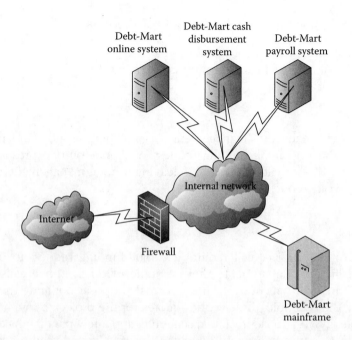

Figure 5.4 Executive Presentation Two

diagrams to show them how Debt-Mart's multiple locations are all accessible over the Internet, and that several of your most critical systems could potentially be exposing sensitive information. You see them each begin to understand the risks as they start to ask their questions.

It may seem overly simplistic, but diagrams like this can help illustrate complex concepts especially if you are able to walk them through any questions they may have. Now that you have gained their interest, you will want to follow up with the next type of report, which is a proposal.

Proposals

Proposals are the types of reports used to sell ideas and projects to others. These are the brochures that espouse the advantages and benefits the new item will furnish. Some of the common intents of this report style include:

- To gain or maintain support for a new product or concept
- To educate people on the new product or concept
- To measure the level of support for a particular concept
- To secure funding

The common audience for this type of report is:

■ Finance department management
■ Subsidiary or business unit management

Scenario

We met with executive management to gain their support and prepare them for the upcoming funding request. Your one-on-one presentations were, of course, wildly successful leaving upper management eagerly awaiting your request for funds.

Analysis

You learn this project will require a capital-funding request to be filed with the finance department. After a couple of quick phone calls to the head of finance, you put together a formal proposal outlining the scope of work, the schedule, three vendor quotes for the project, a rough project timetable, a five-year depreciation schedule, and a few paragraphs describing all of the advantages and benefits this effort is expected to provide.

Status Report

Status reports illustrate the current state of any initiative. The scope of these reports can range from updates on a specific issue, to the status of your entire information security program. Some common types of intent for this report style include:

■ To demonstrate the effectiveness of your program
■ To report any problems or issues noted to date
■ To provide general project information

The common audience for this type of report is:

■ Senior management
■ Middle management
■ Internal audit

Scenario

You've come a long way with your external assessment. You secured funding, selected the right vendor to perform the test, started the project, and are receiving preliminary testing results. Because this initiative has high visibility, you are going to issue a status report to senior and middle management. The intent of this report is to inform them of the progress of the assessment to let them know of any issues that may have come up along the way, and to inform people of the results of the assessment.

Analysis

Because Debt-Mart has implemented a series of policies regarding the implementation of externally facing systems, you have decided to reconcile any findings received against these policies to illustrate areas where you are strongest, and highlight areas where improvement is needed. After reviewing the project plan for the assessment, you learned the project is comprised of five major steps. As a result, you prepare the project status report shown in Table 5.2.

Table 5.2 Debt-Mart Security Assessment

Debt-Mart External Security Assessment	
Week One	
PROJECT STATUS:	
Phase One—Reconnaissance	90 percent
Phase Two—Enumeration	10 percent
Phase Three—Identification and Research of Vulnerabilities	0 percent
Phase Four—Exploitation of Vulnerabilities	0 percent
Phase Five—Documentation and Reporting of Security Findings	0 percent
SECURITY FINDINGS NOTED: Debt-Mart's online system appears to have a number of excessive TCP/IP services running on it, which is in violation of our UltraMegaHard Application Server Policy. The security consultants believe that several of these vulnerabilities are exploitable, and will be running further tests to validate this next week. However, no modems or unauthorized Internet connections were found, which demonstrates our success in implementing our MaxiInvisiStealth Network Policy.	
NEXT STEPS: The security consultants will continue port scanning this Thursday and Friday, and will begin to run some audit tools to enumerate the systems they've identified so far. We expect no system impact during these tests, but will keep you informed as things progress.	

Internal Marketing Documents

Internal marketing documents are used to highlight the value of your information security program to the entire organization. Some common types of intent for this report style include:

- To gain publicity for your program
- To raise awareness of security issues
- To explain the services that your program offers

The common audience for this type of report is:

- All employees in your organization
- All applicable audiences outside your organization

Scenario

You recently concluded your penetration test and the results are in. The findings revealed there were two high-risk vulnerabilities present in the organization. The good news was you were able to fix these vulnerabilities quickly and with little expense. With these items corrected, the infrastructure was rated to be the most secure of any of the companies in your industry — sounds like a great marketing opportunity.

Analysis

Based on these results, you meet with your marketing and public relations personnel and put together a small article for your customer newsletter describing your information security program, its mission, its high-level goals and objectives, an overview of your recent successes, and a photo of you and Debt-Mart's executive management team.

White Papers

White papers are research documents that publish the findings and opinions derived from the study. They are designed as an education tool and are often public domain. Some common types of intent for this report style include:

- To gain notoriety for your program
- To raise awareness of security issues
- To contribute knowledge to the security industry
- To allow certified professionals to earn continuing professional education credits

The common audience for this type of report is:

- Security industry peers who can be located both within your organization and outside
- Employees and co-workers who are interested in the information

Scenario

One month has passed since you declared your external security assessment a success. During this time, you reflected on the effort and determined it was a far more complex initiative than originally anticipated. This sounds like an opportunity to write a white paper on your lessons learned to aid fellow security professionals in planning their similar initiative.

Analysis

You work with your legal department and public relations personnel and determine that you may publish a white paper on the topic, just as long as you don't mention anything about Debt-Mart's proprietary rack-em-up credit scoring application. You and your team put together a 12-page report illustrating the challenges you faced with this assessment, the steps you took during it, and the lessons you learned. Because these report types are often public domain, a quick search on the Internet will turn up hundreds of samples.

Summary

Each of these types of administrative reports can be mixed and matched to achieve the desired result. We presented a series of guidelines to aid you in their application. Keep in mind these are only guidelines, not strict rules. How you get there is somewhat inconsequential — remember always form follows function. Now you are familiar with some of the more frequent administrative report types, we will now move to operational reporting.

Operational Reporting

Operational reporting pertains to information about the effectiveness of your security infrastructure. The goal of these reports is to show how effective the various controls placed in operation are protecting your enterprise. There are two variances of these reports and each of them has a slightly different message. These two types include point-in-time and real-time reporting.

Point-in-Time or Security Audit Reporting

Security audit reports are those reports that take a snapshot of your control environment as of a single point in time. Common examples of this include user listings, password policy settings, and audit log configuration settings. Unlike administrative reports, these reports can vary quite a bit in form depending on the reporting tools and systems you implemented. Your options will increase further based on the amount of customization you made to them. Some common types of intent for this report style include:

- To proactively detect configuration changes in your control environment
- To help illustrate the effectiveness of your control environment
- To demonstrate policy or audit compliance prior to an audit
- To fulfill internal and external audit requests

The common audiences for this type of report are:

- CISO/ISO
- Internal auditors/compliance officers
- Government agencies/independent auditors/regulators
- Technical engineers

And you thought Debt-Mart was gone…

Scenario

Based on the successes you enjoyed during the past year with your program, executive management has given you new responsibilities and several new team members. These members are to perform one primary function, which is to ensure compliance with your program's information security policies by performing spot checks on the various controls you implemented. You and your team determine a layered approach to viewing security controls that will allow you to identify the tools you can use to spot-check policy compliance across your technical security layers.

Analysis

You perform an inventory of the security tools capable of point-in-time reporting you have in place and find a large variety of available options:

- A database auditing tool for your Web systems (ISS database scanner)
- A database reporting functionality within your mainframe security system (RACF: Resource Access Control Facility)

- Operating system audit tools for both your mainframe (RACF) and your Web servers (Microsoft Baseline Security Analyzer)
- An open-source network scanner (Nessus)
- An open-source Web application scanner (Nikto)
- A card key access system controlling access to your computer room

Using the technical security layers document introduced in Chapter 4 Execute, we will illustrate what tools can report within each layer (see Figure 5.5).

Armed with this knowledge, your team begins to develop a reporting strategy for spot-checking policy compliance throughout the enterprise. The first three reports you identify as needing to run are:

- Global password requirements including password length, expiration intervals, password complexity rules, and intruder detection and lockout settings. These reports will be run monthly for the operating system, application, and database layers.
- Users and groups who haven't logged on within 90 days. This report will be run monthly for the operating system, network, application, and database layers.
- Users with administrative access. This report will be run monthly for the operating system, network, application, and database layers.

Summary

Point-in-time reporting can be a very effective tool for determining the organization's security posture and evaluating change within the environment. Over time, these types of reports can provide trending information that will illuminate consistent areas of improvement or deficiency.

Real Time or Transactional Reporting

Transactional security reporting pertains to those reports that show security-related activity over a period of time. These reports are a collection of data queried from a database of transactions monitored in real time by a logging system. Common examples of this include: system logs, event logs, user account activity, Internet activity, viruses detected and cleaned by your anti-virus systems, unauthorized network-based access attempts, and inbound access attempts blocked by your firewall. Like point-in-time audit reports, these reports can vary quite a bit in form depending on the reporting tools and systems implemented and the amount of customization made to them. Some common types of intent for this report style include:

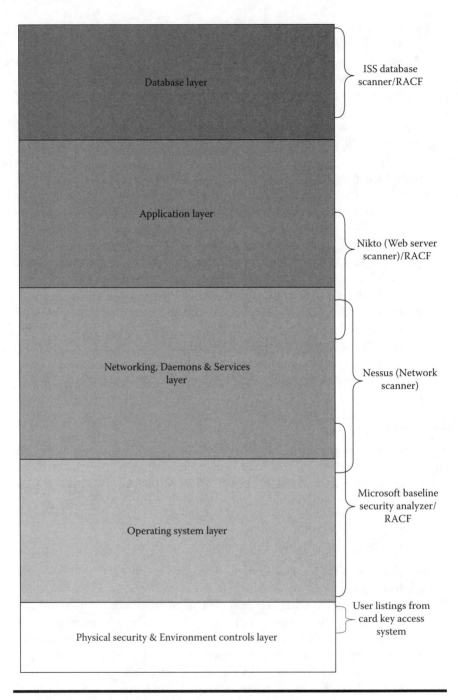

Figure 5.5   Security Audit Tools Mapped to Control Layers

- To proactively monitor security events in your control environment
- To identify potential security breaches
- To identify trends that could potentially lead to a security breach
- To help illustrate the effectiveness of your control environment
- To demonstrate policy or audit compliance prior to an audit
- To fulfill internal and external audit requests

The common audiences for this type of report are:

- CISO/ISO
- Internal auditors/compliance officers
- Government agencies/independent auditors/regulators
- Technical engineers

Let's continue with our Debt-Mart scenario.

Scenario

The second operational responsibility for which your new team members are accountable is to monitor your environment for potential security events and to alert management in the event there is a potential breach. You and your team continue to analyze the security tool arsenal using a layered model.

Analysis

You perform an inventory of the security tools capable of real time monitoring and transactional reporting you have in place and find you have the following tools at your disposal:

- A database logging tool for your Web systems (SQL event logs)
- A database logging and reporting functionality within your mainframe security system (DB2 and RACF)
- Operating system logs for both your mainframe (RACF) and your Web servers (system, application, and event logs)
- An open-source intrusion detection system (SNORT)
- A card key access system that monitors and logs controlling accesses to and from your data center

Figure 5.6 helps to show how these tools match up against your environment.

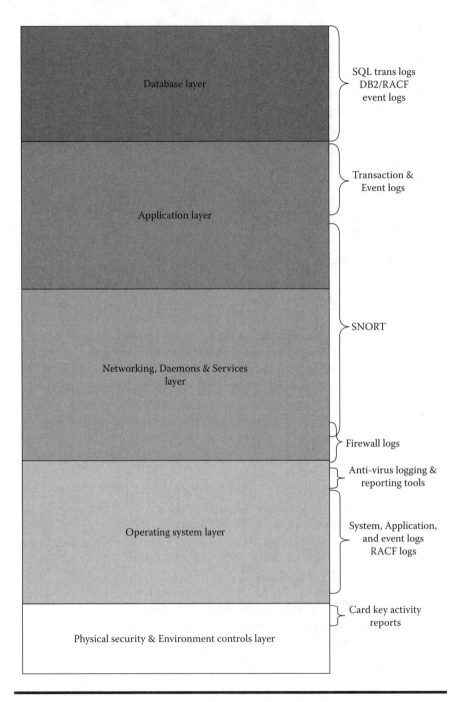

Figure 5.6 Security Transaction Tools Mapped to Control Layers

Based on this analysis, you quickly identify there are two tools that can provide the most real-time information about potential security events within your environment — RACF for your mainframe systems and SNORT for your networks. You work with your team to develop a strategy to obtain and review the following information from these two tools:

■ All mainframe log-on violations to be reviewed daily
■ All mainframe file access violations to be reviewed daily
■ All suspicious inbound network activity detected by SNORT

Summary

Real-time reporting focuses on threats rather than the specific security posture of an organization. It can be very valuable in providing detailed information that exposes the types and quantity of threats that your organization faces for a specified time interval.

Now that we covered the various packaging options available, we will discuss the various methods for delivering the information.

Types of Delivery

Creating content is only half the equation when attempting to deliver a specific message. The manner in which it is delivered is equally as important as the way in which it is packaged. The various methods for delivering information are affected by the big three: the desired intent, the desired audience, and the desired response. To address these factors, we will apply the big three to each of the common means of delivering information. Let us begin with the most used means of distribution: one-on-one meetings.

One-on-One Meetings

These meetings are the most frequent occurrence in any organization. They can take the form of a scheduled meeting or a chance encounter in the hallway. Regardless of the venue, the objective and techniques should be the same.

■ Common intent
  – Gain allies for a larger issue.
  – Test the reaction of a sample group.
  – Gain insights into potential areas for support or objections.

- – Provide a perceived safe environment for candid discussions.
- – Prepare for a larger meeting.
- – Encourage feedback.
- ■ Applicable types of reports
  - – Proposals
  - – Status reports
  - – Executive reports
  - – White papers
  - – Real-time security event logs

Group Meetings

For the purpose of this discussion, we will define a meeting as a gathering of more than two people. Everyone has been at a meeting at some point in their careers and will probably attend at least one more. We want you to try to approach meetings with the big three in mind.

- ■ Common intent
  - – Convenient method of distributing information to a large number of people
  - – High degree of control over the audience interpretation of the data
  - – Strong method for getting others to commit to a deliverable
  - – Provides a high degree of political cover
- ■ Applicable types of written reports
  - – Status report
  - – Proposals
  - – Internal marketing documents
  - – White paper
  - – Executive reports

Presentation

Presentations are simply the verbal walk-throughs for a type of report. They may include additional tools such as multi-media or audio, but they are still reports. Approach them in exactly the same manner with the same considerations.

- ■ Common intent
  - – Convenient method of distributing information to a large number of people
  - – High degree of control over the audience interpretation of the data

- Promotes audience involvement
- For the audience to understand a complex topic
- High efficiency
■ Applicable types of written reports
- Status report
- Proposals
- Executive reports

E-Mail

E-mail has the potential to be a misused and abused method for distributing information, usually due to its expedient nature. As a result, it is also the most risky method at your disposal. Although it can provide an audit trail for messages, information sent in this manner can be easily misinterpreted. Be careful when choosing this method and stick as closely as possible to the outlined intents.

■ Common intents
- Political cover
- Ensure delivery
■ Applicable types of written reports
- Status report
- Internal marketing document
- White papers

Training Classes

Training classes provide an excellent forum for delivering information that conforms to the big three. It provides a pulpit from which you can drive your intent to a desired audience to illicit a desired response. This type of delivery mechanism is extremely powerful because the class begins with the assumption that the instructor is an expert with information to transfer to the students. The means of delivery for a class is the lesson plan: a combination of white paper, marketing document, and status report. We didn't mention this in the packages above because it is uniquely applicable to training classes.

■ Common intents
- Education and awareness
- Security control measure
- Prepares an organization for future changes to mitigate the potential of culture shock

Summary

The method you choose for delivering your message is a critical component of the total message. When determining your reporting and communication strategy, you must remember to consider both the packaging and presentation.

Now that the message has been delivered, we need to ensure it was received correctly. We will address this issue in the next section.

Follow up on the Message

Whenever you go to the trouble of planning the distribution of a message, make sure you always follow up to ensure your efforts to attain the desired result are complete. You may not achieve the objective, but you must do everything possible to try to reach the goal.

Communication between humans is flawed due to its dependency on individual interpretation. The follow up gives you an opportunity to clarify any misconceptions or apprehensions.

Follow ups are usually the most effective when conducted in a one-on-one environment. This will allow you to focus on the individual and his specific issues. It also provides you with the single, most important aspect of the follow up — measuring the desired results to the actual interpretation.

As we alluded to in the beginning, the end game for the entire reporting process is to attain a desired result. Throughout the follow-up process, you will gain the necessary information to determine whether your approach and efforts were fruitful. It will also furnish you with an opportunity to fine-tune your approach to potentially turn a maybe into a yes. The last aspect of the follow up we want to discuss is the element of credibility.

Nothing is more rare in this world than someone who states what he intends to do and then actually does what was stated. The simple act of follow up on a message will put you in esteemed company. It creates a perception of thoroughness and dedication that leads to a perception of integrity and credibility. This perception is like any other victory; it will feed on itself providing momentum for future endeavors.

The last step in the process to discuss is closing the deal.

Close the Deal

There isn't much to say regarding this topic except this is what you have been working toward. Whether it is an idea or product, you embarked on this effort for a specific purpose; don't stop short of the desired objective. Also, don't assume something is done until it is verified as completed by all parties. This period of time represents the highest risk to the undertaking; this is when you have to get other people to state what they will do and then do what they stated. As we said before, this is a very rare trait.

Chapter Summary

We covered all of the information for this chapter as a single iterative process that can be used for any type of reporting. All that is needed is to identify the necessary inputs into the formula accounting for the desired intent, desired audience, and desired reaction (the big three). Let's review each of the steps one more time:

- Identify the need.
- Determine the intent.
- Establish the desired reaction.
- Determine the target audience.
- Determine the appropriate delivery mechanism (both packaging and presentation).
- Follow up on the message to measure the actual reaction to the desired reaction.
- Close the deal.

The application of this repeatable process will improve your probability of achieving your desired objectives. Take the time and plan your message in a strategic manner. Like everything else we have discussed in this book, energy expended in preparation pays massive dividends in achieving the final objective.

This chapter marks the end of the methodology for building your information security program. However, we are not quite finished with you yet. The final chapter will impart some additional thoughts and considerations in putting it all together.

Chapter 6

The Final Phase

Overview

It has been a long journey to get to this point, but your work has only begun. As with any methodology, reading and understanding is only the start. The work comes from the application of these practices to your unique situation.

If you followed all the processes and completed all the checklists, you should have a strong outline for a fully functioning information security program. To get you to the final phase of the methodology, we need to quickly revisit the major objectives and accomplishments that brought you to this point, starting with the assessment of the business.

The assessment phase of the methodology was focused on gaining an understanding of the business, the players, and the environment. Think of it as a getting-to-know-your-company exercise. It should have produced the foundation for everything that was needed to plan your information security program.

The goal of the planning phase of the methodology was to determine the best structure for your information security program based on the constitution of your enterprise. This included critical concepts like:

- Operational versus non-operational
- Centralized versus de-centralized
- Program size
- Integration within the security pipeline

■ Inclusion of additional responsibilities [business continuity planning (BCP) and physical security]
■ Constituency of the team (staffing)

These decisions helped to forge the basis of your information security program, what it looks like, and its role in the organization. From this point, we moved into the design phase.

The primary objective of the design phase was to take the newly created information security program and align it with the business needs of the enterprise. In this chapter, we covered:

■ The definition of the security policies
■ A gap analysis of the existing environment to the security policies
■ Prioritizing areas of non-compliance
■ Building a security project portfolio
■ Building a communication plan

We left this chapter with a security project portfolio that provided a framework for accomplishing the initiatives deemed necessary to make your program successful. The next step was to begin executing these initiatives.

The execution phase of the methodology was all about getting things done. It provided a philosophy as well as a repeatable, mechanical approach for completing the initiatives within your portfolio. The critical ideas incorporated in this chapter included:

■ Project execution
■ Building security into projects
■ Vendor analysis
■ Gathering ammunition for the communication plan

Following execution, we moved to the chapter on reporting.

The reporting phase discussed the tools and techniques for communicating various messages from your information security program. We covered the big three (desired intent, desired audience, and desired reaction). We discussed achieving these objectives using the report construction process. Below are the steps that constitute the process:

■ Identify the need.
■ Determine the intent.
■ Establish the desired reaction.
■ Determine the target audience.

- Determine the appropriate delivery mechanism (both packaging and presentation).
- Follow up on the message to measure the actual reaction to the desired reaction.
- Close the deal.

That brings us to where we are now. What do you do next? Where do you go?

Back to the Beginning

If you operated in a static environment, at this point your work would be complete and it would be time to move on to a new company. But the nature of business is fluid and dynamic; that is how it survives and adapts to an ever-changing world. Further, the nature of the threats your organization will face are constantly evolving. These two factors suggest you will never truly be finished, which leads us to the last conclusion.

The final phase of our methodology...drum roll please...is to start at the beginning and re-assess the enterprise when it is applicable for your organization (see Figure 6.1). This may be an annual event or it may be

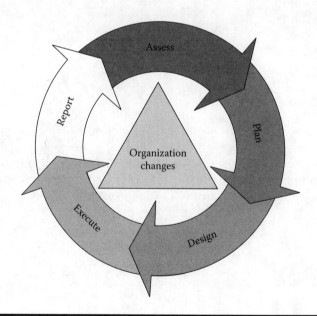

Figure 6.1   Start at the Beginning

the result of major organizational change. Whatever the case, you need to be aware of the issues and events that may trigger the need to re-assess the current business. We suggest you set a recurring event to enter your assessment phase. This is usually an annual event.

The net result of this final element of the methodology is the program essentially recreates itself through the processes, procedures, and methodology you established for the enterprise.

Parting Thoughts

In closing, we want to congratulate you on undertaking this journey, one that will create a unique program tailored specifically to your organization! We hope we provided some valuable insights and tools that will aid you during this process.

Good luck with your new security program!

Lastly, since information security is an ever-changing discipline, please visit our Web site (www.cisohandbook.com) for more tools, and to let us know how things are working out for you. We are interested in your comments and feedback.

Via con dios!

Appendix A

Design Chapter Worksheets

	Existing Controls				
Policies	Preventative	Detective	Residual Risk	Exposure	Priority

Policy Gap Analysis Worksheet

Project Analysis Worksheet

Residual Risk	Exposure	Priority	Project Name	Project Type	Description

Quantitative Project Analysis

Priority	Project Name	Project Type	Description	Number of Occurrence			
				High	Med	Low	Total

Cursory Project Scoping Document			
Project Title:		*Date:*	
Objective Statement:			
Background Information:			
Est. Work Effort:		Est. Duration:	Est. Cost:

Printed Name   Authorizing Signature

Appendix B

Report Creation Process Worksheet

Report Planning
Report Name
In one sentence, identify the *Need* for this report
In one sentence, identify the *Intent* of this the report
List the *Desired Reaction Statement* for this report

Identify the *Desired Audience* for this report	
Identify the *Delivery Mechanism* for this report	
Select the *Packaging* type for this report	
Executive Report	White Paper
Proposal	Point-in-Time Report
Status Report	Real-Time Report
Internal Marketing Document	Other
Select the *Presentation* Style for this report	
One-on-One Meeting	E-mail
Group Meeting	Training Class
Presentation	Other
Scheduled Report Delivery Date	xx/xx/xxxx
Post Report Information	
Report Follow-up	
In a couple of sentences, identify any feedback that has been received for your report	
Identify any report follow-up action items	

Close the Deal
Did you meet the objective of this report?

Appendix C

Requirements Sample

Anti-Virus Project Requirements

Prepared by Jim Johnson
Version 3.04, 10/8/05

Vision

To implement an anti-virus solution that reduces risk and increases operational efficiency for the enterprise.

Objective Statement

- The objective of this project is to implement an anti-virus product for all systems on the enterprise network.
- This project will include the evaluation, selection, and implementation of the solution into the existing technology infrastructure.

Business Requirements

- Must not negatively impact any business critical processes of the enterprise
- Must decrease enterprise security risk

- Must comply with all related regulatory requirements
- Must protect from business outages
- Must protect against the disclosure of information

Functional Requirements

Solution Oriented:

- Must provide virus protection, detection, and removal capability.
- Must support the ability to automatically update.
- Must utilize minimal system resources.
- Must support the ability to enable scheduled system scans.
- Must have configurable reporting functionality.
- Must support both server and workstation class systems.
- Each client must support the ability to integrate with an enterprise reporting architecture.
- Must prevent and detect unauthorized access of systems and servers.
- Must comply with all security policies, standards, procedures, and guidelines.

Operational:

- Must have the ability to be installed and maintained by in-house personnel
- Must be easily installed and maintained
- Must support remote deployment

Vendor Oriented:

- Company selling the solution must be financially stable
- Company selling the solution must be an industry leader
- Company selling the solution must provide a high quality level of support for their solution
- Company selling the solution must have the ability to provide local support
- Company selling the solution must have the ability to provide appropriate training to staff
- Company must offer their solution for use in our test environments at a highly discounted rate
- Company must provide timely updates for specifically identified threats

Technical Requirements

Solution Oriented:

- Must be a signature-based anti-virus technology
- Must support the following desktop based systems:
  - Go-Fast 3400 Desktops
- Must support the following server class systems:
  - Go-Fast 8500 servers
  - Go-Fast 3500 systems
- Must support the following desktop operating systems:
  - Microsoft Windows 98
  - Windows 2000
  - Windows XP
- Must support the following server operating systems:
  - Microsoft 2000 Server
  - Microsoft 2003 Server
- Solution must utilize no more than 2 percent of the overall system resources at any given time
- Must allow system scans that can be automatically scheduled:
  - Daily
  - Weekly
  - Monthly
  - Following user log-offs
- Must provide the following logging capabilities:
  - Viruses detected on the system
  - Viruses prevented on the system
  - Viruses cleaned on the system
  - Viruses unable to be cleaned on the system
- Solution must support the following remote installation functionalities:
  - Scripted installs
  - Packaged installs
  - Distributed installs

Vendor Oriented:

- Vendor must provide daily signature updates.

Appendix D

SDLC Checklist

Systems Development Life Cycle Project Documentation

Project Name: _____

Project Sponsor: _____

Date: _____

SDLC Information Security Checklist Questions	Yes	No	N/A	Information Security Policy, Guideline, or Standard (as appropriate)	References to Supporting Documentation
Physical Security and Environmental Control Considerations					
Are <u>all</u> of the servers and network devices supporting this system to be housed within a policy-compliant data center? **NOTE:** If YES, then all other items under this category can be answered as N/A.					

SDLC Information Security Checklist Questions	Yes	No	N/A	Information Security Policy, Guideline, or Standard (as appropriate)	References to Supporting Documentation
2. Are <u>any</u> of the components of this system to be housed outside of a policy-compliant data center? If so, please complete the following:					
Will there be adequate management and control for electrical power to the servers and network devices supporting this system? These include such items as: ■ Diesel generators ■ UPS systems ■ Power surge protectors					
Will there be adequate air conditioning and cooling for servers and network devices supporting this system?					
Will there be adequate fire and water prevention and detection equipment in place for servers and network devices supporting this system?					

SDLC Information Security Checklist Questions	Yes	No	N/A	Information Security Policy, Guideline, or Standard (as appropriate)	References to Supporting Documentation
Will physical access to these systems be appropriately restricted to only authorized personnel?					
Will there be a process to ensure that physical access to these systems is periodically reviewed?					
Operating Systems					
Are all servers and workstations supporting this system compliant with our anti-virus policy?					
Will the operating system have the latest service patches or security fixes applied before implementation?					
Is there a process in place to ensure that all servers and workstations supporting this system are properly patched and updated after implementation in accordance with our server policy?					

SDLC Information Security Checklist Questions	Yes	No	N/A	Information Security Policy, Guideline, or Standard (as appropriate)	References to Supporting Documentation
Have any unnecessary user, service, and default application accounts been removed?					
Is the local Guest account disabled?					
Is the local Administrator account renamed to a non-obvious account name?					
Have password controls been adequately configured for all user, system, and default accounts in accordance with policy? Password control includes the following: ■ Passwords must be expired upon first use (for initial passwords given to users). ■ Passwords must be changed at least every __ days. ■ Password history must be maintained for at least __ password changes.					

SDLC Information Security Checklist Questions	Yes	No	N/A	Information Security Policy, Guideline, or Standard (as appropriate)	References to Supporting Documentation
■ Users must be locked out after no more than __ invalid login attempts over a period of __ minutes. ■ Passwords must not be written down or shared with others. ■ All vendor supplied or default passwords must be changed upon installation. ■ Passwords must be at least __ characters in length.					
Are all local administration role and profile assignments (i.e., local administrator, root, etc.) appropriate based on the user's job requirements?					
Are all special privileges (i.e., security, audit, SECOFR, and ALLOBJ) appropriate based on the user's job requirements?					

SDLC Information Security Checklist Questions	Yes	No	N/A	Information Security Policy, Guideline, or Standard (as appropriate)	References to Supporting Documentation
Has the system administrator's roles and responsibilities been adequately defined and assigned? This may include such items as: ■ Changing global security options and environmental variables ■ Adding, changing, and removing access levels ■ Periodically reviewing user and group profiles ■ Removing inactive user accounts ■ Reviewing audit logs					
Are the access permissions for sensitive files or directories used by the <u>operating system</u> appropriately restricted?					
If applicable, are the access permissions to files or directories containing <u>application source and executable program code</u> appropriately restricted?					

SDLC Information Security Checklist Questions	Yes	No	N/A	Information Security Policy, Guideline, or Standard (as appropriate)	References to Supporting Documentation
If applicable, are the access permissions to files or directories containing <u>database system or data files</u> appropriately restricted?					
Has system auditing been enabled and configured in accordance with policy? Items that may need to be logged include: ■ Successful and unsuccessful login attempts ■ Failed attempts at privileged resources ■ Privileged use ■ Critical transactions ■ Changes to security levels					
Is there a process for ensuring inactive accounts are reviewed and disabled if no longer required?					
Networking, Service, and Daemons					
Will this system require new network segments to be created?					

SDLC Information Security Checklist Questions	Yes	No	N/A	Information Security Policy, Guideline, or Standard (as appropriate)	References to Supporting Documentation
Are there any single points of failure in between the components of your system?					
Can the network infrastructure supporting this system handle its bandwidth requirements?					
Will this system utilize an existing Internet connection or require a new one?					
Will this system utilize FTP to transfer data over the Internet?					
Has a data flow diagram for the system or application been defined and does it include the following: ■ Data sources and destinations ■ Required TCP and UDP ports and Services ■ Interfaces with all related application systems ■ Communications between systems and networks ■ Logical location of all servers (DB, Apps, Web, Authentication, log)					

SDLC Information Security Checklist Questions	Yes	No	N/A	Information Security Policy, Guideline, or Standard (as appropriate)	References to Supporting Documentation
■ Gateway access points ■ Networking protocols, ports, and services ■ Disaster recovery requirements ■ Encryption points ■ One- and two-way trusts between systems					
Are all networking ports and services used by this system documented?					
Are all unnecessary ports and services disabled on each server supporting this system?					
Have any unnecessary user, service, and default network software/firmware accounts been removed or disabled?					
Have password controls been adequately configured for all user, system, and default accounts in accordance with policy? Password control includes the following:					

SDLC Information Security Checklist Questions	Yes	No	N/A	Information Security Policy, Guideline, or Standard (as appropriate)	References to Supporting Documentation
■ Passwords must be expired upon first use (for initial passwords given to users). ■ Passwords must be changed at least every __ days. ■ Password history must be maintained for at least __ password changes. ■ Users must be locked out after no more than __ invalid login attempts over a period of ___ minutes. ■ Passwords must not be written down or shared with others. ■ All vendor supplied or default passwords must be changed upon installation. ■ Passwords must be at least __ characters in length.					
Are all profile, role, and group assignments appropriate based on the user's job requirements?					

SDLC Information Security Checklist Questions	Yes	No	N/A	Information Security Policy, Guideline, or Standard (as appropriate)	References to Supporting Documentation
Have the network or domain administrator and manager accounts and roles been adequately defined and assigned?					
Are network monitoring services (i.e., SNMP) required for this system? If so, will they require the use of non-standard network ports?					
Will this system require changes to existing firewall objects and rules? If so, will the appropriate teams be included in the development and test process for this system?					
Will network encryption be required for this system? If so, are all of this system's encryption requirements compliant with our encryption policy?					
Will all network interface cards (NICs) be configured in accordance with our network security policies?					

SDLC Information Security Checklist Questions	Yes	No	N/A	Information Security Policy, Guideline, or Standard (as appropriate)	References to Supporting Documentation
Will this system require changes to our domain name services (DNS) and Windows Internet naming services (WINS) records? If so, will all host names and IP addresses be given to the appropriate teams prior to system implementation?					
Will this system require remote access? If so, are all remote access components compliant with our remote access or network policies?					
Has system auditing been enabled and configured in accordance with policy? Items that may need to be logged include: ■ Unsuccessful login attempts ■ Failed attempts at privileged resources ■ Privileged use ■ Critical transactions ■ Changes to security levels					

SDLC Information Security Checklist Questions	Yes	No	N/A	Information Security Policy, Guideline, or Standard (as appropriate)	References to Supporting Documentation
Are the servers supporting this system being deployed in the appropriate network zones for their purpose (i.e., Web servers in a DMZ, development servers in the test network, etc.)?					
If this system will utilize wireless technologies, do they comply with our policies, standards, and guidelines?					
Is there a process for ensuring inactive accounts are reviewed and disabled if no longer required?					
Applications					
Have any unnecessary user, service, and default application accounts been removed?					
Have password controls been adequately configur-ed for all user, system, and default accounts in accordance with policy? Password control includes the following:					

SDLC Information Security Checklist Questions	Yes	No	N/A	Information Security Policy, Guideline, or Standard (as appropriate)	References to Supporting Documentation
■ Passwords must be expired upon first use (for initial passwords given to users). ■ Passwords must be changed at least every __ days. ■ Password history must be maintained for at least __ password changes. ■ Users must be locked out after no more than __ invalid login attempts over a period of __ minutes. ■ Passwords must not be written down or shared with others. ■ All vendor supplied or default passwords must be changed upon installation. ■ Passwords must be at least __ characters in length.					
Are embedded passwords used in scheduled batch jobs or job streams? If so, what compensating controls exist to ensure that they can not be read by users?					

SDLC Information Security Checklist Questions	Yes	No	N/A	Information Security Policy, Guideline, or Standard (as appropriate)	References to Supporting Documentation
Are all profile, role, and group assignments appropriate based on the user's job requirements?					
Are all special privileges, such as security administrator, application administrator, and manager appropriate based on the user's job requirements?					
Has the application administrator and security administrator roles and responsibilities been adequately defined and assigned? This may include such items as: ■ Changing global security options and environmental variables ■ Adding, changing, and removing access levels ■ Periodically reviewing user and group profiles ■ Removing inactive user accounts ■ Reviewing audit logs					

SDLC Information Security Checklist Questions	Yes	No	N/A	Information Security Policy, Guideline, or Standard (as appropriate)	References to Supporting Documentation
Have access privileges <u>to</u> the following objects and resources been documented and reviewed for appropriateness? ■ Input and transactions screens ■ Administrative tools and screens ■ Audit logs ■ System exits and command shells					
Have access privileges <u>for</u> the following system resources been documented and reviewed for appropriateness? ■ Users and groups ■ Service accounts ■ Administrator and guest accounts ■ Scheduled processing or batch jobs					
Have all of the interfaces to and from other systems and platforms been documented in a data flow diagram and reviewed?					
Have adequate input controls been built into the system to prevent incorrect or incomplete data from being entered? These include such items as:					

SDLC Information Security Checklist Questions	Yes	No	N/A	Information Security Policy, Guideline, or Standard (as appropriate)	References to Supporting Documentation
■ Edit checks and routines ■ Onscreen confirmations ■ Batch total reconciliations ■ Batch approval and update authorization ■ Controls over uploads from users					
Have adequate output controls been built into the system to prevent unauthorized or uncontrolled access to system printouts and data exports? These include such items as: ■ Approved report and data file distribution lists ■ Controls over data extracts and downloads ■ Controls over report creation and delivery ■ Data classification of report output ■ Independent report reconciliations or data analysis					

SDLC Information Security Checklist Questions	Yes	No	N/A	Information Security Policy, Guideline, or Standard (as appropriate)	References to Supporting Documentation
Have the global security options and environmental variables been adequately configured to provide a secure operating environment? These may include such items as: ■ Authentication mechanisms (active directory, LDAP, RACF, proprietary) ■ Support for two and three-factor authentication mechanisms (i.e., SecureID tokens, biometrics) ■ Encryption of data files					
Has system auditing been enabled and configured in accordance with policy? Items that may need to be logged include: ■ Unsuccessful login attempts ■ Failed attempts at privileged resources ■ Privileged use ■ Critical transactions ■ Changes to security levels					

SDLC Information Security Checklist Questions	Yes	No	N/A	Information Security Policy, Guideline, or Standard (as appropriate)	References to Supporting Documentation
Have all the ports and services used by the application been documented in a data flow diagram and reviewed?					
Is encryption used to protect sensitive data transmitted over unsecured public networks?					
Have the controls over vendor and third party access to the application been documented and reviewed?					
Is there a process for ensuring that inactive accounts are reviewed and disabled if no longer required?					
a. Have security testing require-ments been documented in the testing plan?					
b. Has security testing been completed and the results documented?					
Are the application server(s) located in a secure network zone?					

SDLC Information Security Checklist Questions	Yes	No	N/A	Information Security Policy, Guideline, or Standard (as appropriate)	References to Supporting Documentation
Databases					
Have any unnecessary user, service, and default database software accounts been removed?					
Have password controls been adequately configured for all user, system, and default accounts in accordance with policy? Password control include the following: ■ Passwords must be expired upon first use (for initial passwords given to users). ■ Passwords must be changed at least every __ days. ■ Password history must be maintained for at least __ password changes. ■ Users must be locked out after no more than __ invalid login attempts over a period of ___ minutes. ■ Passwords must not be written down or shared with others.					

SDLC Information Security Checklist Questions	Yes	No	N/A	Information Security Policy, Guideline, or Standard (as appropriate)	References to Supporting Documentation
▪ All vendor supplied or default passwords must be changed upon installation. ▪ Passwords must be at least __ characters in length.					
Are all profile, role, and group assignments appropriate based on the user's job requirements?					
Have the DBA and DBO roles been adequately defined and assigned?					
Have access privileges <u>of</u> the following system resources been documented and reviewed for appropriateness? ▪ Roles ▪ Users and groups ▪ Service accounts ▪ Administrator and guest accounts ▪ Stored procedures ▪ Extended stored procedures ▪ System stored procedures ▪ Statements					

SDLC Information Security Checklist Questions	Yes	No	N/A	Information Security Policy, Guideline, or Standard (as appropriate)	References to Supporting Documentation
Have access privileges to the following objects and resources been documented and reviewed for appropriateness? ■ Tables ■ Audit logs ■ Stored procedures ■ Extended stored procedures ■ Packages ■ Views					
Have the global security options and environmental variables been adequately configured to provide a secure operating environment? These may include such items as: ■ Table space configuration ■ Remote execution of stored procedures ■ Query timeout settings ■ Buffer cache size ■ Recovery options ■ Encryption ■ Initialization parameters					

SDLC Information Security Checklist Questions	Yes	No	N/A	Information Security Policy, Guideline, or Standard (as appropriate)	References to Supporting Documentation
Has system auditing been enabled and configured in accordance with policy? Items that may need to be logged include: ■ Unsuccessful login attempts ■ Failed attempts at privileged resources ■ Privileged use ■ Critical transactions ■ Changes to security levels					
Have the controls over vendor and third party access to the database been documented and reviewed?					
Is there a process for ensuring that inactive accounts are reviewed and disabled if no longer required?					
Are all database servers located in a secure network zone?					

Appendix E

Recommended Reading

Web sites

- www.cisohandbook.com
- www.isc2.org
- www.sans.org
- www.securityfocus.com
- www.csrc.nist.gov

Books

- Tipton, Harold F., and Micki Krause. *Information Security Management Handbook,* Fifth Ed. Auerbach Books.
- Machiavelli, Niccolo. *The Prince.* Easton Press, 1513
- Carnegie, Dale. *How to Win Friends and Influence People.* BBS Pub. Corp., 1936.
- Byham, William C., and Jeff Cox. *Zapp! The Lightning of Empowerment.* Ballantine Books, 1988.
- Covey, Stephen F. *The 7 Habits of Highly Effective People.* Simon & Schuster, 1989.
- Brinkman, Rick, and Rick Kirschner. *Dealing with People You Can't Stand.* McGraw-Hill, 2002.
- Buckingham, Marcus, and Curt Coffman. *First, Break All the Rules.* Simon & Schuster, 1999.

■ Hammer, Michael, and Steven A. Stanton. *The Reengineering Revolution*. HarperBusiness, 1995.

■ Baird, Michael L. *Engineering Your Start-Up*. Professional Publications, 1999.

■ Dobyns, Lloyd, and Clare Crawford-Mason. *Think About Quality*, Random House, 1994.

■ Bridges, William. *Managing Transitions*. Perseus Books, 1991

■ Yourdon, Edward. *Death March (The Complete Software Developer's Guide to Surviving "Mission Impossible" Projects)*. Prentice Hall, 1997.

■ McCarthy, Jim. *Dynamic of Software Development*. Microsoft Press, 1995.

■ Beckwith, Harry. *Selling the Invisible (A Field Guide to Modern Marketing)*. Warner Books, 1997.

■ Beckwith, Harry. *What Clients Love (A Field Guide to Growing Your Business)*. Warner Books, 2003.

■ Peters, Tom. *Reinventing Work: The Brand You 50,* Alfred A. Knopf, 1999.

■ Shonka, Mark, and Dan Kosch. *Beyond Selling Value: A Proven Process to Avoid the Vendor Trap*. Dearborn Trade Pub. 2002.

■ Peters, Tom. *Re-Imagine*. Dorling Kindersley Pub. 2003.

■ Manning, Tony. *Making Sense of Strategy*. AMACOM, 2001.

■ Buckingham, Marcus, and Clifton, Donald O. *Now, Discover Your Strengths*. Free Press (Simon & Schuster), 2001.

■ (ISC)² Common Body of Knowledge.

■ Maxwell, John. *The 17 Essential Qualities of a Team Player: Becoming The Kind Of Person Every Team Wants*. Thomas Nelson, 2002.

■ Wood, Charles Cresson. *Information Security Policies Made Easy: A Comprehensive Set of Information Security Policies (Version 9)*. 2004.

■ Covey, Stephen, Roger A. Merrill, and Rebecca R., *First Things First*. Fireside (Simon & Schuster), 1994.

■ Snead, G. Lynne, and Joyce Wycoff. *To Do Doing Done!: A Creative Approach To Managing Projects and Effectively Finishing What Matters Most*. Fireside (Simon & Schuster), 1997.

■ Fisher, Roger, and Alan Sharp. *Getting It Done: How To Lead When You're Not In Charge*. Harper Business, 1998.

■ Musashi, Miyamoto. *The Book of Five Rings (Gorin No Sho): A Guide To Winning Strategy*. Bantam New Age Books, 1982.

■ Roberts, Wess, *Leadership Secrets of Attila the Hun*. Warner Books, 1990.

■ Tzu, Sun. *The Art of War* [Translated by Thomas Cleary]. Shambhala Pub. 1988.

■ Benton, D.A. *Executive Charisma*. McGraw-Hill, 2003.

Index

A

Accessibility Compliance for Federal Agencies, 25
Adding security into properly structured program, tools for, 209–210
Administrative cleanup, 183
Ambiguities, defining, 142–143
Annual budget
    approval, 34
    process, 34
Annual portfolio review, 158
Anti-virus program requirements, 285–288
Architects, 94
Architecture, 81–83
Assessment of information security needs, 1–54
    analysis, 22
    assessment checklist, 46–53
    assessment methodology, 16–17
    business, grasp of, 4–6
    business risk reduction, 3–4
    checklist, 47–53
    consultative sales skills, 2
    critical knowledge, 4
    driver of program, identification of, 17–46
    enterprise business, 31–33
    enterprise culture, 14–15
    enterprise differentiators, 8–17
    enterprise's view of technology, 15–16
    external drivers, 26–27
        identification of, 22
    financial environment, 33–35
    industry, 42–46
    internal drivers, identification of, 27
    legal, regulatory environment, 9–10
    new business opportunities, enabling of, 2–3
    organizational dynamics, 11–14
    organizational structure, 10–11
    political climate, 27–29
    rationale overview, 17
    regulatory/audit environment, 22–26
    risks, understanding of, 6–8
    skills required, 2–4
    stakeholder types, 18–21
    stakeholders, 18
    team, 29–30
    technical environment, 35–41
Attributes per employee, concentration of, 101–102
Audience, researching, 241
Audit environment, 22–26
Auditors, 96

B

Bad news, proactivity with, 242
Belief in product, 155
Benefits of program mentality for information security program, 170
Brand perception, 230–231
Budgeting, 171

Building requirements, 187–188
Business
    continuity/disaster recovery manager, 99
    functional technical requirements,
        188–193
    grasp of, 4–6
    requirements, 129, 131
    risk reduction, 3–4
Business-sensitive processes, 32
Buyers, roadblocks, identification of, 156
Buying offerings, 156

C

Cable maps, 38
Capital budgeting, 153
Centralized authority model, 77
Change, 244
    attitude toward, 15
Change in scope, 174
Charts, graphs, use of, 240
Chief Information Security Officer, 97–98
Children's Online Privacy Protection Act, 24
CISO. *See* Chief Information Security Officer
Clarity of mission, 88–90
Clearance level, 143
Closing of deal, 219–220
Color-coded cabling, 38
Commander, 94, 168
Communication, 168, 253
    channels, 159–161
    effective, tips for, 239
    plan, 125, 158–161
Company technology profile, 207
Competition, 221
Computer Security Resource Center, 61
Conferences, 43–44
Consensus-building tools, 186–187
Construction effort, blueprint for, 186
Consultants, 94, 222
Consultative sales skills, 2
Contract between program, organization,
        186
Control layers
    security audit tools mapped to, 264
    security transaction tools mapped to, 266
Control result chart, 7
Control timing, 120
COPPA. *See* Children's Online Privacy
        Protection Act

Corporate responsibility/code of conduct,
        127
Corporate spending controls, 34
Cost efficiency, 90–91
Cost estimation, 152
Critical knowledge, 169–177
Cursory program scoping document, 280

D

DDA. *See* Disability Discrimination Act 1995
De-centralized authority model, 78–79
    reasons for choosing, 80–81
De-commissioning processes, 40
Deal closing, 105–106
Death March, 201–202
Debt-Mart security assessment, 259
Decision makers, 12
Defensive posture, 245
Define phase, 210
Deliverables, defining, 221
Dependencies, 91, 150
Design of information security program,
        111–164
    ambiguities, defining, 142–143
    analysis, 132, 142
    analytical skills, 112
    annual portfolio review, 158
    approval of security program portfolio,
        153–155
    belief in product, 155
    build communication plan, 158–161
    business requirements, 129, 131
    buyers, roadblocks, identification of, 156
    buying offerings, 156
    capital budgeting, 153
    checklist, 161–163
    communication plan
        channels for, 159–161
        development, 125
    constraints, 126–127
    corporate responsibility/code of
        conduct, 127
    critical knowledge, 115–124
    design checklist, 161–163
    detective controls, 121
    discovery, 112
    enablers, 127–128
    enterprise drivers, incorporation of,
        125–128

evaluation, 112
examples, 118–119, 129–131, 142
financial planning, budgeting, 114–115
formulation, 114
functional requirements, 130–131
  methods for creating, 132–133
gap analysis, 121–123, 133–135,
    140–141, 143–145
guidelines, 118
in-person presentations, 157
information security policies, drafting of,
    136–138
laws, regulations, 127
methodology, 124–161
opportunity cost, 115
organizational skills, 114
people programs, 123–124
policies, 116–117
portfolio, security program, 140–158
pressure, to individuals not buying,
    157
preventive controls, 119–121
preview, 124–125
prioritization logic, 155
process programs, 124
product knowledge, 155–156
program portfolio development, 125
program scoping, 151–152
programs *versus* core, 152
purchases by others, 156
qualitative evaluation, 148–151
quantitative evaluation, 146–148
ratification of security policies, 138
requirements, 128–133
requirements summary, 133
risk, exposure statements, 145
risk rating, 145–146
sales, 114
scheduling, 152–153
security control types, 119
security documents, 115–116
  development, 125
  summary, 139
security policies, 135–139
security programs, 146
selling, 157
  through momentum, 157
  through others, 157
skills, 112–115
  summary, 115
SMART statements, 123

standards, 117
  procedures guidelines, 138–139
strategy, 112–113
technology programs, 124
theory of security policies, 135–136
types of programs, 123
vulnerabilities, 118–119
Design phase, 211
  objective of, 274
Design processes, 40
Design worksheet, 162–163
Designated areas, 143
Desperado, 200–201
Detail, accuracy of, 244
Detailers, 96–97
Detective comparison, 20
Detective controls, 121
Development flow, 184
Development methodology
  structure, 178–180
  summary, 183
Differential diagrams, 211–212
Disability Discrimination Act 1995, 24
Document hierarchy, 117
Documentation, quality of, 38
Driver of program, identification of, 17–46

E

E-Government Act of 2002, 23
e-mail, 269
Educators, 95
EGOV. *See* Privacy Compliance for Federal
    Agencies
Enablers, 127–128
Enabling tools, 210–211
Enforcement of policies, 14–15
Enterprise business, 31–33
Enterprise culture, 14–15
Enterprise differentiators, 8–17
Enterprise drivers, incorporation of,
    125–128
Enterprise risk factors, 8
Environment best-of-breed or
    homogenous, 38
Execution of information security program,
    165–224
  adding security into properly structured
      program, tools for, 209–210
  analysis, 169

benefits of program mentality for
information security program, 170
budgeting, 171
building phase, 212
business, functional technical
requirements, 188–193
commander, 168
communication, 168
critical knowledge, 169–177
define phase, 210
design phase, 211
development methodology structure,
178–180
execution of program, 178
executors, 167–168
formalized program plan, 198–199
governance model, 196
incorporation of security into programs,
208–209
lull, identifying, working through, 199
management support sponsorship,
196–197
marketing
metrics, 193–195
preparation of materials, 223–224
methodology, 178–223
missing components, program with, tools
for adding security into, 214–217
people program guidelines, 205–206
preview, 166–167, 178
problem programs, 200–203
process programs, guidelines, 206–207
program guidelines, 204–205
program management
methodologies, overview of, 169–172
triangle, 172–175
program type, 204
summary, 208
research, 168–169
security opportunities, 181–183
shared vision, 197–198
skills, 167–169
summary, 169
success factors for program, 183–188
tactician, 168
team, establishing, 197
technical control layers, 175–177
technology programs guidelines, 207–208
test phase, 212
vendor evaluation/selection, 217–223
warning signs for programs, 200

working through lull, 199
Executive presentations, 256–257
Executive reports, 255
Executive summaries, 228
Executive updates, 159
Executors, 96
Existing security posture, 40–41
Expertise, purchase of, 221
External drivers, 23, 26–27
identification of, 22
External recruiting, 103

F

Final phase, 273–276
Financial authority, delegation of, 34
Financial environment, 33–35
Financial Modernization Act of 1999, 23
Financial planning, budgeting, 114–115
Five layer control model, 176–177
with example, 192
Foreign operations, 27
Formal requirements, benefits of, 186–187
Formalized program plan, 198–199
Functional requirements, 130–131
methods for creating, 132–133
Funding, 150, 153
accessibility of, 34–35

G

Gantt charts, use of, 198–199, 212
Gap analysis, 102–103, 121–123, 133–135,
140–141, 143–145
Governance model, 196
Gramm-Leach-Bliley Act. *See* Financial
Modernization Act of 1999
Group meetings, 268

H

Hail Mary, 202
Health Insurance Portability and
Accountability Act of 1996, 23
HIPPA. *See* Health Insurance Portability and
Accountability Act of 1996
Hoover, 201

I

In-person presentations, 157
Incorporation of security into programs, 208–209
Industry experts, 43
Industry organizations, 44–45
Industry self-regulation, 26
Industry stereotype, 45–46
Influencers, 12–13
Internal audit function, 84–85
Internal drivers, 28
    identification of, 27
Internal financial processes, 6
Internal marketing documents, 260
Internal recruiting, 102–103
Interviewing, 105

J

Job security, 87

L

Lab equipment, 219
Large program considerations, 85–88
Legal, regulatory environment, 9–10, 127
Lulls
    graph, 199
    working through, 199

M

Maintenance, 40, 83–84
Management overhead, 88, 90
Management support sponsorship, 196–197
Mandate flow, 65
Mandate of program, 63–68
Marketing, 58
    function, 158–159
    material, preparation of, 223–224
    metrics, 193–195
Middle management, 242–243
Missing components, program with, tools for adding security into, 214–217
Missing policies, 133–135

Mission, 239, 241, 243, 245, 252
Mission statements, 64–68
    translation, 67–68
Monitoring, attitude toward, 15
Motivation, 238

N

National Credit Union Administration, 23
National Strategy to Secure Cyberspace, 24
NCUA. *See* National Credit Union Administration
Negative press, sensitivity to, 244
Negotiating skills, defined, 57
Negotiations, 219, 221–222
Negotiators, 96
Network scanners, 213
New business opportunities, enabling of, 2–3
Newsletters, 160
Nonoperational program structure, 68–74
Nonoperational security office, 71–74
    model, 72

O

Obstructionist identification, 205
Obstructionists, 12–13
OCC. *See* Office of Comptroller of Currency
Office of Comptroller of Currency, 23
One-on-one meetings, 267–268
Operation security office model, 70
Operational program structure, 68–74
Operational security office, 70–71
Operational teams, 74–75
    capacity for impeding, hindering initiatives, 75
Organizational dynamics, 11–14
Organizational skills, 114
Organizational structure, 10–11
OuiNukem controls, 144

P

Packaging, 195
Peers, 43

People, types of, 12
People programs, 123–124
  guidelines, 205–206
People vendors, 220–222
Personnel, 143
Philosophical debates, avoiding, 246
Phone interviews, 218
Physical security specialist, 99–100
Planners, 96
Planning for information security, 55–110
  architecture, 81–83
  attributes, critical, 93–97
  body of knowledge, 59–60
  building mission statement, 66–68
  centralized, 80
    decentralized, contrasted, 75–81
  checklist, 107–109
  checklist for, 106–109
  critical knowledge, 59
  critical skills, 56–62
  de-centralized model, reasons for
    choosing, 80–81
  gap analysis, performance of, 102–103
  information security program structure,
    influence on staffing by, 101–102
  information security program structure
    summary, 92
  inspection, 84–85
  large program considerations, 85–88
  maintenance, 83–84
  mandate of program, 63–68
  marketing, 58
  methodology, 62–106
  mission statements, 64–66
  negotiation, 57–58
  nonoperational program structure,
    68–74
  operational program structure, 68–74
  political climate, 74–75
  program structure, 68–75
  security industry resources, 60–62
  security pipeline, 81–85
  security responsibilities, 91–92
  security roles, responsibilities, 97–101
  size of enterprise, 74
  size of program, 85–92
  skills required, 58
  small program considerations, 88–91
  staffing issues, 92–106
  strategic planning, 57

  summary, 106
  talent assessment, 58
  talent evaluation, 103–106
  team members, defining roles,
    responsibilities of, 93
  visioning, 56–57
Policy, requirements for, 134
Policy analysis worksheet, 147
Policy gap analysis worksheet, 277
Policy gap analyst worksheet, 141
Policy phrasing example, 138
Policy types, 116
Political climate, 27–29, 74–75
Politics, 150
Portfolio, approval of, 153–155
Potential solutions, 228–229
Pragmatic perspective, 244
Presenters, 94
Press, negative, sensitivity to, 244
Pressure, to individuals not buying, 157
Preventive controls, 119–121
Price *versus* quality, 222
Prioritization logic, 155
Privacy Compliance for Federal Agencies,
    25
Problem programs, 200–203
Problem statement, 228
Process evaluation, 41
Process programs, 124
Process programs guidelines, 206–207
Product knowledge, 155–156
Product vendors, 217–218
Program analysis worksheet, 278
Program dependencies, 153
Program guidelines, 204–205
Program management methodologies,
    overview of, 169–172
Program management triangle, 172–175
    summary, 174
Program mission, determination of, 64
Program portfolio development, 125
Program requirements, 185–186
Program scoping, 151–152
Program structure, 68–75
Program types, 203, 208
    intricacies of, 204
Programs *versus* core, 152
Proposals, 257–258
Purchases by others, 156

Q

Qualitative analysis, 151
Qualitative evaluation, 148–151
Quality control, 230
Quantitative program analysis, 146–148,
    279
Quantitative security program portfolio, 149
Quick Sand, 202

R

Ratification of security policies, 138
Recruiting, 88
Regulations, 127
    guidelines, 24
Regulatory environment, 9–10, 22–26
Report, 225–272
    administrative reporting, 254–261
    backgrounds, 250–251
    branding, 230
    closing of deal, 270–271
    components, 228–229
    creation process, worksheet, 281–284
    critical knowledge, 227–229
    customers, clients, 252–253
    damage control, 231–232
    delivery mechanisms, 229, 253–271
    delivery types, 267–270
    executive management/board of
        directors, 239–245
    external audiences, 250
    government agencies/independent
        auditors/regulators, 250–252
    intent, determination of, 235–236
    internal audiences, 238–239
    internal audit/regulatory compliance
        office, 248–249
    marketing, 229
    message follow up, 270
    metrics, 231
    mission, 250
    need, identification of, 234–235
    operational reporting, 261–267
    presenter, 227
    reactions, 236–238
    report construction process, 233–253
    reporting, primary principle of, 227–228
    skills required, 227
    stockholders, owners, 252

    target audience, 238
    target audience summary, 253
    technical engineering staff, 245–248
    writer, 227
Reporting phase, objective of, 274–275
Requirements flow, 188
Requirements gathering, 194
Requirements sample, 285–288
Research, 168–169
Researchers, 96
Resource requirements, 90
Resources, 153
    in security industry, 60–62
Resume review, candidate interviews, 221
Resumes, 104–105
    review tips, 104
Risks
    exposure statements, 145
    rating, 145–146
    understanding of, 6–8
Roles
    attributes, 100
    variety required, 101

S

Salesperson, 95
Salvageable policies, 133
SANS. *See* SysAdmin-Audit-Network-
        Security Institute
Sarbanes-Oxley Act, 22
Scheduling, 152–153
    constraints, 154
SDLC checklist. *See* Systems development
        life cycle program documentation
Security analyst, 98–99
Security architect, 98
Security audit tools mapped to control
        layers, 264
Security checklist, 211
Security committee, 160
Security consultant, 98
Security control types, 119
Security documents, 115–116
    development, 125
    summary, 139
Security opportunities, 181–183
Security pipeline, 81–85
Security policies, standards, procedures
        guidelines, 135–139

Security program portfolio, 140–158
Security responsibilities, 91–92
Security roles, responsibilities, 97–101
Security transaction tools mapped to
        control layers, 266
SecurityFocus, 61–62
Self-determined *versus* inflicted budgets, 34
Selling, 157
    through momentum, 157
    through others, 157
Senior management, 241
Shared vision, 197–198
Size of enterprise, 74
Size of program, 85–92
Small program considerations, 88–91
SMART statements, 123
Staffing issues, 92–106
Stakeholders, 18, 137
    motivations, 19
    types, 18–21
    updates, 159
State of knowledge, determination of, 40
Statement of facts, 228
Status report, 258
Structure, factors for determining, 69
Success factors for program, 183–188
Superfluous information, 242
Support, offering, 246
SysAdmin-Audit-Network-Security Institute,
        60–61
System centricity, 116
Systems development life cycle program
        documentation, 289–311

T

Tactical mindset, 244
Tactician, 168
Talent assessment, 58, 103–106
Talent scouts, 95
Team members, defining roles,
        responsibilities of, 93
Teams, 29–30
    establishing, 197
Technical control layers, 175–177

Technical environment, 35–41
    elements of, 35
Technical gurus, 95
Technical material, avoiding, 242
Technologies, facilities, 37–39
Technology, enterprise's view of, 15–16
Technology culture, 35–37
Technology lifecycle, 39
Technology processes, 39–40
Technology programs, 124
    guidelines, 207–208
Technology review, 41
Theory of security policies, 135–136
Trade publications, 43
Training, 219
    classes, 269
    specialist, 99
Transactional reporting, 263–265
Trended information, 240
Triangle elements, focus on, 241
Types of programs, 123

V

Vendor evaluation/selection, 217–223
Vendor material, 217–218
    reconciliation of requirements with, 218
Vendor orientation, 287
Vendors, 44, 222–223
Visionaries, 93–94
Volume of work, 86

W

Warning signs for programs, 200
White papers, 260–261
Wiley Coyote, 201
Work effort, 152
Working through lull, 199
Workload distribution, 86–87
Worksheet, 277–280
    report creation process, 281–284
Writers, 94